Technologies in the Second Language Composition Classroom

Joel Bloch
Ohio State University

Michigan Series on Teaching Multilingual Writers

Ann Arbor
THE UNIVERSITY OF MICHIGAN PRESS

This book is dedicated to the memory of
Milton and Ida Bloch and to Lan and Hannah Bloch.

ISBN-13: 978-0-472-03210-5

Contents

 Michigan Series on Teaching Multilingual Writers

Series Editors
Diane Belcher (Georgia State University) and
Jun Liu (University of Arizona)

Available titles in the series

Series Foreword

When we, the series editors, first began to envision this series, we knew immediately that it should include a book on the implications of technology for teaching and learning composition in an additional (or any) language. We soon discovered, however, that finding someone willing and able to accept the challenge of writing such a book was no easy task. We should not have been surprised. Considering how increasingly expansive, varied, and fraught technology-as-topic is, it presents a daunting, rapidly moving target for any would-be commentator. It morphs itself faster than most of us are able to write. For Joel Bloch, however, the challenge of this topic seems to have been a large part of its charm, a view resulting, one might speculate, from his extensive personal engagement as a teacher and researcher with second language writing classroom innovations utilizing technology.

The fast-paced nature of technological change, as Bloch has observed (this volume), is exactly the reason why teachers of writing need a book that will encourage and support their exploration and evaluation of the role of technology, or technolog**ies,** in the writing classroom. Neither a techno-optimist who views technology as the solution to all our writing pedagogy problems nor a pessimist persuaded of the inevitable dangers posed by technology to literacy learning, Bloch is a techno-realist who sees the growing presence of technology in academia and elsewhere as calling for an informed, critical, and reasoned approach to understanding its impact on and place in the writing classroom. Grounded in applied linguistics research and composition theory and practice, Bloch is able to bring a hands-on, intellectually engaged perspective to his topic—from the theoretical underpinnings of and ongoing debates over technologically enhanced writing and writing pedagogy to the potential "enhancements" themselves (e.g., networking, hypertextuality, computer-mediated discourse, concordancing). Whether new or long-accustomed to considerations of the pedagogical use (or misuse) of technology, readers are likely to find much that is thought- and action-provoking in Bloch's discussion of numerous applications and implications of evolving technologies and literacies that are changing, or at the very least challenging, the way we think about, teach, and enact composing.

Diane Belcher,
Georgia State University

Jun Liu,
University of Arizona

Introduction

At one of the first CALL interest action meetings held at the international TESOL conference in the early 1980s, someone asked a panel of "experts" whether there was any evidence that computers really helped students write better papers. The "experts" responded that there was not, in fact, any such evidence and that some students even wrote shorter and less well-developed papers on the computer. Clearly frustrated by the answer, the woman responded that she could not ask her dean for money to buy computers without any evidence that they helped students write better.

Looking back on this story after more than 20 years has passed, this question seems almost ancient. As Nydahl (1991) argued in the early 1980s, there was a tremendous amount of enthusiasm about the potential of the computer in the composition classroom but little, if any, empirical evidence that this enthusiasm was justified. Even when the research began to be published on the effects of word processing, it was often inconclusive and contradictory. Today, there is still little evidence that technology creates better writers (Hyland, 2002a).

However, the spread of computers, and later development of the Internet, throughout every aspect of our society has made the use of these technologies almost inevitable. For many teachers, the question itself is irrelevant since there is little evidence to "prove" the significance of any classroom practice. Kemp (1998) has argued that very little that is done in the composition classroom, including the use of technology, has been proven to create "better" writers. All such classroom practices are often too "messy" to be examined in quantifiable and replicable studies. What also makes this research in technology messy is not only that new technologies are being constantly introduced but also that old technologies are constantly evolving. Each of these changes in the technology or in how it is being used can require a different form of implementation. As each implementation varies, the positive or negative results may not be generalizable because in its next instantiation, the nature of the technology, how it was implemented, or the background of the users may have changed, all of which can affect the introduction or the effectiveness of its use.

From the stand-alone computer to the development of the Internet, teachers have struggled with these issues of implementation in the composition classroom. Advocates of the use of computer technology in the classroom have argued that technology can alter the writing process, the nature of the writing environment, and the types of literacies found in these environments all in positive ways. Technologies such as computer networks, hypertext, computer-mediated discourse (CMD), and concordancing have extended the role of technology far beyond that of the stand-alone computer and the word-processing programs that first sparked the interest of L2 composition teachers in the use of technology. Even the traditional word-processing program, which was once only thought to be a tool to help students draft or edit papers, can now be integrated with the Internet and other technologies to create a more complex tool for the writing classroom that can be used by teachers and students at any time and anywhere.

The introduction of these technologies has not been without controversy. The ability of students to communicate at any time and anywhere has sometimes meant that students may expect their teachers to be on call 24 hours a day, seven days a week. The growth of the Internet has challenged traditional ideas of authorship, the ownership of online intellectual property, and the relationship between creativity and the free flow of information (Barlow, 1993; Lessing, 2001; Stallman, 1999). Teachers have often had to become experts in intellectual property law to understand how they can legally use the vast trove of information available to them on the Internet. Students who have been uploading and downloading music files may have different ideas of what constitutes "stealing" than do their teachers. Given the long history of the interrelationship between intellectual property, authorship, and plagiarism, the growing importance of the Internet may greatly affect how composition is taught in ways we cannot imagine. Unfortunately, it is often difficult for both teachers and students to understand which materials they can legally use. Traditional concepts that have governed the use of materials for educational purposes, such as fair use, are often difficult to understand even for lawyers (Crews, 2001) and are continually being attacked by copyright holders (Lessing, 2003). New concepts of how intellectual property can be used, such as "copy left" ("What Is Copyleft?" 1999) and "creative commons" (Lessing, 2003) have inspired people to post materials on the Internet that others can use and modify, often with specific guidelines on how these materials should be acknowledged.

The introduction of technology into the classroom has always been accompanied by warnings about the dangers of overestimating the usefulness of technology, a point of view that sometimes has been referred to as techno-utopianism, a belief that technology is revolutionizing society, and that digital technology in particular would increase personal freedom by freeing people from the big government bureaucracy (see Wikipedia). The old controversy over whether technology will replace teachers has evolved into new controversies over the role teachers play in a technologically enhanced classroom and the quality of education that may result from the introduction of these new technologies. Neil Postman (1992) warns that technology is not a panacea for solving pedagogical problems but can worsen the problems by limiting what teachers can do with the technology to only what the technology itself can do.

In online education, technology has become the central focus of the educational process. Not everyone has felt that such a focus is a positive development. Online programs have been dubbed "digital diploma mills" that have relegated teaching to be a minor part of the course package (Noble, 1998, para.

31). Controversial assessment programs such as the Intelligent Essay Assessor™, which has been used for evaluating the content of essays (Landauer, Laham, & Folte, 2003), and e-rater® (Burstein, 2003), which has been used by the Educational Testing Service (ETS) for evaluating the essays on its standardized tests, have raised old questions about replacing humans with machines for some of the more mundane tasks associated with composition. Other programs, such as Write~Now (2003) and Smart Thinking *(www.smartthinking.com)* take advantage of technologies by providing outsourcing services for grading online compositions.

The ease by which students can cut and paste entire texts or pieces of texts from the Internet has raised a concern over whether the Internet has aided in what has been called by many a "plagiarism epidemic." Online texts are easier to cut and paste than print ones, and there has been a proliferation of sites (e.g., *www.schoolsucks.com* or *www.sparknotes. com*) that are dedicated to such practices. On the other side, teachers have increasingly turned to using tools like the search engine Google™ or proprietary websites like Turnitin.com (e.g., Marsh, 2004) to check whether their students have plagiarized. The passion many teachers feel about plagiarism has turned the Internet into a virtual battlefield between teacher and student over how to deal with plagiarism. The CCCC intellectual property caucus *(http://ccccip.org/files/CCCC-IP positionstatementDraft%209%2016%2006.pdf)*, for example, has argued that plagiarism detection websites "can compromise academic integrity (para. 3). On the other hand, defenders of Turnitin.com argue that this program can be a valuable tool for identifying instances of plagiarism and can save teachers hours of work (Bruton, 2006).

Plagiarism is one of many areas where technology has affected literacy. As Postman (1992) argues, we have learned from Plato's warning in his dialogue *Phaedrus* that literacy can undermine memory, and the use of one technology can negatively impact the uses of other, potentially more useful technologies. He warns against what he calls a "technopoly" where educational decisions are primarily determined by the available technologies. He argues that new technologies can alter the structure of objects, the symbols used to think about them, and, perhaps most important, our awareness of the implications of these changes. It is difficult if not impossible to predict the directions these changes will take. The result, as Cuban (2001) warns, is that there have been numerous failures in the implementation of technology in education, which should warn us about being overenthusiastic about the use of any technology. The same fear is evident with regard to concerns some have as to whether our handwriting has become worse or whether we are paying less attention to grammatical correctness (cf. Crystal, 2001). When the financial costs of implementing a technology are added in, it is no wonder that any discussion of technology will encounter resistance.

The result of all this controversy has been that many teachers, even those who want to use technology, are frightened away from becoming involved in the implementation and evaluation of technology in their classrooms. In addition, then there are all the considerations regarding implementing a technology. Therefore, a fear of failure is quite understandable. Selfe (1999) writes that some of the failures in the use of technology can often be attributed to a lack of understanding of how technology functions within the political, social, and economic forces of educational institutions in which they are implemented. As a result, she argues that teachers interested in using technology need to be lifelong learners not only of the uses of technology but also of the theoretical perspectives in which the technologies have developed. All of these factors, in fact, make it more important for teachers to become involved. Therefore, technology needs to be approached like any other issue in the teaching of composition. In her book on the controversies in L2 composition, Casanave (2004) urges teachers to always be engaged in the discussions that are occurring in their fields of interest, which is important in the use of technology where all the controversies existing in the composition field may be compounded.

The Goals of This Book

The primary goal of this book is to help L2 composition teachers to become participants in this discussion of the potential for the use of technology. The major challenge this book addresses is that teachers interested in using new technologies often have to make choices not only about whether a technology or technologies are appropriate in a given learning environment but also how these technologies should be implemented. As Agre (2001) argues, it can be difficult, if not impossible, to generalize about the effects of technology on the writing process without taking into account issues regarding both implementation and training. We have found that technologies are inherently workable or not. A technology that works in one context may not work in another; conversely, what fails in one context may be remediated or integrated with other technologies to work in a different context.

To help teachers understand these issues, this book attempts to provide the reader with ideas for using technology in the L2 composition classroom, a theoretical perspective that can be useful for deciding which pedagogies to use, and an approach for investigating the effectiveness of various technologies in different writing contexts. The book attempts to combine theories about composition teaching, the use of technology both inside and outside of the language classroom, and reflections of our own uses of technology. This combination of theory and pedagogy is important for showing teachers (1) how their use of technology is connected to how they teach composition, (2) the nature of the technologies themselves, and (3) how these technologies fit into the larger social, political, and economic contexts.

While any book on technology risks a certain degree of obsolescence as older technologies are better understood and newer technologies are introduced, it is hoped that this book will provide a theoretical perspective that allows teachers to adapt to the challenges in balancing theory and practice. Because of the growing complexity of technologies that L2 composition teachers may have to use, it is not enough to offer "tips" in how to use a technology in the classroom. It is also important for L2 teachers to understand the complex series of relationships underlying the nature of the technology itself, its relationship to other technologies, and its relationship to the writing environment in which it is used.

This understanding can help teachers implement technologies to the specific needs and goals of their classes as well as remediating problems they may encounter in the implementation. In this way, teachers can adjust their uses of the technologies to reflect the contexts of their classroom and the uses and problems they want to address. For example, most teachers believe in the value of classroom discussions, but they seem to be continually fighting the same battles over getting students to talk. However, the introduction of a technology, such as a listserv or a blog, can dramatically change how such problems are viewed. How we conceptualize technology as an environment for forming groups could help such teachers solve their problems.

Adapting a technology, however, to fit a certain problem is not always simple. Research into the use of technology is inherently chaotic, particularly when jumping from older technologies to newer ones without completely understanding the old technologies. This chaos results from the nature of technological development as well as from the nature of research into using these technologies. As Feenberg (1999) argues, technology does not develop linearly from one stage to another but frequently develops branches into new areas and then may return to the original point of development with a new perspective. How to respond to these new perspectives and subsequent new needs can be hampered by the lack of a concentrated focus by researchers on the problems that these developments may entail. As Baron (1999) argues, there is a danger in the fact that most research focuses on cutting-edge technologies while ignoring the technologies that are most prevalent in the composition classroom, which can be confusing and frustrating for teachers and students who are told to implement a new technology before they have mastered the previous one. The result is that both teachers and students often have to balance learning about new technologies and trying to master existing ones.

Thus, a middle ground has emerged that assumes that technology is neither transparent nor deterministic, neither inherently good or bad. This position is often referred to as "technorealism" ("What Is Technorealism?" 1998, para 22); technorealists share with the determinists the concept that "technology is not neutral," which assumes that there are positive consequences to the use of technology yet demands a critical approach toward its role. Integral to this perspective is an understanding that the current tide of technological transformation, while important and powerful, is actually a continuation of changes that have taken place throughout history.

> In truth, technologies come loaded with both intended and unintended social, political, and economic leanings. Every tool provides its users with a manner of seeing the world and specific ways of interacting with others. It is important for each of us to consider the biases of various technologies and to seek out those that reflect our values and aspirations ("Technorealism," 1998, para 7).

This book focuses on both old and new technologies from theoretical and pedagogical perspectives. It is the ultimate goal of this book to explore how technology can both aid and affect our goals for helping what Mike Rose (1989) has called "the richness of the composing process."

Chapter 1

Issues in Using Technology in the L2 Composition Classroom

Theoretical Concerns in the Use of Technology

The Relationship between Theory and Practice

For teachers who feel they only want to know what to do with a technology in class on a Monday morning, theoretical issues concerning the use of technology may seem irrelevant. However, technology can be so overwhelming and fast changing that it is critical for teachers to have the theoretical basis to adapt, evaluate, and redesign the technology, often without any outside help. Many of the issues relating to technology today have, in fact, been relevant since the inception of writing. It is important, therefore, to understand that since the beginnings of literacy, there have been parallel developments in the technologies that have been used in relationship to those literacies: from innovations in writing spaces, such as turtle shells and clay tablets to rice paper, papyrus, and the Internet, to innovations in tools such as the pen, the printing press, the typewriter, and the computer.

Questions have been long been raised concerning how technology may affect literacies: Is it only an aid in the writing process, or can it also alter how individuals learn to write and the nature of writing itself? Is the use of technology only a means of helping students become better print writers, or is it part of pedagogy to help students achieve what has been called "technological literacy"? Are the goals for using technology universal for all writers, or are some technologies of interest to L2 composition teachers or different groups of L2 writers?

For some, however, writing online is simply an alternative to writing or typing on paper and has little if any effect on the nature of writing itself. Haas and Neuwirth (1994) refer to this viewpoint as being "transparent," meaning that there is no effect on the writing because of the technology being used. For others, the introduction of new technologies can be seen as dramatically altering the nature of literacy itself (e.g., Bolter, 2001) in the same way the invention of the printing press altered how the book was viewed (e.g., Eisenstein, 1979).

Haas and Neuwirth refer to this viewpoint as "deterministic," meaning that the nature of the technology itself strongly affects the type of writing produced, which complicates the teaching of L2 composition. Writing online, for example, may differ from writing on paper, which means that the introduction of a new technology can dramatically alter the nature of literacy—something that has been argued in discussions of hypertext (e.g., Bolter, 1991, 2001; Landow, 1997) or blogging (Blood, 2000; Gilmour, 2004; Lydon, 2004). Some believe that technology can restructure the entire communication network or even the political and social structure of a society (e.g., Negroponte, 1995), and others believe technology can alter the social process by which knowledge is created (e.g., Brown & Duguid, 2000).

Technological Literacy and Print Literacy

Every new form of literacy has changed how information is accessed which some feel may change our perceptions of the world (Ong, 1982). As Ong points out, unlike oral texts that have to be memorized, writing in a fixed medium allows information to be more readily indexed and accessed, which can change the nature of the reading and writing processes. The Internet not only has allowed readers to access even more information but also has provided new ways of connecting pieces of information that are not yet fully understood.

Technological change has also greatly expanded and changed the reading audience. The introduction of writing in ancient Greece and Rome dramatically affected the nature of the audience as a illustrated by how writing could preserve Plato's oral forms of discourse. Writing expanded the potential audience, which then had an effect on the types of rhetorical strategies found in texts (Enos, 1988). Later the invention of the printing press would further change both the social and cognitive relationships between reader and writer. As Eisenstein pointed out, the invention of the printing press made it possible for anyone who could afford to buy a book to have access to the information contained in the book, which then destroyed the stranglehold that a few individuals had over texts like the Bible.

This view of the relationship between technology and literacy has often raised questions about the effects literacy may have on patterns of thought and on the social and cognitive development of an individual (c.f. Goody,1977; Heath, 1983; Olson, 1995; Ong, 1982; Scribner & Cole, 1981; Street, 1984). While claims about strong dichotomies between oral and literate cultures have been moderated, some researchers on literacy have continued to argue that literacy can have a profound effect on this cognitive development but also there is a hierarchy of literacies where some forms of literacy have a greater effect than others (e.g. Goody, Olson, Ong). For example, does writing a research paper restructure information, and therefore help writers learn the information in more complex ways, rather than taking notes or having discussions about that information? Others feel, however, that this view devalues the importance and complexity of the variety of kinds of literacies different groups of people possess (Heath; Scribner & Cole; Street).

While the debate is far more complicated than can be presented here, it deserves mention because if literacy is thought of as a technology, as Ong (1982) suggests, then the same issues under debate regarding print literacy can be extended to technological literacy. Is, for example, creating a hypertext different from creating a linear text (Bolter, 1991, 2001; Landow, 1997)? Do digital texts involve different cognitive skills and social relationships than print texts? Does hypertext force both readers and writers to restructure information in different ways than is possible with print literacy? This is the same question that some (Goody; Olson; Ong) have asked about the relationship between oral and written forms of discourse.

Multiple Print and Digital Literacies

However one might view this debate, the continual development of technologies and new forms of literacy have already redefined what it means to be a literate person and will continue to do so in the future. To be a literate person today, it is necessary to possess multiple print and computer literacies that themselves can vary greatly and can vary across a variety of contexts (Barton, Hamilton, & Ivanic, 2000; Gee, 1996, 2000; Street, 1984). Selber (2004) identifies three aspects of computer literacy that can be incorporated into the classroom—functional, critical, and rhetorical—that, in combination, can be used as a basis for thinking about using computer technology in the classroom.

If we speak of multiple literacies with regard to print texts, then we also need to speak of multiple literacies in terms of digital texts. For example, discussions in real time, such as in a chatroom, may require different types of literacies than discussions on a listserv or by email. Email programs, for example, allow the writer to send a paper to a teacher or classmate the moment it is finished and the reader to return it as soon as he or she has read it, which in turn changes the space and time constraints that exist in a traditional classroom. Online discussions can also occur without regard to time and place, which can change the dynamics of language interaction from what it may be inside the classroom. The ability to produce discourse at the learner's own pace can be important for students who feel insecure with their language abilities. They also may need to master various registers of language, as they always have, but to learn how they can vary. Email, for example, can either be formal or informal, depending on the writer's perception of the audience (Bloch, 2001).

Today's new technologies are having an equally dramatic effect on literacy, which in turn affects writing pedagogy. As previously discussed, hypertext has changed how texts are read as well as how they look. New forms of online discourse such as blogging, which will be discussed in more detail in Chapters 2 and 4, have been thought to provide not only new forms of discourse but also new ways for that discourse to be read. New technologies have been created that have changed how information is organized and connected to each other (Siemens, 2005). Blogs often contain what are called RSS (Really Simple Solution) feeds that allow them to be aggregated together into one space (e.g., Bloglines.com) so that information personally chosen by the user can be accessed at the moment it is posted on the Internet and archived for future use. Podcasting allows for a greater integration of oral and written texts. New types of communities can be formed, sometimes referred to as *folksonomies,* by tagging or connecting information in different ways. New forms of publishing information to the Internet, such as on Wikis, which is the Hawaiian word for quick, allow individuals to read and edit what they have read in different ways. New ways to search, such as that developed by Technorati™ *(www.technorati.com),* can allow the user to access the information contained within the blog by topic so that the user can find all the writing on a topic of interest.

One of the more significant consequences of the rise of new technologies has been the number of different opportunities one has for writing in a technologically enhanced context. Taken in conjunction with research on print-based "multiliteracies" (Graff, 1987) or the concept of "situated literacies" (Street, 1984), technologically enhanced literacies have added both opportunities and problems for second language writing. For example, our research on blogging has attempted to look at the relationship between a more oral and expressive form of writing and more formal forms of classroom-based writing (Bloch, 2004; Bloch & Crosby, 2005). We have focused this on the particular problems that Blanton (2005) has identified with students who do not have well-developed first or second language literacy skills.

Historical studies of literacy have found that what it means to be literate is continually changing (Graff). Achieving technological literacy has always required the use of an ever-expanding variety of technologies. For example, Castells (2001) calls this new period "The Internet Galaxy," a play on McLuhan's (1962) term "the Gutenberg Galaxy," and compares the importance of the Internet today to technologies like television that have been thought to have altered the relationships between people.

Technology as a Form of Literacy

Therefore, the use of a technology only as a tool to help develop traditional print literacy skills may not be enough to help students understand fully the potential of these technologies. This discussion about the relationship between technology and literacy raises important pedagogical questions: Should writing in a technological environment be considered a literacy that is taught like other forms of literacy? How do different forms of technology affect literacy in different ways? There may be no specific answers to these questions; some may depend on the perspective from which the technology is viewed. If, for example, technology is considered to be only transparent, there would be no such thing as technological literacy that goes beyond knowing how to turn the computer on since there is nothing to learn about writing on a computer beyond how to use it efficiently as a tool to help with one's print-based writing. On the other hand, if technology is seen as reconceptualizing the nature of literacy, then more focus needs to be placed on the nature of technology literacy itself and how it may differ from traditional forms of print literacy.

These considerations are complicated by the fact that there is little consensus on defining what different technological literacies entail. Applying the term *literacy* to technology is problematic in that the use of technology involves a variety of skills from being able to turn the computer on to understanding what de Pourbaix (2000) refers to as the social practices involved in using technology.

Technology literacy covers the same wide range of social and cognitive uses that print technology has traditionally covered.

In fact, if the word *technological* is added in front of the word *literacy,* the meaning of the sentence would not substantially change. The pedagogical implications are that teachers have to consider the specific nature of the technology across a wide variety of literacy events. Using technology in specific literacy environments, such as an academic writing course, can often call for a unique set of literacy skills that can change over time (e.g., Gee, 2003): Using the technology in a course that stresses personal writing may require a different set of skills. The use of the same technology may differ in different types of writing classes. Blogging in an academic writing class that stresses generating ideas for an academic paper may look different from blogging for a personal writing class where the blog may be the primary form of writing.

Integrating technology into the composition classroom can, therefore, require teaching the students a whole variety of skills beyond simply knowing how to use the technology. Simply reading and writing on the Internet require that students, for example, must increasingly be able to evaluate what they find, follow links from one site to another, and understand how visual images relate to the texts, all of which they may be able to best learn only through designing web pages for themselves. The growing importance of multimedia in writing has changed many aspects of how literacy in general is viewed (Kress, 1998, 1999). To understand this aspect of literacy, students may need to design a multimedia project, such as a digital story (Lambert, 2003), to better understand the interrelationship between different forms of media. In this sense, the use of multimedia in the composition classroom is not just an aid for improving student writing but also a means of teaching new forms of writing.

Therefore, the goals of integrating technology can encompass a wide range of literacy activities that exceeds its use as a tool. As Selfe (1999) argues, "technological literacy refers to a complex set of socially and culturally situated values, practices, and skills involved in operating linguistically within the context of electronic environments, including reading, writing, and communicating" (p. 11).

While the advantage of obtaining any form of literacy has sometimes been overstated (Graff, 1987), the ability to use these technologies can allow for the acquisition of what Bourdieu (1997) calls "cultural capital." Bourdieu defines cultural capital as the type of capital one can receive from obtaining often institutionalized educational qualifications. Understanding the use of these various technologies can give students the cultural capital needed to survive first in the classroom and later in both inside and outside the workplace.

Th acquisition of such capital is never a static process. Often more "capital" is needed by both the teacher and the student to just stay in place. Teachers are increasingly demanding higher levels of technological skills, and higher levels of technological skills are often being demanded of teachers by students who have been using these technologies most of their lives. These new demands are not always met with the additional resources or training needed to meet the challenges they entail. A lack of a computer, access to the Internet, or adequate support can negatively affect a student's classroom performance or a teacher's ability to use the technology.

The social context in which technological literacy exists means that it shares with print literacy what (Graff, 1987) calls the "myth of progress." The acquisition of technological literacy does not guarantee a better life and, in some cases, can make life more difficult. Technology has often been thought of as something that will make our lives simpler—the washing machine and dishwasher among the most notable examples; however, in reality, technology can just as easily make our lives more complicated, and these effects are often difficult to predict. Brown and Duguid (2000), for example, describe the complications office workers face when they are given a laptop to take home: They become more dependent on the technology in their home, frequently having to update it in order to do their work; they feel obligated to check their email on vacation days; and sick days often become a day to sit in front of a computer at home instead of at an office. Teachers may feel the same way when tied to a computer to grade papers or when expected to respond to email at all hours. They may have to deal with a new set of problems associated with familiarizing students with the use of computers and the Internet as well as new issues that can result from actual or perceived problems with the technologies. Teachers must therefore be prepared to deal with a whole range of problems that cannot be anticipated when creating a syllabus.

A historical viewpoint shows that the introduction of a technology has always involved a degree of disruption, a high degree of cost, and sometimes elusive results. Those who romanticize the past to a time before computers (e.g., Birkerts, 1995), often seem to forget that the pen, the printing press, and the typewriter were all at one time considered radical new technologies that disrupted what had previously been considered to be literacy.

Likewise, the development of new technologies for writing has greatly complicated what composition teachers have to consider when making decisions about whether a technology should be used and, if so, which technology is the best tool for addressing the pedagogical issues the teacher is facing. The lack of transparency of technology has meant that now every factor must be taken into account in evaluating implementation and outcomes. The research has consistently shown how even the smallest changes in the implementation process can have dramatic changes on the use of the technology.

Changing the nature of the hardware can have similar effects. Haas (1989) found that differences in the computer hardware, such as the size of the computer screen, can similarly affect the writing process: Students who wrote on small-screen computers drafted and edited their papers differently from those who wrote on large-screen computers, thus making the answer to the question about whether students write "better" on the computer raised at the beginning of this book impossible to definitively answer.

The rapid development of new technologies has further complicated these decisions. Researchers and teachers are continually finding new uses for existing technologies while new technologies are being promoted for their pedagogical potential. But new technologies and existing technologies interact in ways that cannot always be predicted.

Despite these limitations, technology has an incredible potential for not only expanding what is meant by literacy but in valuing different forms of literacy, which may be the most important reason to introduce technology. There has been much discussion about how certain forms of literacy have become dominant in specific historical periods and social environments, such as in the university (e.g., Bartholomae, 1985, 1997; Bizzell, 1982, 1986). As Bartholomae put it, students who do not possess these forms of literacies are "on the margins." By expanding the number of literacies available to the student, the Internet may be one of the most important tools challenging the domination of any one form, thus allowing its users to express themselves in different ways with different forms of language. We can see this challenge in Warschauer's (1999) study of Hawaiian speakers or in my study of Chinese speakers (Bloch, 2004). On the Internet, the power of gatekeepers to determine which form of literacy is preferred has been greatly diminished or in many contexts completely eliminated, something that has always been the intention of those who have created it. Tim Berners-Lee (2000), the principal designer of the World Wide Web, has said that it was his primary goal to make it as easy as possible for individuals to post their own materials without having to be judged or controlled by an arbitrary set of gatekeepers. Teachers may still be gatekeepers, but students at least have a greater chance to supplement the traditional literacies with new ones.

While some teachers and students may find this abundance threatening and difficult to evaluate, others have seen the possibilities of new forms of publishing online, which can give audiences the opportunity to sample new ideas they would not normally have access to, a phenomenon known as "the long tail" (Anderson, 2006). As Anderson argues, the idea of a long tail was first applied to activities such as the selling of music, books, and movies and the rental of DVDs over the Internet. The long tail refers to the fact that companies that sell over the Internet can offer customers a much greater selection of items, a great number of which will sell little but can still add greatly to the goals of the seller and the buyer.

The long tail can extend the audience for student writing and change how they view their audience. It can also affect professional writing since it gives authors new avenues for publishing their ideas. As with every other aspect of technology, there are also new challenges. Besides the need for new ways of evaluating this proliferation of information, Anderson argues that there need to be more effective ways of evaluating and filtering to guide the audience to the materials they are most likely to want.

Despite the challenges, these new technologies offer students more opportunities to publish their own writing as well as to participate in the gatekeeping process, which means that, as consumers of information, students have to learn how to utilize these new resources to evaluate what they find.

Teachers can contribute to but never control the direction of computer literacy. There have been many aspects of what Lessing (1999) calls the code or architecture of the Internet that have been developed specifically to further that goal. The development of HTML (the computer language used to develop many web pages) has been made widely accessible and relatively easy to use, and computer tools have simplified the process to give more people the ability to put their ideas online. The tremendous hype today around blogging has resulted in part from the ease by which it is set up and posted to with little or no technical background or financial commitment.

As Hawisher and Selfe (2004) argue, computer literacy can be seen as emerging, interacting, competing, or fading in its relationship with print literacy, which in an ESL or EFL context, would include both the students' L1 and L2 print literacies. This challenge can be both liberating and challenging for L2 composition teachers.

Issues Affecting the Use and Implementation of Technologies

Interactivity in Technology Use

One of the primary factors in understanding the relationship between the social context and the architecture of a technology is the extent to which the technology can foster interactivity. No issue has been more central to the development of technological literacy than how social interaction can be affected by what is called the architecture of the technology. In general, architecture has been said to conform to the institutional norms in which the architecture is situated; for example, the distinctions between master bedroom and other bedrooms in a house reflect society's concept of family structure (Agre, 2001).

Today, this relationship between architecture and social structure can be seen in how we interact on the Internet. People log on to the Internet to look for information or to have some form of social interaction. How they do this is then facilitated by the design of the Internet. As Berners-Lee (2004) pointed out, the Internet has made an important contribution to social interaction as a result of fundamental design choices with regard to its architecture. One of the most important choices was that the Internet was created using a distributed network of computers rather than a centralized location. The uses of technologies are often similarly affected by the institutional goals in which they are implemented. Decisions about the types of networks, the use of course management systems (CMS), the nature of the hardware and software, the choices about computer languages underlying the technology, the nature of the interface to the technology, the availability of the technology, and even how the technology is arranged in a room can impact the interactions that occur.

One of the best examples of how the architecture facilitates interaction is email. What makes email difficult to control, whether it be from friends or from spammers, has been the decentralization or distributed nature of the Internet—that is, it was designed to run on millions of servers, not just one. The decision to use a distributed architecture in the design of the Internet has meant that email can be sent fast and easily and can be readily accessed from anywhere using a variety of devices. All these factors have contributed to making email one of the most powerful and popular applications. Similarly, decisions regarding individual technologies affect how they are used in the classroom or other contexts. Bruckman (2001), the designer of MediaMOO *(www-static.cc.gatech.edu/~asb/ MediaMOO/)*, one of the first MOOs (see Chapter 4), discusses how she came to realize that the architectural decision to have visitors share their real names and personal experiences on a MOO made for more engaging discussions. Local decisions can in the same way affect how the architecture affects a particular context. Lessing (1999) gives an example of how the decision regarding whether an email system allows the users to send email anonymously can impact the nature of the email being sent. Pedagogical decisions can be affected as well. A teacher choosing between using a closed architecture, such as a listserv or a threaded discussion board on a CMS, and using an open architecture like a blog is making a decision about the social context of the architecture that can greatly impact the types of writing the students will produce. Such a decision can determine who will read the student's writing, which can affect the type of writing or the student's attitude toward it. Some students may find a closed architecture more comforting and feel freer to write more personally; others may feel more challenged writing to a larger audience.

As these examples illustrate, interactivity in composition courses can take on many forms as writers connect with each other in different ways throughout the writing process. One of the most interesting changes for composition teaching has been the way writers can use the Internet to easily publish their work, giving them an opportunity to interact with a larger audience than is usually possible in the classroom. This ability to contribute information, as well as having access to it, was the primary aim for the design of the Internet (Berners-Lee, 2004). Berners-Lee refers to interactivity as a connection between reading and writing, including the ability to click on links to make decisions about the paths reading will take and the ability to contribute personal ideas and information to what has already been posted online. The ability to exploit the interactivity of the Internet is consistent with constructionist approaches to education that emphasize "learning by exploring" (Shank & Cleary, 1995). Even the use of the term *surfing the web* can frame how a user must continually read and evaluate the often overwhelming amount of information encountered on the Internet.

Interactivity can also apply to how students and teachers have to integrate various forms of technologies so that the technologies themselves can interact with each other. As Haas (1999) argues, different technologies should not be understood as isolated from each other but rather as interconnected. A student may be able to write a paper on a computer, send it to peers or teachers over the network, discuss it using synchronous or asynchronous forms of discourse, use a concordancing program to help make decisions about grammar usage, and then post the paper on a personal web page or in a blog to reach a wider audience. The nature of these connections must be linked to a pedagogy of interactivity, which means that technologies must be evaluated in conjunction with their pedagogical uses.

The concept of what is meant by interactivity has also been changing as the Internet has changed. Interactivity no longer simply means making decisions about whether to click on a link. Terms such as *convergence* have been used to describe how different technologies are used together to do different things. We can communicate through email and Instant Messenger over the Internet. Now we can also communicate using text messaging or cell phones. What are the differences? Which one do we choose? O'Reilley (2005) has popularized the term *Web 2.0* to reflect some of the changes that have been occurring on the Internet. Blogging is seen as an evolution over hypertext. Wikipedia *(http://wikipedia.org)* is similarly seen as an evolution over other online encyclopedias. New terms such as *Web 2.0, Push/Pull, Just-in-Time,* and *Read/Write* (O'Reilley) all reflect ways in which the Internet has been continually reconceptualized as a new form of learning environment where students can decide what they need to do, when they need to do it, and what tools they need to use.

Technology and Composition Theory

Underlying any form of implementation are the approaches to teaching composition used in the classroom. As composition theory and practice evolved to include a variety of pedagogies, the use of technology evolved as well. Early research on the use of technology integrated a variety of approaches for teaching composition, both expressive and cognitive. As Kemp (1992) has pointed out, the early uses of word processing for grammar and style checking raised the hope that the technology could help solve nagging grammar issues that could easily be picked up by the computer and then corrected by the writer. The ability, for instance, to easily and instantaneously correct errors on screen seemed to support a focus on grammatical correctness that permeated what is called the current-traditional approach to composition teaching. The current-traditional approach focused primarily on the style and organization of a paper, with the writer perhaps creating a short outline of its organization and revising some grammar errors and typing mistakes (Young, 1978).

The current-traditional approach also focused extensively on organizational patterns (e.g., Bander, 1978). At the same time, commercially available programs such as ThinkTank, seemed to support a highly structured approach to composition that focused primarily on organization. Moreover, these outlining programs were limited to allowing users to do little more than they could do with paper and pencil. As will be discussed in greater detail in Chapter 2, the development of cognitive process approaches in the late 1970s (Emig, 1978; Flower & Hayes, 1981; Hayes & Flower, 1980) and expressionistic process approaches in both L1 and L2 composition (Coles, 1978; Elbow, 1981; Raimes, 1983; Zamel, 1983) would eventually change the use of technology in the composition classroom.

These approaches emphasized how the individual created meaning through the expression of a personal vision (Berlin, 1982), and composition teachers began to see the potential for computers to foster the notion that what was on the screen was not permanent and could be revised at any time. This focus on revision was one of the fundamental premises of the process approach that was developing at the same time.

The central focus of this approach was the importance given to the generation of ideas, what at that time was referred to as the prewriting stage of the writing process. Young and Liu (1994) state that one of the key factors that distinguished current-traditional from the process approaches was the attention paid to the role of invention. While the current-traditional approach had its own form of invention, it had little to do with the way writers actually generated ideas for their writing (Young & Liu). The relationship between composition theory and technology continued to evolve as new theories were proposed and new technologies developed. The number of invention-based programs reflected the importance given to prewriting approaches but were also mimicking approaches to invention that were already being accomplished with paper and pencil. As technologies evolved, new forms of relationships could be developed that did not have the vestiges of traditional approaches.

The use of technology began to dramatically change as composition teachers began to focus more on the social aspect of writing. Writers were no longer seen as being isolated; now they are part of larger networks. Early approaches to using local area computer networks (LANs) focused on having students share in the development of their ideas (Batson, 1993), an approach that held great potential for English language learners (ELLs) who may have felt more comfortable writing than speaking.

Over time, L2 composition theory has incorporated genre, post-process, critical pedagogical, and cross-cultural approaches to teaching. LeCourt (1998) has argued that the technology itself can help implement a critical pedagogy by raising issues about how differences can be valued and oppressive power relations transformed. As composition pedagogy evolved to include a more collaborative component, there was a growing sense of the importance of networking and later intertextuality and the new writing spaces on the Internet.

The development of hypertext, with its ability to foster the linking of many texts, similarly reflected changes in the importance composition theory placed on intertextuality and the nature of authorship. Computer-mediated discourse elevated writing as the primary means of communicating in the virtual world. More recently, new approaches to teaching L2 composition, such as genre-based approaches to teaching academic writing, have necessitated shifts in how grammar is taught, which, in turn, have resulted in new ways of thinking about grammar (e.g., Hyland, 2002b, 2002c). As these new approaches to grammar teaching have been incorporated into the curriculum, technologies such as concordancing have replaced traditional "drill and kill" programs to support the teaching of grammar within specific genres (e.g., Cobb, 1997; Gaskell & Cobb, 2004; Hewings & Hewings, 2002).

The spread of new technologies has also created new rhetorical contexts that the L2 composition teacher can use in the classroom. Writing no longer simply takes place on a piece of paper or even on a computer screen but in email, listservs, blogs, chat rooms, MOOs, and even cell phones and other mobile devices (e.g., Rheingold, 1993; Sun, 2004). These latter devices allow the transmission of text, using either aural or written modes, into a blog on the Internet. While these devices are not widely used in education at this time, they represent possible new directions for thinking about the relationship among oral, written, and visual forms of texts.

The interaction between these devices can affect traditional issues such as the relationship between oral and written forms of language. While for a long time online discourse was primarily written, oral discourse has become increasingly important. Bloggers, for example, can post their oral discourse directly into written discourse on their blogs. Podcasts, which are recorded files that can be posted on the Internet and aggregated like blogs or downloaded to personal listening devices, can be created orally or first written down and later recorded. Videocasts are similar but add visual dimension to the podcasts. While some of these devices are not widely used in composition courses at this time, these new forms have accelerated the growing importance of oral and visual discourse in relationship to written discourse means that may result in new directions for thinking about the relationship between oral and written as well as visual forms of texts.

These multiple forms of digital literacy give teachers numerous opportunities for incorporating different forms of language into the composition classroom. By including web page design in the L2 composition classroom, for example, teachers can give students the opportunity not only to reflect on their writing as being both intertextual and visual but also to think of the effects of publishing their writing for a wider audience than just themselves, their classmates, and their teachers.

Technology and Language Learning

The use of technology in the L2 composition classroom has its roots in the more general area of computer-aided language learning (CALL). CALL has been applied to a variety of technology-enhanced forms of language learning that have addressed both general classroom issues and the needs of language learners. While research in the use of technology in L2 composition classrooms has been heavily influenced by L1 composition research, it still has its own traditions that often reflect differences between L1 and L2 composition, not only in terms of teaching methodologies but also the backgrounds of the teachers and students. Levy (1997) argues that L1 research cannot always be relied on since what works for L1 learners or writers may not work for L2 learners.

CALL was first developed for mainframe computers in the 1960s and was introduced to the general ESL community in late seventies and early eighties with the introduction of microcomputers in education (Chapelle, 2001). CALL has been a major focus in second language learning and foreign language education since the 1970s and was formally incorporated into TESOL as a special interest group in the early eighties (Stevens, 2003). Over the years, the field of CALL has covered a wide variety of software applications ranging from the design of dedicated software for the L2 classroom to the adaptations of Internet technologies for language learning (e.g. Chapelle, 2000; Egbert & Hanson-Smith, 1999).

The initial uses of CALL for language learning, as is true for L1 composition, were dominated by teachers trying to create their own software. Later, commercial interests and research groups began to explore large-scale projects (e.g., Reid & Findlay, 1986). Many of these projects, despite their failures, have laid the groundwork for some of the developments in technology currently used. Hawisher, LeBlanc, Moran, and Selfe (1996) point to the importance of these large-scale projects both as introducing the potential of new types of software and providing teachers who were not skilled programmers with the ability to write their own software. Some of these technologies failed to deliver the desired results but led to the development of newer technologies while raising questions that would later be addressed in technologies that could be better understood and exploited. Other technologies lay dormant but were later transformed to be more relevant in the classroom. For example, what Levy (1997) calls language data processing has evolved in its relationship to corpus linguistics, which will be discussed in Chapter 5.

In the tutor/tool distinction (Levy), early CALL programs mostly reflected the former role. One of the earliest debates among ESL teachers was whether CALL programs should focus on aspects of language learning that a teacher may not be able to spend time on in class or on reinforcing the kinds of communicative or process-based approaches used in the classroom. Computers were thought to be able to do some of the labor-intensive drilling of students since they were intrinsically more "patient" in delivering as many examples as could be programmed so that the "real" communicative functions could be done in the classroom (Reid & Findlay, 1986). Early CALL programs often used traditional drill and practice techniques, a practice that contradicted the growing importance of pedagogical theories regarding communicative competence in the language classroom.

Regardless of how these drill and practice programs are viewed today, they have played an important role in the development of current uses of technology. Many teachers, like myself, became involved with CALL through wanting to design their own computer programs. Despite the limitations of these programs, designing them was the beginning of their interest in computer technologies. In addition, these programs raised issues about the relationship between learning and technology that are still discussed today. Chapelle states that traditional CALL research in areas of software evaluation and sociocultural concerns can be used by teachers and researchers to implement and evaluate new technologies. For example, issues such as the task's authenticity, the nature of its content, the types of feedback and its appropriateness for a given learner have always been the basis for evaluating CALL programs (Chapelle, 2001), and they are as relevant today in the implementation of new technologies.

Like the research in technology and composition, the evolution of CALL has focused not on isolated applications but on creating integrated environments where the technological dimension is part of the learning process (Egbert, 2005). CALL research has focused on the learner process and on the user or language learner. One of the most promising areas of intersection between CALL and L2 composition can be found in research on human-computer interaction (Agre, 2001; Belotti & Edwards, 2001; McCullough, 2001), which has examined ways that computer users interact with technology and the implications of this interaction for the design and implementation of the technology. Human-computer interaction covers a variety of issues, such as how the use of a technology can be affected by learner differences in language ability and how the attitudes of users toward the technology and their degree of understanding it can also affect their use of a technology.

Such research is important for obtaining feedback about what has happened when a technology is introduced and how the technology can be modified (Belotti & Edwards). For example, students bring a wide variety of experiences, competencies, and attitudes to the use of technology. As a result, CALL research has been an important source for ideas about the relationship between the nature of the learner and the design of the technology. This relationship has been particularly true in the use of the Internet. Chun and Plass (2000) identify four aspects of the Internet that are conducive to the language learning environment: the availability of authentic materials, the ability to communicate through networking, multimedia, and the nonlinear organization of knowledge.

There remain significant differences between how technology is perceived in L1 and L2 composition classes, however. Composition classes often address different levels of students with different backgrounds, language levels, and needs. For instance, the apparent resistance to visualizing these technologies as forms of writing rather than as tools for language learning is significant and a major focus of this book. Surprisingly, technology has rarely been seen as the object of study for its own sake. ESL/EFL students, for example, have rarely been asked to design CALL programs or write programs as part of their study of the language. If they are asked to create materials for the Internet, the objective is more likely to develop writing skills in general, but not with the primary goal of achieving digital literacy.

The traditional view of CALL has been as a tool for helping students learn a language, often necessitating a more utilitarian approach to the use of technology resulting from the differences in the types of classes where the technology is used. However, there has been a growing interest in L1 in using some of the newer forms of audio and video technology in more advanced professional writing classes where digital literacy is the primary goal. L2 composition research, on the other hand, has been concerned primarily with more basic-level writing courses or with courses to prepare students for writing in other courses in high school, college, or graduate school. The result has been that the tool metaphor has dominated how technology is viewed, although the situation is gradually changing.

Technology and Intercultural Rhetoric

One of the biggest differences between the perspectives of L1 and L2 research has been the role of culture in technology. The role of culture in the writing process, what has often been called contrastive rhetoric or intercultural rhetoric (Kaplan, 1966), has been one of the longest and most controversial debates in L2 composition. Without going into the details of that debate here, the question to concern us is, if cultural differences are critical factors in writing in a second language, how should they also be considered in the study of technology in the L2 composition classroom?

Intercultural rhetoric has been seen as a method of examining the effect of what Connor (2004) has called "small culture" (p. 292) on the second language writing process by drawing upon research from a variety of fields including anthropology, rhetoric, second language acquisition, and discourse and genre studies.

Of significance in answering this question is how concepts of authorship vary across cultures, which can vary across different media. Intercultural rhetoric can be an important factor in any discussion of the Internet because of the Internet's growing globalization. Today, anyone with a computer and Internet access can publish anything in virtually any language or form of language without having gatekeepers determine what is standard and what is not. In this context, what is considered standard and which forms of rhetoric should be focused on in intercultural rhetoric research is highly problematic. One continuing problem is that many of us do not even understand all the new technologies emerging. In his study of social networking among Asian youth, Harold Rheingold (2003) found extensive usage of text-messaging among Asian youth point to the ongoing development of new technologies that in the future need to be taken into consideration in the second language composition classroom.

The Internet may provide us with a rich potential area for research into intercultural rhetoric that develops an understanding of the potential of technology to be appropriated by different cultures for their own local needs, as well as the potential for the technology to further what Phillipson (1992) calls the "linguistic imperialism" resulting from the globalization of English. The controversy over high-tech companies such as Google™ and Yahoo® in China providing filtering software or names of users who would later be arrested has triggered much discussion of how the implementation of technologies may reflect the unique political and social context of the society in which they are used (e.g. Zittarin & Edleman, 2003).

At the same time, there have been many issues in different cultures that were once repressed but can be discussed online. One well-known example was a woman who blogged about her sex life *(www.danwei.org/archives/000785.html)*, which in a Chinese context is a more direct challenge to the dominant social norms than it would be in other countries where sex is talked about more openly. This blog raised other political issues that have long been repressed. Another woman posted a comment that blogging would be a good way to expose the men in her department who sexually harassed her, a situation where women often have little protection. In Singapore, Ibrahim (2006) reports on how blogging was used to mount a protest against capital punishment that would provide an alternative to the position found in the government-controlled media.

Numerous political blogs in China have raised issues about government cover-ups and political corruption, as has been the case in the West, but often with a much different focus. There have been well-publicized cases where blogging played a significant role in Chinese politics, such as in exposing the government's repression of SARS data or about the death of a graphic designer in a jail, illustrating the variety of ways that blogs and the Internet have been used in the political contexts of the society. Other websites such as Oh My News *(www.ohmynews.com)*, which is a blog written in Korean and English, allows individuals to become "citizen-journalists" and publish items that the major news media may not have covered.

For the study of intercultural rhetoric, these examples provide an important cross-cultural perspective of what is meant
by such terms as *civic literacy* in the digital world as well as
what is the potential for using these technologies as forums for
expression in the composition classroom (Bloch, 2006).

The consideration of intercultural rhetoric is also important
for the study of technology because the issues regarding its
use have become globalized. My own research into this area
has been tentative and is not meant to be definitive. In my
study of a Chinese Usenet group, I saw how passionately the
participants felt about accusations they considered racist and
how they used the Usenet group to organize a response (Bloch,
2004). I found that the Internet provided its users a means to
create a hybrid form of rhetorical systems that both incorporated traditional forms of Chinese rhetoric with new forms of
Internet discourse. Any shift in the rhetorical context in which
intercultural rhetoric is studied has the potential for revealing
new perspectives that cannot be found in other contexts.

Intercultural rhetoric has been a major area of research in
L2 composition study for more than forty years. The study of
digital literacies, therefore, can add a new dimension to the
traditional study of intercultural rhetoric by adding new perspectives on the effect of the writing environment on how ELLs
utilize the rhetoric of their home cultures: How do factors such
as collaboration, intertextuality, and authorship interact in a
digital environment? Digital literacy can provide another way
of showing that the rhetoric of a culture is not "hard-wired"
but can change along with changes in technologies that support literacy. Intercultural rhetoric needs to account for these
multiple forms of literacy that are in a constant state of flux.

Students write email, post to listservs discussion boards and
blogs, or create web pages in ways that might not be the same
as they create print texts. A consideration of these possibilities provides new areas for exploiting the students' rhetorical
backgrounds in both their first and second languages. In the
teaching of L2 composition, teachers can have the opportunity to utilize these alternative forms as a part of the language

learning process and as a way of valuing the students' own languages. Understanding the cultural context of technological usage will better help teachers understand the literacies of their students as well as prepare students for the future in the same way it has helped us prepare our students to deal with more traditional forms of rhetoric and discourse.

Discussions about the visual nature of online forms of writing, such as hypertext, can also be significant because multimedia is increasingly being discussed in cultural terms. Kress (2003) argues that visual design in a global environment can be as much influenced by cultural differences as text is. These cultural differences make teaching visual literacy as much of a challenge for L2 composition teachers as teaching written literacy. The possibility of cross-cultural differences in the use of visual imagery, as well as other aspects of hypertext design (e.g., Kim & Papacharissi, 2003), allows us to think about multimodal literacy as a form of intercultural rhetoric. Whether these differences are the result of differences in architecture or differences in implementation is not clear. Nevertheless, these issues raise interesting questions for the study of intercultural rhetoric and the effect of shifting writing contexts and shifting concepts of authorship on the types of discourses being produced.

Thinking about multimedia and other forms of online discourse in the context of intercultural rhetoric raises additional questions about the design of web pages, the types and layout of images, the colors used, and even the different font types and sizes. These factors combine in influencing how a web page is understood or how the text on the page is interpreted, and therefore they need to be studied in the same way paragraph organization has traditionally been studied in intercultural rhetoric research. This issue is not just important in teaching composition, but it is also important in our increasingly globalized economy in which communication across borders is increasing and can be facilitated by new technologies in any number of languages. English remains the *lingua franca* of cyberspace, so if a blogger, for example, wants to communicate to readers who do not speak her language, she will usually blog in English; however, a writer can blog or post to sites such as Wikipedia in many languages. In this way, learning to use the technology, even in English, can be transferred to writing in other languages. As in traditional intercultural research, there has been great interest in the organization of discourse, but in an Internet context, the concept of organization can refer not only to the arrangement of sentences in a paragraph or paragraphs in a text but also to how much text is placed on a page, how pieces of texts are arranged, and the relationship between text and images.

Authorship and Technology

No discussion on the use of technology on the Internet would be complete without a discussion of what it means to be an author in the digital age. Until recently, the Internet has been primarily a space for writing. The earliest manifestations of the Internet were completely written. Communication acts that were oral in nature when conducted face to face became written when performed on the Internet. The ease of publishing on the Internet without gatekeepers allowed for greater participation and more open discussions than were possible in face-to-face contexts.

Although this increase in the amount of published material has made it more difficult to judge its quality, the Internet has allowed writers who would never have the opportunity to be published to publish and be read by others. The tremendous popularity of blogging today epitomizes both the positive and negative aspects of this opportunity. Blogging has created millions of new authors who can now can publish publicly what they could only publish privately in the past, although much of it is of little interest to anyone and some of it may even be detrimental to the author.

This ability to make information public so easily has affected how authorship is considered. The traditional romantic view about how information is the sole possession of a few geniuses has been challenged by the sheer number of individuals who publish. The ease by which information can be published on the Internet has been matched by the difficulty individual authors or their publishers have in controlling what they write and who has access to it, a conflict that lies at the heart of the often bitter debate over intellectual property (Lessing, 2001).

The tension between the public and private nature of the Internet can also be seen in the ability of the Internet to facilitate the adoption of alternative personae (Turkle, 1995). Turkle's ground-breaking work on the notion of multiple selves and the ability to shift among these selves was encapsulated in the famous *New Yorker* cartoon of the dog sitting in front of the computer saying, "On the Internet, no one knows you are a dog." Turkle and others have looked at issues such as the distance between reader and writer and the possibility for anonymity to explore how an author can construct his or her own persona and how readers can construct the persona of the author.

Internet users can hide their private self and express an alternative public self, which challenges concepts of authorship developed in the print world. Turkle (1995) argues that the Internet facilitates not necessarily false identities but the ability to try out different aspects of one's identity and see how they sound. A man can play the role of a woman, or the young can be "adult." Liaw (1998) found instances of this gender switching in an online ESL discussion list. L2 students can, in effect, change their identities as well as lose their accent, though not necessarily their level of grammatical fluency in online discourse.

The ability to slip between different selves, in fact, may be of great importance for students to deal with the social and cognitive constraints on their writing. As Atkinson (2003a) has argued, being able to fulfill these demands of classroom assignments is constrained by possible cultural differences in "'voice,' 'critical thinking,' 'originality,' 'clarity,' and [concepts of] 'plagiarism'" (p. 6.).

By creating these types of alternative writing spaces, students may be able to express themselves in ways not always seen in the classroom. We have found that students who are reticent to express their opinions in their classroom papers often freely express them in listserv groups or blogs (Bloch & Panferov, 2003; Bloch & Crosby, 2006).

It can be argued that the architecture of different technologies fosters a different sense of authorship. It has long been argued that hypertext, for instance decenters the nature of the author (Bolter, 1991). Bolter has argued that websites cannot always be read in a linear way but allow readers to follow a link that allows them to choose the way they will connect different sites. Listservs, which share an architecture similar to email, are often highly interactive since many writers can contribute to the development of an idea, which may be why they are most often centered around a topic.

Blogs, on the other hand, can be topic- or author-centered. Blogs can share with listservs a collective nature. We have extensively used class blogs as a way of collectively aggregating the opinions and ideas of our students. Although there are a number of differences here between blogs and listservs in terms of permanence, accessibility, and ease of set up, their purposes in the classroom can be seen as being similar. At the same time, blogs can be set up in different ways that can change the relationships between the individual blogger and the community. On the one hand, blogs have been shown to foster a new sense of online communities as individuals can comment on and aggregate other writers' blogs (White, 2006), thus allowing each individual writer to create their own personal network. On the other hand, blogging seems to engender a stronger sense of authorship (Shirkey, 2003). Blogging has brought fame and sometimes fortune to a small but growing number of bloggers. The most popular blogs, such as DailyKos *(www.dailykos.com)* or InstaPundit *(http://instapundit.com),* are often identified with a single author.

The same thing can be true about the blogs that only have a small number of readers. Using the concept of a long tail, the publication of blogs is comparable to the publication of music: There are a few musicians who sell a large number of albums and many more little-known musicians who can post their music to the Internet and be heard by a few but often devoted circle of listeners (Anderson, 2006). Bloggers, like these musicians, are all contributing to the abundance of expression on the Internet. All of these forms of expression can be linked together through a variety of technical devices that can be used to form different kinds of communities. Blogs.Free-ESL.com is an example of a blog that attempts to create a community of ESL teachers using a blogroll, which is a list of blogs placed in a column alongside the main text.

The idea that blogging fosters a different form of authorship is complicated by the fact that the concept of authorship itself may not be the same in the blogosphere. This view of the relationship between the individual blogger and the community challenges the dichotomy that seems to exist between the individual and the community. Although as White (2006) points out, individual bloggers can exercise a great deal of control over the communities that may form around their blogs by shutting down the blog or by limiting or censoring comments. The ability of blogs to be linked together and aggregated on a single web page can help both writers and readers connect in a larger social network while still exhibiting the same qualities that writers and readers may demonstrate with print texts.

What may emerge is a more collective form of authorship, consisting of a network of individual authors, where the dichotomy between the individual and the group may be erased. This network can have important pedagogical implications for giving students the opportunity to write using different forms of literacy, all of which can be valued and used in student writing. Canagarajah (2006), for example, has argued for the importance of allowing students to "shuttle" between different forms of discourse. Blogging is one technology that teachers can use to create different rhetorical contexts for these different forms of discourse between which writers can shuttle.

Some forms of blogging, on the other hand, seem to foster a greater sense of authorship. In the blogosphere, readers tend to identify blogs by authors they like reading rather than by topics they are interested in, which is often the case with websites, listservs, and Usenet groups. In the United States, for example, the most well-known blogsites are usually single authored. Even sites that are authored anonymously are sometimes centered on the personalities and ideas of that author, often transferring unknown writers into what are called "A-list" bloggers. In this way, the blogosphere can give ordinary people access to the famous, make famous the not so famous, and allow everyone else to publish whatever and whenever they want. However, only a small percentage of blogs are read by a large percentage of the readers, and most blogs are hardly read at all; this is what Shirkey (2003) refers to as the long tail of the blogosphere. Bloggers with far fewer or even no readers still create a presence on the Internet as authors.

The concept of authorship in the blogosphere is not mono-lithic. Some forms of blogging sites like myspace.com *(www. myspace.com),* a highly controversial site popular among teen-agers and young adults, is a social community where people network based on common interests. Posts are often short, almost like text messaging, unlike the longer, more elaborated posting found on other blogging sites; like the traditional web-sites, the written texts share the space with images and audio files. Despite the controversy, websites like OurStory *(www. ourstory.com)* can be used by teachers to create these kinds of communities as well as have students learn to make new kinds of connections across different types of information.

Only technologies such as wikis not only allow individuals to post their ideas but also allow others, with some controls, to modify these ideas. In this way it can be a group or a com-munity, rather than one or two individuals, who can control the flow of ideas. Wikipedia, for example, is a collaboratively written "open-source" website where contributors can eas-ily publish encyclopedia-style entries, most of which are extremely useful but some contain false or inaccurate information. (Wikipedia initially allowed anyone to post and edit information; however, a number of incidents of deliberate falsification forced individuals who wanted to post and edit them to register.)

Wikipedia exemplifies how this new concept of Web 2.0 facilitates a social environment for writing. Wikipedia has thousands of volunteer contributors and peer reviewers who check everything from grammar to the overall appropriateness of an entry. Jimmy Wales (2006), the founder of Wikipedia, has said that Wikipedia has "a total commitment for free knowledge and respect for community." Once a piece of writing is published to Wikipedia, these peer reviewers may choose to edit the writing, which can then be reedited according to guidelines set up by Wikipedia (see *http://en.wikipedia.org/wiki/Wikipedia:How_to_edit_a_page*).

Wikipedia presents a different kind of reading/writing environment for English language learners to negotiate. For example, one assignment we have given to advanced-level students is to post to Wikipedia about either personal or academic topics. In this example about animal-assisted therapy *(http://en.wikipedia.org/wiki/Animal-Assisted_Therapy),* the student's post was first evaluated as lacking links and later discussed with minor corrections and links added. Within minutes of posting, many of the students received comments ranging from threats to delete their post for not using the correct format to asking for more information or more links to other texts. We left it up to the students to decide whether to respond to these comments. While this was a small assignment, it is indicative of how these new forms of online discourse can help solve long-time issues L2 composition teachers have faced in getting students to see themselves as writing to an audience outside the classroom on topics that have meaning to them. Creating these kinds of online materials, such as Wikipedia postings, hypertexts, or blogs, can facilitate the students' writing development and also help them develop an awareness of themselves both as producers and users of online information.

Perhaps a more controversial area is that these smart mobs force their readers to redefine what is meant by expertise. Being an "expert" is no longer confined to a few who have been designated to be experts by gatekeepers but can be anybody who takes it upon themselves to share their knowledge with others. The veracity of the information is no longer checked by a small group but by a larger community who can bring to bear their own expertise for evaluating and rewriting the information, which raises questions concerning whether sources such as Wikipedia should be used by students since some consider the information not as reliable as that published in traditional encyclopedias. While there is some evidence that Wikipedia is as reliable as these encyclopedias (Giles, 2005), such questions reflect the lingering distrust over the reliability of these kinds of open-source sites.

One of the most controversial aspects of authorship can be found in the growing concern for Internet plagiarism. I have argued, perhaps prematurely, in a cross-cultural study of how plagiarism in China and the West is viewed that the Internet itself may affect how plagiarism is viewed in L2 composition (Bloch, 2001) so that there was a growing convergence between the conventions found in both cultures. This claim was predicated on how the Internet was breaking down the traditional dichotomy between the individualistic nature of authorship and the collectivist nature of authorship (Boyle, 1996). As Benkler (2006) has argued, the Internet allows individuals to work collectively in loosely associated groups that can break down traditional social boundaries. What particularly interested me was how this breakdown mirrored ways that individualism and collectivity were traditionally seen in Chinese rhetoric (e.g., Mao, 1995). From this perspective, I argued that the Western concept of plagiarism was moving toward the traditional Chinese view. Although some have argued for this kind of new approach to thinking about plagiarism (e.g., Angélil-Carter, 2000; Howard, 1999), clearly there is evidence that the reverse is happening as Chinese attitudes toward plagiarism become more Westernized. There have been several reports on how Chinese academics were punished for plagiarizing in ways that in the past may have been ignored (e.g., Li & Xiong, 1996).

Despite the limitations and the controversies, all of these spaces create possible writing environments for students. The ability to create these alternative writing environments may be beneficial for students who may be at risk in traditional L2 composition classrooms because they do not share the concepts of authorship that dominate an institutional context. As Harklau (2001) has argued in her discussion of Generation 1.5 writers in the United States, these students often have to navigate through multiple and unstable identities since their identities can be a mixture of their home culture and their English language culture. Some of them have had their literacy development in both their first and second languages "interrupted" (Blanton, 2005, p. 105) and therefore do not have the range of literacy skills that students who are fully literate in the first language have. We have found that an online environment may allow these students to manipulate these identities and express themselves in ways they may not be able to in a classroom context (Bloch & Crosby, 2005).

Therefore, it cannot be expected that these technologies will liberate the L2 writing student from the traditional, dominant cultural practices of print cultures. As Herring (2001) argues, these technologies are still the products of the dominant culture in which they were produced, just like print literacy. Nevertheless, they can create an alternative form of literacy practice that will affect all students and benefit some. It is therefore left to the composition teacher to design effective environments that can exploit the possibilities of digital literacy to help students create images of themselves as authors in both the print and digital worlds.

Training and the Implementation of Technology in the L2 Composition Classroom

All of the issues discussed so far illustrate how the technology can be implemented in the classroom at a variety of different levels. For example, a macro-level technology, such as a CMS like WebCT *(www.webct.com),* can reflect the institutional goals of a school or university for creating an easier method for faculty who do not have the experience or the time to put materials online to create a larger pool of courses. The architecture of the CMS can, in turn, affect more micro-level activities such as how computer-mediated discourse (CMD) is used or whether it is private or public. The closed nature of WebCT, for example, means that only those who have been invited can post messages or read them. There can be advantages to limiting access in order to better protect the privacy of the users, which is particularly important in teaching writing to young children or to anyone who may not feel comfortable posting publicly.

These types of concerns can affect decisions about what type of technology is used. New types of blogging sites, such as Vox *(www.vox.com)* or Blogger *(www.blogger.com)*, give the ability to control the level of privacy of each post to the website so that the user can still post some things to an open audience and restrict other things to a more limited audience. On the other hand, an open architecture like most blog sites, as will be discussed in Chapter 4, can allow anyone to read the postings and, in some cases, comment on them. This change in the architecture can affect the relationship between reading and writing in the classroom. Teachers can choose whether they want to use an open or closed architecture based on pedagogical or economic factors, the ease of use of the technology, or the familiarity and facility of the users with a technology.

Similarly, departmental or individual decisions about which pedagogies should be used can affect which technology is chosen and how it is implemented. For example, decisions about how grammar is taught can influence whether a traditional grammar book is used or a concordancing program (see Chapter 5) is used. The choice of using a concordancing site or designing one's own concordancing materials can reflect departmental or teacher decisions on specific approaches to grammar teaching. Teaching general principles of grammar may be best suited for a more general concordancing program like Collins Cobuild *(www.collins.co.uk/Corpus/CorpusSearch.aspx)*. On the other hand, a choice to teach a more genre-based grammar may require a more specialized use of concordancing.

In fact, every pedagogical choice can influence choices about technology. As Brown (2002) notes, there has been a shift away from examining the isolated usage of a technology toward how technologies allow people to interact with each other, including the teacher-student and student-student relationships. Therefore, the individual writing alone at a computer is no longer the main focus for implementation. But there has been a shift to examining how different technologies can be integrated to facilitate linking with other writers both inside and outside the classroom.

Along with social context and the architectural structure of the technology, another important factor is the technological background of both the teacher and the students. No technology can simply be taken out of the box and immediately used. As Bloch and Brutt-Griffler (2001) found, teachers must be able to both understand how to use the technology and modify or fine-tune its implementation process to respond to problems as they arise. We found that teachers can remediate some of the weaknesses of a software program once they understand the nature of the software itself and the kinds of problems the students are having using it. Therefore, no technology is intrinsically "good" or "bad," but its effectiveness can heavily depend on how the teacher implements it.

The implementation process includes a variety of factors concerning teachers and students:

- what attitudes they bring to the use of technology
- what skills they have
- what levels of access they have
- how teachers and students are instructed in using the technology
- how the users relate to the context that is chosen for the implementation
- how user backgrounds and goals affect decisions about which aspects of the technology will and will not be used
- how a curriculum can be designed or modified to be used with a specific technology

The sometimes large number of factors that need to be considered inevitably makes the implementation process complex. Although the initial planning for implementing a technology is crucial, the implementation process needs to be seen as an ongoing one that requires collaboration between teachers and students in monitoring and researching how the technology is being used.

Teachers are often expected not only to understand all the factors related to the implementation of the technology but also to make a commitment to see the implementation through, often with little or no technical support. Teachers are constantly bombarded with new technologies before they even have the chance to understand the old ones. Thus, decisions about implementing a technology, or even whether to use it, are often based on an imperfect understanding of all of the factors discussed. Without proper implementation, the use of technological innovations in the classroom can be severely compromised.

However, teachers cannot be expected to be able to do all this on their own. As Alan Kay (1996) has noted, the complexity of how a technology operates in the classroom is not always well known. Kay argues that if music teaching was introduced into the classroom in the same way as technology has been, a piano would be given to every class and untrained teachers would be given two weeks of training before beginning to teach. Teachers, therefore, cannot simply consider the practical aspects of what to do with a technology on Monday morning; rather they must conceptualize the technology so that they can understand how to adapt to the ever-changing needs of the composition classroom.

Reflection Questions

1. What is your history of technology use? What kinds of technologies do you like to use? What kinds of technology do you not like to use?

2. The book discusses a great deal about the relationship between the use of technology and composition theory. What are your theories about how composition should be taught? What kinds of activities do you like to do in the classroom? How could technology be used in conjunction with these activities? For what activities may technology not be useful?

3. The book uses terms like *nonneutrality, transparency,* and *determinism* to describe how technology can affect the writing process. What do these terms mean to you in terms of your own use of technology, both in your teaching and in your personal life? How has the use of a technology changed the way you do things? Have you found new ways for using the technology beyond the ways in which it was originally intended to be used?

4. The book talks a great deal about *implementation.* Think about a particular context where you want to implement a technology, perhaps a type of writing assignment or a particular kind of course. What are the features of this context that may affect the choice of a technology and the way you want to use it? For what aspects of a writing assignment might you want to use a technology?

5. The term *literacy* has been used to cover many activities beyond reading and writing. We talk a lot about *multiple literacies.* How would you define literacy? What kinds of literacies do you associate with the computer? With the Internet? How do they differ from the kinds of literacies you associate with print texts?

6. Interactivity is another controversial concept in technology. What do you think interactivity means? What kinds of interactivity would you like to see in the classroom? How do you think technology can aid in achieving a higher level of interactivity in the classroom?

7. How have you used technology in your own language learning activities? When has it been useful? When has it not been useful? Why do you think the technology was useful in one area of language learning and not the other?

8. Another controversial area is whether the use of technology varies across cultures. The book gives some examples, such as differences in web page design or the political ways blogs are used, but, frankly, we know very little about such differences and whether they really exist. What do you think? Are there really differences in how different cultures use a technology? Does a technology have to be designed differently for different cultures? What does thinking about technology in these ways tell you about the idea of intercultural or contrastive rhetoric in general? Is it an important factor in how students learn to write in a second language?

9. What does the term *authorship* mean to you? What does an author do? How do you think of yourself as an author? Does the term mean the same thing in every situation? Have you ever published something online? Did publishing online change how you think of yourself as an author?

10. Think of a situation where you want to use a technology in your classroom. How would you introduce the technology to your students? List the steps you would use to introduce the technology. What kinds of activities, handouts, or tutorials would you like to create?

Chapter 2

The Potential of New Technologies

It is impossible to address every technology that has potential for use in the L2 composition classroom in this book. It is not possible to know whether some of the newer technologies will eventually become useful for composition teachers. Chapter 2 looks more closely at the variety of technologies currently seem to have the greatest promise.

The development of the personal computer as an educational tool was both a cause and a result of a dramatic change in how technology was viewed. The image of the Homebrew Computer Club, the first group dedicated to building personal computers, or Steve Jobs and Steve Wozniak designing the Apple computer in a garage, replaced the more menacing image of the mainframe computer, perhaps best personified by HAL in the film *2001, A Space Odyssey*. It was, therefore, not a coincidence that the first meeting of the CALL interest section at the TESOL 1984 conference in Toronto occurred at the same time personal computers began to take hold across many educational fields. The expansion of access to computers and then the growth of computer networking, which led to the development of the Internet, have greatly expanded the possibilities for using technology for language learning purposes. As Felix (1999) points out, the Internet provides language learners a variety of content, teaching approaches, and media—all of which create authentic language and learning experiences and are often available for little or no cost.

The growing prominence of the Internet in language learning has meant that the computer is now only one point along a network of technologies available to the language teacher.

But deciding which technology to choose and solving the kinds of problems inherent in implementing the technology require a theoretical conception of what writing in the digital age entails. Using any technology in any situation can require some such conceptualization. However, Levy (1997), whose work has focused primarily on language learning, has argued that there has been a lack of a conceptual framework for the development of CALL because of the lack of a theoretical orientation regarding the use of the technology in language learning. Citing a study by Henry and Zerwekh (1994), he argues that a formal evaluative process is of central importance because there is an inevitable conflict among what the technology was designed for, what features teachers and students want, and what the final outcomes of its usage should be.

This theoretical framework has often been lacking in research on the use of technology in L2 composition. However, it has become even more important to understand how the use of technology is related to both the theory and pedagogy of L2 composition. This lack of a theoretical framework has become more problematic in L2 composition since many of the technologies used were not designed for a composition classroom and therefore require a greater emphasis on how they are implemented. Kemp (in Hawisher, 1994) has argued that all technologies in composition classrooms encompass some theory of writing pedagogy. However, often in the rush to implement a technology, teachers lose sight of the principles on which these writing practices are based; so the implementation of any technology must be integrated into these practices. While most of the early technologies in English language learning were developed for specific aspects of language learning, such as the learning of specific grammar items, almost all the new technologies have had to be adapted to meet the specific goals for teaching writing. Therefore, understanding these technologies in relationship to the composition classroom has become the greatest challenge for teachers who want to implement them.

Chapter 2 develops a conceptual framework for implementing these various technologies by focusing on the theoretical issues related to the use of technology in L2 composition pedagogy.

I examine five areas of concern for implementing technology in the L2 composition: (1) word processing, (2) writing and networks, (3) writing and the Internet, (4) computer-mediated discourse (CMD), and (5) corpus linguistics. Some of these technologies are cutting edge; others are not. My discussion will draw on what has already been accomplished with the older technologies while exploring the potential of the newer ones.

Word Processing

In many L2 composition classrooms, word processing is the primary use of technology. It has had what some consider a radical influence in composition pedagogy (Porter, 2002). The introduction of personal computing occurred during the same time as an equally dramatic shift occurred in composition theory away from the current-traditional approach, which was dominant in the 1970s, to what was called the process approach. In combination with the development of more available and affordable personal computers, there was great excitement among ESL teachers over their potential in the writing classroom, as well as tremendous fears and doubts.[1] Word processing was a tool that teachers could use to accomplish more easily many of the new approaches to teaching composition advocated by process approaches. Students could produce multiple drafts more easily with a word processor than paper and pencil. At the same time, some teachers feared the possibility of being replaced by the computer in the classroom. Regardless of their concerns, the introduction of computers into the educational system raised a number of new questions. The introduction of word processing also meant that teachers needed to make decisions about when students should use pencil and paper, when they should use the computer, or when to take the students to a computer lab. These decisions often had to be made by teachers who had little personal experience or training.

---

1. One of the first CALL sessions held at the 1983 International TESOL conference in Toronto was by invitation only, so participants could discuss CALL without having to debate it or defend it.

Today, with the tremendous role of the Internet and the growing mobility of technology, these decisions are not as crucial. Today's generation of teachers and students are used to writing and revising online and making their own decisions about when to work online or when to use pencil and paper. In many situations, computers are so ubiquitous that there is often no need to take students to a lab, although in other contexts, labs provide opportunities for helping students learn to use the computer and provide opportunities for accessing it.

Changes in the architecture of the word processing programs themselves have also contributed to their increased value for writing. The earliest word processing programs, which forced writers to enter strings of characters to format texts, not only made writing difficult but also limited the number of people who had enough technical ability and patience to use the program. As Baron (1999) points out, it was not until the development of "What you see is what you get" (WYSIWIG) programs, where the screen mirrors what is seen on paper, that word processing began to have a major impact.

With the tremendous increase in computer memory and processing speed, a new generation of programs could be developed to better reflect changes in composition theory. The design of the early software programs dedicated to composition teaching clearly reflected the importance of invention in the process approach. Early software programs designed specifically for writing classes, such as TOPOI (Burns, 1984), SEEN (Schwartz, 1984), and WANDAH (Blum & Cohen, 1984), all incorporated the various modules to help with generating ideas.

Designers of these programs have attributed the architecture employed directly to the influence of process-based research. Helen Schwartz, the developer of SEEN, acknowledged the importance of the theories of pioneers in process writing, such as Janet Emig (1971) and James Britton as well as the work in rhetorical invention by Ross Winterowd (1975) and Richard Young (1978) in the development of her program. In the development of WANDAH, Blum and Cohen (1984) similarly acknowledge the work of Emig

(1978) as well as Flower and Hayes (1981). TOPOI, which provided questions for writers to answer before beginning to write, clearly reflected the research of Flower and Hayes (1980).

Other forms of the process approach, such as expressionistic methodologies, which often relied less on such structured heuristics and a greater degree of spontaneity (Faigley, 1986), could take advantage of the technology in different ways. One simple method, which did not even need a special proprietary program, was for the writer to turn off the monitor so that he or she could not see what was being typed (Marcus, 1990). In this way, the writer would not be tempted to stop typing to edit mistakes while at the same time generating ideas.

Although recent research has shown that students may write better on computers (Pennington, 2003), the widespread use of computers today has made this argument about its effectiveness irrelevant, especially for students in academic contexts. Even test-taking involves using the computer. Students taking TOEFL® or SAT® must complete a written essay that must be done on the computer.

The growing use of computer technology has changed both student attitudes toward its use and how it is being implemented. For students who lack this technological capital, there can be problems. Often, these students are non-traditional immigrants whose lives may have been interrupted by forced migrations, and the problems these students typically have with their writing assignments (e.g., language errors) can be compounded by the lack of familiarity with the technology, thus increasing the frustration they may feel with their writing.

The fact that technology can be an aid to some students and a detriment to others is illustrative of the non-neutrality of the technology. Changes in hardware can have an equally great effect. As Baron (1999) pointed out about the development of screen layout, changes in the nature of the technology can have a major impact on the writing process. Haas (1996), for example, discussed how changes in screen size can affect the writing process. She found that with larger screens, writers could view more of the text at one time, which would help them make more global changes than when using a smaller screen. This non-neutrality can also be seen in the decisions writers make about how to use the computer. For example, Haas (1996) also identified a number of issues that writers need to consider: She found that some writers do better if they edit hard copies of their papers rather than edit them online. However, it should be noted that in many of the writers in her study had had a great deal of experience using typewriters and editing hard copy, a situation that may be less relevant today since many students have, in fact, grown up learning to compose on computers.

The use of the computer also has impacted how the writing process is viewed. Word processing was not simply a different form of typing but a new way of manipulating text. The ability to continually and easily revise texts, in fact, had an immediate effect on the "steps" in the writing process. Rather than having four distinct steps, the process was a continual and recursive one of inventing, drafting, revising, and editing. The ease with which one could make changes or incorporate new ideas made it clear how all of these aspects of the writing process were now integrated.

Change can also be seen in the shift from viewing writing as a personal effort produced individually on an isolated computer to a social effort produced on a computer network. Word processing is a more inherently social process than using a typewriter or writing by hand. The typewriter was somewhat antisocial because of its noise, while handwriting could often be difficult for others to read. Although the social-epistemic aspect of writing with computer networks has long been discussed, the computer itself created a more collaborative atmosphere for the production of knowledge, which could promote more social interaction. Computers were quieter than typewriters so they could be arranged in a lab without creating a cacophony of individuals typing, and their arrangement could be configured so their monitors could be easily read by others besides the writer.

As more and more users gained access to computers, the use of the technology evolved similarly to the composition theory (process) underlying its usage. This evolutionary process can be further seen in how changes in the architecture of the Internet have changed how writers can collaborate. Designers of a computer lab change the level of interaction, for example, by clustering computers into pods instead of rows (Palmquist, Kiefer, Hartvigsen, & Goodlew, 1998). The growing importance of computer labs, as with word processing, reflected changes in composition pedagogy toward incorporating a more collaborative approach to writing.

Changes in the nature of the computer itself have also affected the writing process. Recently there has been a growing interest in laptops since they give the teacher even more flexibility in organizing a class (Warschauer, Turbee, & Roberts, 1996). Choosing laptops instead of desktop computers may also reflect differences in theory and pedagogy. Windschitl and Sahl (2002) found that decisions about implementing laptops rather than desktop computers reflected differences in the teachers' views about learning, in institutional views of good teaching, and in students' perceptions about the role of technologies in their lives. For example, the use of laptops allows students to move around more freely, increasing their ability to work in groups, which can increase the possibility of student interactions, although as Cuban (2006) warns, in practice, laptops may have little effect on teaching practices. Research has also indicated that laptop use can be distracting to students. In a study of laptop use at Carnegie Mellon University, Fay (2006) found that while students spent more time working when they had laptops, they did not always use their time effectively, and furthermore, sometimes became over-dependent on computers.

More recently teachers and researchers are beginning to examine Wi-Fi, which allows computers to connect to the Internet as easily from inside a classroom or café as a means of adding further flexibility to the composition classroom (Dean, Hochman, Hood, & McEachern, 2004). The growing availability of wireless communication allows users to escape the confines of a classroom and a computer lab to work anywhere there is access to a network (Dean et al.).

Wi-Fi allows students to access information from the Internet in response to something that was said in class. Although some teachers may find this distracting and feel they may lose control of their classes, the use of Wi-Fi can allow students to connect what is said in class to information outside of class at the precise moment it may do the most good. Others may find that the new mobility technology is frustrated by the nature of the spaces where the laptops are used. These changes in mobility can create new types of interconnections that will force changes in the design of buildings in which we learn (Mitchell, 2003).

One of the newest changes in word processing is the migration from computer-based word processing programs to Internet-based programs. Free online programs such as Google™ Docs & Spreadsheets *(docs.google.com)*, ZOHO Writer *(zohowriter.com)*, Writeboard™ *(www.writeboard.com)*, and thinkfree *(www.thinkfree.com)*, provide writers a basic word processing program that allows documents to be published either online or to a blog. As with email and blogging, students from anywhere in the world can collaborate on a single document.

These sites can free the writer from being tied to a particular computer or having to carry files around since files can be accessed from wherever a computer connected to the Internet can be found. New types of writing spaces like Wikis can also be used for students to collaborate. In connection with social bookmarking sites like del.icio.us *(http://del.icio.us)*, which allows individuals to share the URLs of all the websites they are using in their writing, these kinds of websites can change how writers can collaborate with each other or use peer review instead of having to work in the same physical space or exchange email back and forth.

Most interestingly for the global teaching of English, these websites, at the time this book was written, had no costs, which can lower the cost of access to the technologies. All of these websites reflect the growing role of the Internet in fostering new forms of collaboration among writers as well as new types of writing spaces and contexts. If these types of sites become more widely used, possible differences in the social context in which texts are created will become an important research topic.

Writing and Computer Networks

The development of the computer network, even when only situated within a room or across a college campus, also significantly influenced the writing process.

In a networked environment, knowledge and cognition are decentralized and ever widening as the network expands and as more people log on. Whereas using a word processing program alone at a computer mirrored the process orientation toward the isolated writer, networked classrooms reflected the realization that all writing was social. The rise of computer networking in the L2 composition class reflected another pedagogical shift toward more social interaction mediated through discourse, which differed from the forms of discourse found in the classroom. As Atkinson (2003a) argues, L2 writing research in the 1990s moved away from the more internally directed process model to a more socially situated approach where students wrote in a variety of social contexts.

This social approach to writing predated the development of computer networking. Bruffee (1983) and LeFevre (1987) had already critiqued traditional process-orientated approaches because they ignored this social aspect. Research on local-area-based writing, such as that found in the ENFI project (Batson, 1993; Kemp, 1993), championed the ideas advanced by these researchers that every aspect of the writing process was social in nature. Discussing a simple local area network (LAN) in a composition classroom, Langston and Batson (1990) used almost science fiction–like imagery of writers melding together over a network to describe the interaction of writers in a network.

These approaches to network-based writing paved the way for the development of software designed specifically to allow students to interact in the composition classroom, such as Daedalus® *(www.daedalus.com)* and CommonSpace (Bloch & Brutt-Griffler, 2001). These programs contained many of the features of the early stand-alone programs previously discussed but could better integrate the traditional features of process-based writing with the more social concerns of network-based writing. While these programs contained a variety of modules to support the phases of the writing process, their main advances were in facilitating the exchange of information and texts across these networks, both between student and student and student and teacher. Although these programs had technical and design problems that would either limit their usefulness or make them obsolete, they still represented an important shift in how writing and technology were viewed in a social context.

However, as with research on word processing, evidence that these social networks improved writing was elusive. Braine (1997) found evidence that L2 students wrote better essays on a LAN, a result he attributed to the ability of the computer network to create a more supportive environment, to give more authentic language contexts, and to provide varied and comprehensible language with real communicative value. However, these findings were not always consistent. In a later study, Braine (2001) found fewer positive results, which he attributed to the limited exposure the students had to using the network. As with earlier research, these sometimes conflicting findings illustrate that even small changes in the environment or in how the technology is implemented can cause major differences in the type of writing found.

Writing and the Internet

The nature of the Internet is such that it has been the most natural environment for this social-epistemic approach to composition teaching because the fundamental design of the Internet was to support collaboration (Berners-Lee, 2000). This connection furthered the evolutionary nature of the writing/ technology relationship in a way that began to resemble the idea of a social-epistemic form of rhetoric that had emerged as an alternative perspective on the writing process (Berlin, 1982). Berlin argued that in what he called a "New Rhetoric," "the message arises out of the interaction of the writer, language, reality, and the audience" (p. 775).

One factor that made the Internet such a powerful tool was the ease with which individuals could access and in many cases post information to the "read/write" web. The development of the Internet exponentially increased the number of people who could interact, far beyond what local networks could. As more and more people were able to access the Internet, the more useful the Internet became, which is the phenomenon referred to as Metcalf's law (Rheingold, 2003). It was not until the Internet became commonplace that this process could be dramatically extended beyond the classroom so that individuals could interact with communities of people all over the world sharing a common interest or problem (Rheingold, 1993).

From a social-epistemic perspective, the Internet facilitates the introduction of students to new "communities of practice" that allow them to search out knowledge in ways that had been difficult or impossible to access. Lankshear and Knobel (2003) believe that such epistemological changes can have a great effect on classroom practice. The greater emphasis on hypertext, the visual elements of a text, and the use of different forms of CMD have introduced multiple forms of literacy in the composition classroom. We have extensively used listservs and blogs, for example, as a means for students to ask questions, raise issues, and respond to each other whenever and wherever they want. The ability of the Internet to provide writers with a variety of types of literacies related to a specific context, or what I have been calling architecture, is consistent with the general ways in which literacy is viewed. Terms like *situated literacies* (Barton, Hamilton, & Ivanic, 2000) or *multiple literacies* (Heath, 1983) are used to discuss how the concept of authorship can shift in different writing environments.

Students need to negotiate multiple literacies as well as the multiple components of each form of literacy. As Kress (2003) argues, the shift from reading print texts to reading digital texts not only changes how the information is accessed but also how the texts are read and written. Because of the ease by which images can be inserted into a text, visual information can be more widely integrated into print texts. The ability to jump from one website to another by simply clicking on a link means that knowledge can be accumulated in chunks rather than in a purely linear process. Individuals have the ability to make their own connections in ways that best suit their purposes. By using this linking process, readers can accumulate the specific pieces of information they need and connect them in any way they want to. Lankshear and Knobel use the term *bricolage,* which refers to taking only something from the immediate environment to solve a problem, as a metaphor for the process of how knowledge is constructed online. The Internet provides users with a vast store of information from which the writer can choose and reconstruct in any way he or she wants.

The greatest impact of computer technology may be found in its ability to create various kinds of "push/pull" environments (Hagel & Brown, 2005) where some online resources are given to the students to use and others are placed in such a way that students can draw on them whenever they are needed. However, there are downsides as well; there are always "dead" links. Unfortunately, information that was used once may not necessarily be available the next time. As with every technology, there will be limitations to the ways it can be used.

Writing Hypertexts

Perhaps the best-known form of Internet writing is **hypertext,** a user interface for displaying documents that contain hyperlinks to other documents. When a hyperlink is selected, the computer displays the linked document that can be static (prepared and stored in advance) or dynamically generated (in response to user input). A well-constructed hypertext system can be used to access static collections of cross-referenced documents and interactive applications from anywhere with the help of a computer network like the Internet. The best-known implementation of hypertext is the World Wide Web.

Ted Nelson, an information technology pioneer, coined the term *hypertext* in 1963. The concept of hypertext is often credited to an earlier article by Vannevar Bush (1945), who proposed a "memex" by which all "books, records, and communications" can be stored and retrieved through "associative accessing." In 1960, Nelson proposed Xanadu®, a model that defined hypertext as nonsequential writing that can branch out to other texts to give readers choices in the information they want to access. Nelson wrote that hypertext would be powerful if it could point to absolutely anything. Every document would exist together in the same information space. (See Wikipedia for more on hypertext.)

Berners-Lee (2000) writes that he was inspired to design the World Wide Web by ideas about interconnectivity from these pioneers. Like many other aspects of these technologies, hypertext is not a completely new concept. It has frequently been said that the Jewish Talmud, with its myriad connections between texts, commentaries on the text, and commentaries on the commentaries, was the first hypertext. Although hypertext is most associated with the World Wide Web, its popularization could be attributed to how a hypertext creation program called HyperCard was bundled with Apple Macintosh computers even before the Internet became widely available. However, the development of the Internet greatly accelerated the growth of hypertext. It was not until Berners-Lee, as well as others, developed protocols to send hyperlinked information from one end user to another that the use of hypertext exploded.

The basic precepts of hypertext can also be found in traditional, print-based forms of writing. The importance of linking on the Internet has mirrored a growing awareness in composition theory of the importance of intertextuality by which all texts contain the essence of previous texts. At the same time, hypertext reduces the power of the author to control the choices the reader can make.

Hypertext can be seen as an extension of one of the primary features of literacy: the ability of texts to reference other texts, what is also known as *intertextuality*. In academic writing one of the important reasons for citations is that they provide the reader with the opportunity to find out more information about a topic than is contained in the paper. However, in print texts, the reader traditionally had to return to the library to find these materials. With hypertext, the materials may be only a click away.

However, the dominance of hypertext over traditional linear forms of literacy has never completely materialized perhaps because the technical difficulties have limited the number of potential authors. The linear, print-based novel has not been threatened by even the most acclaimed hypertext novels from authors such as Michael Joyce (e.g., *Afternoon, a Story, www.eastgate.com/catalog/Afternoon.html*) and Stuart Malthrop (e.g., *Victory Garden, www.eastgate.com/catalog/ VictoryGarden.html*). These forms of hypertext were designed to allow the reader the freedom to create his or her own story-lines. For Umberto Eco (1996), hypertext can be conceived as a detective story where readers have the ability to create their own story line. By giving the reader this freedom to enter and leave the text at any point, the author gives up the dominant position that authorship usually entails. However, this condition is not absolute since the amount of freedom is still limited by the number and type of links inserted.

Educators, including composition teachers, have also seen the value of hypertexts coming from the social construction-ist approaches to learning that reading and writing hypertexts entail. The mystery that results from moving from one link to another forces both the writers and the readers of hypertext to construct pathways through the interlinked texts. How they do this depends greatly on the background and needs of both the reader and the writer. The general relationship between the production and the consumption of knowledge has been explored in great depth in constructivist approaches to educa-tion (e.g., Shank & Cleary, 1995; Spivey, 1997; Spiro, Feltovich, Jacobsen, & Coulson, 1995; von Glaserfield, 1995). Constructiv-ism refers to how information is "constructed" differently by each individual, depending on backgrounds or interests (von Glaserfield). As Petraglia (1998) points out, for advocates of a constructivist learning environment, hypertext creates for the learner an authentic, information-rich environment that stresses both the connections between knowledge and the existence of a variety of perspectives on the same topic.

Both the creation and use of a hypertext produce different and sometimes more complex demands of the reader and writer than are found in traditional print media (Kress, 2003). The interaction of all of these elements makes hypertext design an excellent example of what Spiro et al. call an ill-structured knowledge domain. As the term indicates, making the decisions necessary in the design of a website cannot be regularized to the extent that it can be taught as a set of prescriptive rules; instead, design requires a process of exploration where designers have to use what Spiro et al. call "cognitive flexibility" to decide the most appropriate feature of design for the specific audience and in the specific context being addressed.

Hypertext has emerged as an important genre of writing that can be taught like any other genre. Kress argues that these various forms of multimodal discourse are not simply extensions of traditional forms of literacy but an emergent genre containing all the complexities related to the teaching of any genre. The types of skills developed in reading and writing hypertexts, however, are not simply limited to online writing. Spiro et al. argue that hypertexts make good models for developing the cognitive skills necessary for any form of writing. By giving up some of the control over how the text is read, the author cedes to the reader some of the decisions normally made in organizing and connecting texts. Hypertexts force the writer to consider what additional information an audience might want, as well as the best source for that information.

The same kinds of constructivist metaphors have been applied to reading hypertexts. Readers can easily leave the text via a link and go in any direction. Readers of hypertexts make decisions about which link to click on, are able to evaluate a variety of sources of information, and make connections between these different pieces of information in ways that differ from how print texts are read. As Charney (1994) argued, the nature of this writing space can cause problems both for the writer who must be able to predict the paths the readers might want to take and for the reader who must make decisions about which paths to follow and evaluate the sites he or she lands on.

Being able to "read" and "write" hypertexts is not simply an extension of reading and writing linear texts but may require the same type of formal teaching as that of traditional forms of reading. In the same way that reading and writing are linked, the ability to read hypertexts is linked to the ability to create them. Evaluating texts can be more complex in an Internet environment than in a print environment, in part because there are no established gatekeepers to screen what is published. Therefore, hypertexts often require a more critical perspective than is necessary with print texts.

Directly teaching the construction of hypertexts can be an important pedagogy for teaching students about both online and print-based forms of literacies. Johnson-Eilola (1997) argues that constructing hypertexts can empower students in a way traditional classroom assignments cannot that in turn can help them see the value of writing in a different way, which may be transferred to print-based writing. Lam (2000) also used the constructionist metaphor to argue that L2 writers can use the computer as a way of constructing alternative social networks and subject positions through the textual media (p. 479) in order to "renegotiate their identities (p. 461)" within the communities of practice to which they belong. Spiro et al. have argued that in working with students to use such ill-structured domains, traditional forms of teaching are not always effective. In order to understand the learning process in such areas, they argue for emphasizing the production or construction of knowledge over passive usage.

While hypertext may contribute to the development of all forms of writing, it still remains primarily an online form of discourse. Hypertext has the ability to, in Bolter and Grusin's (1999) terms, "remediate" the basic concepts of literacy, especially those aspects that may be different from other forms of communication. One clear difference is the greater skill necessary for evaluating hypertexts since there are no traditional gatekeepers to judge the texts and eliminate those of lesser quality. Stapleton (2005) found a great deal of variance in the quality and genre of websites students cited in their research papers. This variance could be due not only to the vast amount of information published online without having gatekeepers but also because many search engines the students tend to use, such as Google™, list websites in an order based on how much money the website owner has paid and not on the quality of the website.

Hypertext also extends the potential audience beyond the one addressed in the composition classroom. Because of the ability of hypertext and the Internet to facilitate online publishing, writers can use hypertext to create a "webfolio" of their writings that can be accessed by anyone at any time, thus forcing the writer to account for a wider variety of audiences with varying amounts of interest or understanding in the text. The unique qualities of hypertext have important implications for L2 composition teaching in that teaching hypertext becomes not simply a means of helping students become better writers in print but teaching web page design as its own genre.

Visual "Literacy"

Also important to hypertext is the visual nature of hypertextuality. Academic writing has always had a visual component for representing information through the use of graphs, charts, and diagrams (Tufte, 2003). The growing importance of hypertext as a writing environment, therefore, has also led to a renewed interest in what some call *visual literacy*. Although Kress (1999) is not comfortable with the use of the term *literacy* as a metaphorical extension of the traditional term applied to print text, he argues that the visual is displacing the central position of written language in communication. He sees these multimodal forms of literacy more as a genre that cuts across a variety of forms of literacy than a type of literacy in itself. The visual aspect of the text is only one of a number of possible non-text dimensions, including sound and video, which can be integrated into a hypertext. Lemke (2004) uses the term *multimedia literacy* to describe how all forms of literacy employ various visual and textual modes.

The visual nature of a web page can add a further dimension to the complications of reading and writing hypertext: The architecture of hypertext has allowed for the incorporation of a variety of colors, images, designs, backgrounds, and animations. The wide availability of images on the Web and the proliferation of graphics programs to create new images have increased the ease by which visual texts can be integrated with online print texts. The tremendous growth of bandwidth, moreover, has meant that images can be transported across the Web more easily, which has also increased their importance (Kress, 1999). In some online writing environments, creators of hypertexts can avail themselves of a wide variety of visual components, including images, colors, fonts, page designs, and textual layouts to integrate with their texts.

The visual nature of hypertext has raised many issues related to both reading and writing. Since text and images can be placed in a variety of positions in relationship to each other, the meaning of a text can vary depending on the relationship between the text and the visual elements that accompany it. Trupe (2002) points out that the choice of colors, fonts, backgrounds, and layouts should reflect decisions as to what information is to be featured and what information can be subordinated. These decisions may facilitate, hinder, or affect how the written text is read and understood (Kress, 1998), which a designer might use as a way of challenging the reader. Siegal (1996) argues that choosing images, as well as colors and design features, is not simply a matter of finding out what might appeal to the audience but also of considering to what extent the audience is willing to be challenged.

The pedagogical implications of this relationship between visual and textual literacy are complex. An instructor cannot expect every student in L2 composition courses to navigate the Internet without extensive training (Crosby, 2004). Many still feel uncomfortable reading large amounts of text on a screen as exemplified by the difficulty of online literature to become well accepted. This fact has important implications for the design of hypertexts. Similarly, the ability to click rapidly from one text to another can be confusing for some readers. The differences between reading digital and print texts, as well as the differences across different kinds of digital texts, can challenge what teachers traditionally tell students about such rhetorical features as organization patterns or writing style.

The importance of visual literacy can be another challenge for both teachers and students. Many years ago, Rudolf Arnheim (1969) lamented that children first learn to communicate through art, but after they learn to read and write, art is relegated to a secondary position in the school curricula, a situation that has not changed much. Visual literacy is rarely stressed in the same way as reading and writing print texts, and, as a result, it is not surprising that few composition teachers have experience with visual literacy. Hawisher and Selfe (2004) have found that many composition teachers have been educated only in print literacies and have received little training in using digital literacies.

The visual nature of these digital literacies can also impact the language learning process. As Lemke argues, the meanings of words and images in a multimodal environment change as the interrelationships between them change. These changes may either help or hinder the language learning process, but in either case, the process of learning and the content of what is learned change. Lemke calls this process "multiplying meaning" (p. 77), since the possibility for meaning grows exponentially as the reader has to consider more features of the hypertext to make sense of it.

Despite its growing importance, hypertext is far from having the status of academic writing in the university context. Although many academic papers, including dissertations, are being published online, few of these works attempt to take full advantage of their hypertextual nature. Few purely online journals have the status of print journals, and many of them retain the look and feel of their print counterparts, perhaps only adding a few links to essentially what is a traditional academic paper. Some journals in the field of composition, such as *Kairos (http://english.ttu.edu/kairos/)* and *Language Learning and Technology (http://llt.msu.edu),* have attempted to explore alternative forms of academic writing and publishing in the online format.

In the constructionist learning paradigm, the complexity of all these factors gives great importance to students' thinking about all these elements while designing their own web pages toward becoming competent users of hypertext. Teachers may, then, want to consider teaching multimodal writing for its own sake as any other form of writing. Having to make choices in their own designs helps students better understand the choices made in the hypertexts they encounter on a daily basis. Thus, integrating hypertexts into the L2 writing curriculum may not only be of value in itself as an aid in learning to write but also in teaching how to read on the Internet.

Computer-Mediated Discourse (CMD)

Computer-mediated discourse has been described as the "killer-app" that made the Internet as popular as it is today. The primary goal for the creation of the Internet was to allow individuals to talk with each other across a decentralized network that could not be disrupted by an attack on a single node. Over the years, CMD has been one of the strongest agents for fostering interconnectivity. CMD can take "a community of practice" and transform it into a "network of practice" (Brown & Duguid, 2000), which can allow those who may be on the "peripheral" of a community of practice to easily connect to those at the center of the community without having to be in the same place. This can reduce differences in status that can exist in these communities (Kiesler, Siegel, & McGuire, 1984).

CMD as a Writing Space

Because of its usefulness in linking both teachers and students from all over the world, CMD has had a great importance in language learning. Herring (2001) defines CMD as "the communication produced when human beings interact with one another by transmitting messages via networked computers (p. 612). CMD has traditionally been divided into two areas: synchronous discourse and asynchronous discourse.

Synchronous discourse refers to interactions in real time that use a variety of technologies including chat-rooms, multiple user domains such as MUDs and MOOs, instant message computer programs (ICQ), and Internet Relay Chats (IRC). MOOs such as Tapped-In® *(http://tappedin.org)* are used by teachers to form communities to exchange ideas or to meet with students. Newer technologies, such as Elluminate® *(http://elluminate.com),* can integrate chat, voice, and video. Virtual worlds, such as Second Life® *(http://secondlife.com),* can create interactive three-dimensional visual environments, similar to game environments, where classes can be taught and individuals can publish their own texts or interact with others using written language.

Synchronous forms of CMD may more resemble oral language and assist in the development of a student's oral language. CMD has traditionally been a form of written language. New technologies allow for both oral and written forms to be used simultaneously (e.g., Elluminate®). The growing popularity of podcasts has given a new importance to oral modes of delivery. Nevertheless, the use of CMD gives the L2 writer practice in writing in English and an opportunity to use alternate forms of literacy in which they may be more proficient. Moreover, the use of CMD can provide students with directed practice in using different types of language. Even a simple email message can exhibit a variety of different forms and registers of language, depending on its purpose. By illustrating these differences in a context students already know, they may be able to better see how language use can vary in different rhetorical situations.

As with other technologies, CMD can have a dual purpose in the composition classroom. On the one hand, it is an alternative writing environment where students can express their thoughts and publish them online for their classmates, and even complete strangers, to read. This makes it a form of literacy in itself (Warschauer, 2000). On the other hand, CMD can be a tool for use in the writing process; one of the most popular ways has been to provide a space for students to collaborate in developing their ideas throughout the writing process (e.g., Weasonforth, Biesenbach-Lucas, & Meloni, 2002).

CMD can be used in a variety of purposes: (1) as a means of extending the class time of a face-to-face class, which is sometimes referred to as a technologically enhanced class, (2) as a substitute for class time, which is referred to as a hybrid class (Sands, 2002), or (3) as the primary means of interaction in a distance learning course, which is the most controversial one. Despite the controversies, L2 composition teachers in both ESL and EFL contexts have shown great interest in CMD because it gives language learners a different kind of writing space with different cognitive and social dimensions. Weigle and Nelson (2004) found that online tutoring provided a better opportunity to use a variety of strategies and greater flexibility in roles of the tutor and tutee. Other research has shown that synchronous discourse may aid in the language learning process (Yuan, 2003) or in the ability of the participants to negotiate meaning (Toyoda & Harrison, 2002). The Internet may, therefore, give students who feel uncomfortable in the classroom or in face-to-face situations an alternative context where they may feel more at ease and productive. In cyberspace, students who may lack fluency in writing are given extra time to compose their questions as ideas. Students who feel uncomfortable or constrained by the classroom setting may feel liberated in cyberspace where some of the classroom-based constraints may be lifted (Bloch, 2004).

The initial appeal of CMD for composition teaching may have come from how users could produce a tremendous amount of written text when using CMD. In his study in a French classroom of the use of Daedalus InterChange®, a composition software program that can be used for discussing and the exchanging of papers, Kern (1995) found that the language students produced contained aspects of written language, such as a preference for certain syntactic forms usually found in written language and a higher lexical density, as well as certain aspects of oral language, such as a familiar style and direct interpersonal address.

CMD may be especially useful for types of writing that emphasize critical thinking. For example, bringing the context online can change the types of critical thinking that students display. The ability of writers to distance themselves from their audiences changes the interactions writers can display. Kern argues that the online discussions are especially effective for expressing multiple perspectives and voicing differences. CMD creates different learning environments, too. Mynard (2003) argued that L2 students demonstrated high levels of learner initiative in the chat room, which she attributed to the less-threatening nature of the CMD environment.

Therefore, CMD has the potential to empower writers in many writing contexts. Issues relating to time and space of the interactions decenter the writing experience in ways that cannot be replicated in the traditional classroom. With CMD, teachers have reduced roles or different roles than they could probably not perform in the face-to-face classroom. The result of this is both liberating and challenging. Faigley (1992) argues that in comparison to face-to-face discourse, online discourse can be chaotic because of lack of any central authority. This chaos is liberating for some students who may feel restricted in classroom situations, particularly those who feel it is inappropriate to voice their opinions, ask questions, or especially take opposing viewpoints. Faigley says that CMD "allows mute voices to speak and gives opportunities for resistance to the dominant discourses of the majority" (p. 199).

CMD creates opportunities for students to use alternative voices. Warschauer's (1999) study of the use of CMD to preserve Hawaiian languages illustrates how CMD can be used to give voice to those with these traditionally "mute voices." Warschauer et al. (1996) found CMD could empower the language learner by giving him or her greater control over the learning process by creating more equitable relationships and providing the student with a unique space to develop thinking and writing skills. The ability to talk in real time to one person or a group of people located anywhere has a great fascination for many students. CMD, therefore, is not simply a substitute for face-to-face interaction, but requires a different perspective on the nature of the conversation and the role of both teacher and student.

Much attention today has been given to the social concepts of online writing. CMD has been recognized for creating virtual communities for social and political purposes (Rheingold, 1993), personal interests (Baym, 1995), and professional interests (Aycock & Buchignani, 1995). In my study of a Chinese Usenet group, I saw how passionately the participants felt about accusations about spying they considered racist and how they used the Usenet group to organize a response (Bloch, 2004a). In my composition classes, I have found that students often produce more fluent and complex evaluative writing online than when given these kinds of assignments.

CMD can have a variety of uses in the composition classroom. It can be a means of communication where students can ask and answer questions, it can extend the classroom discourse beyond the time and space of the face-to-face class, or it can replace certain or all aspects of the classroom discussion.

There are cognitive elements in the writing process that are also affected by the use of CMD. Writers at all levels who need to take more time composing their ideas may prefer asynchronous forms of discourse that allow them to compose at their own pace, a concept that is reminiscent of process writing (Elbow, 1981). As the level of the writer increases and students are better able to clearly express their ideas in writing, issues such as fluency become less important as CMD is more integrated as part of the writing process—for example, as a space to discuss ideas or as a way of creating texts that other students can use in their own writing.

CMD also provides the composition teacher with a great deal of flexibility in creating different contexts for writing. CMD can be used in a variety of individual, pair, and group situations, providing learners with the opportunities to use and practice writing, but in a much different social context. A number of factors have been identified as unique to CMD, such as the distance between reader and writer (Sproull & Kiesler, 1991) or the ability for the user to take on an alternative persona (Turkle, 1995).

As a writing space, CMD complicates both our conception of the nature of writing and the nature of language, which is consistent with new approaches to teaching composition. In post-process approaches to composition teaching, it is more difficult to pin down what constitutes "writing" (Olson, 1999). Should online chats be considered writing, or just different from traditional forms of writing? Should email writing be held to the same rules as print texts (Crystal, 2001)? Thinking about CMD differently allows some students who may have been marginalized by traditional classroom discourse a powerful means of expressing themselves.

CMD, such as chat or email, exemplify what Olson (1995) calls the more dialogic, exploratory, and personal ways of writing that predominate in post-process approaches. Writing online problematizes traditional concepts of authorship, originality, and textual ownership. These issues, as Atkinson (2003b) argues, can be problematic in the L2 composition classroom. Having such an alternative space can help "students trust their voices and gain experience in formulating their ideas clearly as they connect to the ideas of others" (Blanton, 1994, p. 122). In a class where academic forms of literacy are dominant, alternative forms of CMD can be incorporated not only as aids in the social and cognitive development of the students' academic literacy but also as a means of helping them gain these voices as authors. Therefore, CMD can be viewed as a genre or type of writing that can be explicitly taught like other forms of writing. Each form of online writing presents the same challenges as other print-based forms of literacies. Although many students are today well-versed in a variety of forms of CMD, others can be encouraged to think about the Internet as a place where they can be a writer after they have completed their writing courses.

Blogging in a Second Language

Chapter 1 mentioned how new forms of CMD, such as weblogs, may be able to foster new forms of online authorship. Weblogs have emerged as one of the most important forms of CMD currently available to the composition teacher. Blogs have been identified as a powerful means of fostering student literacy and exploring ideas, giving blogs an important epistemological function in the writing process (Bloch & Crosby, 2005). Blood (2000), for example, describes this epistemological function she finds in her own writing. As she wrote her blogs and found links, she began to discover new interests. She writes about blogging:

> This profound experience may be most purely realized in the blog-style weblog. Lacking a focus on the outside world, the blogger is compelled to share his world with whomever is reading. He may engage other bloggers in conversation about the interests they share. He may reflect on a book he is reading, or the behavior of someone on the bus. He might describe a flower that he saw growing between the cracks of a sidewalk on his way to work. Or he may simply jot notes about his life: what work is like, what he had for dinner, what he thought of a recent movie. These fragments, pieced together over months, can provide an unexpectedly intimate view of what it is to be a particular individual in a particular place at a particular time. (para. 21)

Blood's comments about her experiences echo the idea of blogging changing authorship. Her list of possible rhetorical purposes, contexts, and relationships with readers places much more emphasis on the choices a blogger can make.

In all these ways, CMD provides a technology for incorporating multiple literacies and multiple forms of discourse into the classroom. However, unless teachers recognize that these literacies can differ from classroom-based discourse, there is a danger that they may simply try to replicate what they would do in a classroom with online writing

(Fanderclai, 1995). Such replication will almost inevitably fail, not because online interactions are inherently inferior to face-to-face ones, but because the differences between them are not sufficiently understood.

Despite the advantages and the tremendous popularity of CMD, teachers may encounter resistance to using some forms of CMD in the classroom. Many students simply seem to prefer face-to-face interactions. I have found that when students have a choice between being tutored online or face to face, they will overwhelmingly choose the face-to-face context. When asked why, many students have remarked that they simply prefer being in the same room as the instructor or peer reviewer (Bloch & Brutt-Griffler, 2001). For others, the resistance may come from a discomfort of having to type quickly. In group contexts, students sometimes feel that they cannot type fast enough to ask questions or read fast enough to keep up with the scrolling text.

In both asynchronous and synchronous discourse, the freedom found in online discussions can also cause problems both inside and outside the classroom. Perhaps the most well known of these problems is "flaming," which refers to the sending of highly inflammatory messages that likely would not have been sent in a face-to-face context. Sometimes these annoyances can escalate because of the lack of traditional safeguards that may exist in the classroom. Janangelo (1991) argues that technology can also provide a space for the suppression of dissident voices. Janangelo tells an anecdote about an L2 student who had criticized her American classmates and as a result was continually sexually harassed on an online class bulletin board.

Another potential annoyance are "trolls," who go online primarily to annoy other members of the group. One of the most well-known examples of this kind of harassment can be found in Julian Dibble's (1998) article "A Rape in Cyberspace," which describes an occurrence of a virtual "rape" and how it upset the women in the online community. (Tapped In®, a leading chat space for education, instituted a feature that allows participants to shut out unwanted guests, which itself is an interesting example, along with spam filters and programs to block pop-up ads, of how technology can respond to the problems it creates.) The reality of these kinds of incidents can conflict with the principles regarding free expression that many on the Internet hold dear. Dibble found this conflict in the often agonizing decisions that participants in the blog where the "rape" took place had to make to ensure this kind of behavior could not be repeated.

Weblogs became popular around 1997. The word *weblog* was coined by Jorn Barger, but began to explode in 1999 with the introduction of free or inexpensive web blogging services (e.g., Blogger, LiveJournal™, mo'time™) that allow blogs to be set up by people with little technical background either for free or for a small fee (Doctorow et al., 2002). In the last few years, blogging has exploded all over the world in a variety of languages. The number of blogs has exploded in many fields, especially journalism, where they have become an alternative source of information in opposition to the growing concentration of the media. They have allowed people on the periphery of public life to participate for the first time in gathering and disseminating information that in the past was controlled only by the established media (Gilmour, 2004). They have become a worldwide phenomenon, written in many languages and providing readers with insights into worlds and issues they could not see elsewhere (Rheingold, 2003).

A blog "is a web page that contains brief, discrete hunks of information called posts," which are arranged in reverse chronological order (Doctorow et al., 2002, p.1). Blogging cannot be viewed as static, but one that is continually developing in much the way other forms of literacy are developing, although probably more quickly. As Gurak, Antonijevic, Johnson, Ratliff, & Reyman (2004) write about the complications of defining blogging:

> At this point in their development, blogs are best described as web sites that are updated frequently, most often with links to other sites and commentary on the other sites' content. The content of blogs combine musings, memories, jokes, reflections on research, photographs, rants, and essays,

though we would argue that it is not the nature of the content that defines it. Blogs can be devoted to only one topic, or they can reflect what the author is interested in at any given time. They can have one author—authors of blogs are known as 'bloggers'—or multiple authors. What characterizes blogs are their form and function: all posts to the blog are time-stamped with the most recent post at the top, creating a reverse chronological structure governed by spontaneity and novelty. (Definition of weblogs section, para 3)

Herring, Kouper, Schiedt, & Wright (2004) identify three types of blogs: (1) *filter* blogs, which express external content such as opinions, (2) *personal* blogs, which express the blogger's inner thoughts, and (3) *knowledge* blogs, which contain information related to the course or discipline. For the writing classroom, the proliferation of online blogs has been seen as one way to foster publishing online to reach out to a wider audience (Lowe & William, 2004). As Mortensen and Walker (2002) assert, blogs straddle the line between the process of writing for publication and writing for oneself. As mentioned earlier, there are some bloggers who want to write for a large audience and even get paid for it, but others who write only for themselves or a small circle of friends or classmates. Nevertheless, all these blogs are published in the blogosphere for anyone to read.

Like websites, blogs can be designed to foster connectivity. The social nature of blogging is one of the latest manifestations of the collaborative nature of writing on the Internet. As Berners-Lee (2004) puts it, blogs are a way to have a conversation with other people. Terms such as *watchblogging* and *mobblogging,* both of which refer to the ability of individuals to share information at any time and at any place, are indicative of how this collaborative nature can be viewed as a new form of participatory democracy (Rheingold, 2003). This democratic interaction has been seen in countries such as the United States where bloggers have raised political issues that the mainstream media ignored or in countries like China where blogs have been used to expose issues the government has tried to repress. Blogging has emerged in countries like China and Iraq (Pax, 2003) where there are strong political undercurrents that cannot be expressed in the mainstream media. This role is not a new one in the history of rhetoric. Berlin (1990) wrote that in times when power relationships are changing, it is not a coincidence that new forms of rhetoric emerge.

As with hypertext, the idea of community in the blogosphere is fostered by the ability of one blog to be linked to other blogs or other web pages; however, they can also be "pulled" or aggregated by readers onto a site like Bloglines.com, which allows readers to access their favorite blogs and see if anything new has been posted. Sites like Bloglines.com can also be used to archive favorite blogs in a way that can be used to create a personal knowledge space. Technologies such as RSS (Rich Site Summary or Really Simple Solution) are used to broadcast when a new posting has been made. These types of applications allow both people and information to be connected in new ways.

There are other types of sites that also allow users to collect information that could later be shared in writing assignments. Social networking sites, such as del.icio.us, allow readers to share their pieces of information, in this case their favorite websites, with others who might also be interested in the same topic. Search engines like Technorati™ can locate blogs either by author, subject, or topic. Teachers and students, for example, can subscribe to each other's blogs so that they are notified whenever someone posts, although there are always privacy issues involved. Blogs can also contain long *blogrolls* that list the designer's favorite blogs and websites, although seldom with any annotation to guide the reader. Not all of these technologies are unique to blogging, but what is unique is how they have been combined to form a vast network of, to borrow the title from Dave Weinberger's (2003) book, *Small Pieces Loosely Joined*. These sites can connect the vast number of blogs available on the Internet to allow readers and writers to interact in ways not available with print texts or even with other forms of CMD.

The integration of images into blogs, which had required more programming knowledge than necessary for setting up the blogs, has been dealt with in the same ways. Photo-sharing websites like Hello™ *(www.hello.com/)* or Flickr™ *(www.flickr.com)* can be used to post images, which can then be pulled to the blog. Other technologies can be used by authors to find who has cited their blogs. Bloggers can add code using a program such as BlogThis to post the blog they are reading to their own blog. Flickr™ allows storage of photos so they can be easily shared and transferred from online albums into blogs.

For many advocates or "evangelicals" for blogging, weblogs have emerged just when some have felt that the Internet "fron-tier" has limited the spirit of creativity and collaboration that has marked it since its beginnings (King, Grinter, & Pickering, 1997). This enthusiasm for blogging as a new form of literacy has interesting parallels in the history of American literacy. As Graff (1987) argues, literacy in the 19th century was con-cerned with the education of the masses for the purpose of perpetuating the dominant norms and values of the society. Blogging has also been seen by its advocates as a mass move-ment with a major focus on the spread of democracy and political involvement, which can promote what has been called "Extreme Democracy" because it can bypass traditional gatekeepers.

One of the interesting questions that has arisen in the debate over blogging is the degree to which it can affect the ability of writers to publish their work and have others be able to read what they have written. Graff has argued that there has always been an attempt by the dominant authorities to con-trol who has access to literacy. While blogging has often been seen as beyond the control of individual authorities, recent controversies over control by U.S. media companies such as Google™ and Yahoo® to block sites in countries where the government feels threatened by them have challenged the openness of blogging.

Control over blogging can also be maintained intentionally or unintentionally by controlling access to the Internet. In a study of Internet access in China, Bu (2004) found significant differences in Internet usage between most urban areas and more rural areas. In a country such as China the control over access is an important factor in the battle over what information can and cannot be viewed. While the digital divide may still exist in some areas, the simplicity of relative inexpensiveness of the Internet has allowed it to become a worldwide phenomenon (Negroponte, 1995).

Blogging, as with other forms of CMD, has also played an important role in changing the power balance on the Internet. While the digital divide is often thought about in terms of access, there are other factors such as gender. Changes in technology over the years have also changed the role of gender on the Internet. The growth of email and blogging has increased the number of women using the Internet. In a study by the Pew Internet and American Life Project (Fallows, 2005), it was found that there were differences between how men and women used the Internet and their attitudes toward the technology. Women tended to use the Internet more for personal interactions, such as sending email, but they were less interested in the technology itself. Men spent more time looking for information. However, there were a number of other factors, such as the amount of time spent online, where the differences are small. Research has indicated that blogs are predominately more often created by women and by a wide margin (Herring et al., 2004); women have been shown to find CMD most useful in establishing and maintaining social relationships. Recent statistics showing that the largest number of blogs are written in Japanese illustrate ways in which English has lost its domination of the Internet.

The nature of the postings and interactions can change dramatically, depending on whether an email list, a threaded discussion board, or blogs are used. Such differences in CMD architecture can also affect the willingness of the students to go through the steps needed to access the postings. This result seems inevitable given that posting to a listserv is like sending email, which people use primarily to communicate with others. Blogging, on the other hand, may be more effective for publishing more polished texts, which could result from the stronger sense of authorship attached to blogging. Teachers need to choose from among these different forms and match them to the types of assignments they create.

These differences are not absolute and may change as the technology changes. Both the use of blogs and listservs can be affected by technological changes in terms of how information can be imported to the Internet. The use of cell phones, for example, to post blogs or send email retains the reading component but not necessarily the writing component. These changes may not greatly affect the nature of the discussion, but they might affect their role in the writing development of the student.

These continual changes raise new pedogogical questions for teachers. Some of the questions have no definite answers: What are the new technologies? What kinds of interaction do they best foster? How can they be best used? What role can they play personally, socially, and politically in both the classroom and the society? The potential confusion over what blogs are, how they can be used, what effect they have on the writing process, and in what direction they will develop can cause problems for writing teachers.

Despite the popularity of blogging, some have argued that the introduction of blogging is not such a radical departure. Grohol (2002) argues that blogs are nothing more than "glorified discussion forums" ("Everything Unique Is Something Old Repositioned," para. 6). As has been found with many other forms of technology, this similarity is the inevitable consequence of not being able to conceptualize using the technology in new and different ways. Herring et al. (2004) argue that in their current state of development, blogs often resemble other forms of print and digital texts.

The role of CMD as a replacement for classroom discussion has been criticized largely because it lacks the intimacy of personal interaction. Noble (1998) ridicules the notion that online interactions can ever be personal, referring to them as part of a process of "drawing the halls of academe into the age of automation" (para. 1). Others have argued that CMD can create a more intimate space between reader and writer. Dreyfus (2001) argues that virtual communities can encourage a passionate commitment that is often discouraged in traditional contexts. Studies of these virtual communities have shown, in fact, that they often become a place for expressing deeply held beliefs. Therefore, great care must be taken both in making definitive judgments about how these technologies should be used and in listening to the judgments of others. As with other forms of technology, the answers to these questions will ultimately depend on how they fit in with how writing is taught in the classroom.

Corpus Linguistics and the Teaching of Grammar

All the technologies discussed thus far have been imported from outside the field of CALL and then adapted for the composition classroom. One technology that has been discussed within the domain of applied linguistics and second language learning is *concordancing,* or in broader terms, *corpus linguistics.* The use of concordancing programs reflects a growing interest in the use of authentic discourse rather than decontextualized invented sentences. Traditional approaches to grammar teaching that use decontextualized and isolated single sentences to focus on one discrete grammar point are not necessarily compatible with the need for understanding both the use and variation of language across and within different genres. Often these invented sentences are based only on the intuition of the materials writer, which Sinclair (1997) argues may not be suitable for understanding usage in actual communication.

Even examples of authentic discourse may not be able to capture the variations within or between genres. Concordancing can allow individual sections of papers to be examined in order to understand possible variations within the paper. Concordancing has also allowed researchers and material designers to examine large number of examples, from which a more nuanced understanding of the usage or meaning often can be gleaned. Single examples may be based on assumptions that may not hold up to a statistical analysis of large samples that concordancing can supply. Hyland (2003) suggests a number of activities where students can examine the meanings of specific words across different genres and writing types. These statistics can be used to complement other ways of studying the use of even discrete items (e.g., Harwood, 2006). As will be discussed in more detail in Chapter 5, concordancing programs can be given to students or adapted for student-specific needs so that they can become investigators and not just consumers (e.g., Lee & Swales, 2006; Yoon & Hirvela, 2004).

A concordancing program is a technology that allows the user to access a sample collection of sentences from a larger group of texts, which is referred to as a *corpus,* according to a predetermined set of criteria. A concordancer can be a program or Web-based interface that allows the user to search the corpus. The criteria for searching the corpus can be a word, a syntactical phrase, or a concept.

Corpus linguistics has traditionally been used in linguistics and the humanities for creating frequency lists (e.g., Academic Word List, *www.vuw.ac.n2/lals/research/awl/*) or studying such works as the Bible or Shakespeare. More recently, it has been used for the development of dictionaries such as the *Longman Dictionary of Contemporary English* and for the development of teaching materials (Hewings & Hewings, 2002; Leech, 1997; Simpson-Vlach & Leicher, 2000; Thurston & Candlin, 2002). Its importance in linguistics and ESL has greatly increased with the development of the Internet, which has simplified the use of concordancing programs and widened accessibility.

Concordancing is one of the latest attempts to incorporate technology into the teaching of grammar in the composition classroom. Since technology was first introduced into the L2 composition classroom, teachers have been fascinated with the possibility of using software to correct grammar errors and help students in general with developing their writing style. Moran (2003) found that there has been a great hope among teachers that computers could relieve the drudgery associated with grammar teaching and correction, as well as with composing and revising. Programs such as GRAMMATIK or Editor5 (Thiesmeyer & Thiesmeyer, 1990) were used to help students correct grammar errors outside the classroom although the "errors" addressed were often limited and occasionally incorrectly identified. Large-scale programs such as Writer's Workbench (Smith, Kiefer, & Gingrich, 1984; Reid & Findlay, 1986) provided students, for example, with data about sentence length and word frequency against benchmarks of papers incorporated into the program.

Teachers hoped that this seemingly "objective" data from a computer program would better motivate students to revise their papers. However, as has often been the case with technology, the practical value of the program never matched its expectations. Early attempts at using programs to catch low-level grammar errors were either over hyped or useless (Kemp, 1992). In a review of Writer's Workbench, for example, Day (1988) found that it could provide some useful advice but was not a cure-all for grammar or style problems, a general attitude that reflected the conclusion that while spell-checking might be a useful technology, technology was not the answer for student problems with grammar and style.

The ineffectiveness of early technologies led to a negative attitude toward the use of technology in the teaching of grammar by teachers. As Kemp has pointed out, these software programs only utilized the current traditional approaches to writing (cited in Hawisher, 1994) that emphasized writing style over content, as opposed to the process and post-process theories. As the current traditional approach came under greater attack from process-oriented theorists, many in composition teaching considered using technology for teaching grammar a waste of money, hoping instead that software, such as the integrated writing programs previously discussed, could be used for higher-level functions, such as invention. The lack of meaningful results, as well as paradigmatic shifts in the teaching of composition, greatly reduced the interest in using technology for the teaching of grammar. However, in L2 composition teaching, interest remained in the approaches these technologies were attempting to use.

It can be argued that the growing interest in concordancing in L2 composition teaching reflects pedagogical shifts in how grammar is taught. Kennedy (1998) argues these shifts reflect a growing interest in the context of language learning rather than simply the isolated forms, which includes the usage of specific lexical and grammatical items, their variations, and their frequencies.

Since the primary goals of corpus linguistics have been to find new ways to describe language and to compare different genres or registers, it fits well with the teaching of genre and the related questions about grammar and vocabulary use. For example, there has been a growing interest in integrating corpus linguistics into the study of the rhetorical context of a paper (e.g., Hewings & Hewings, 2002; Hyland, 1998; Hyland & Tie, 2004; Lee & Swales, 2006). Lee and Swales attempted to integrate concordancing into an advanced-level L2 composition course by helping students learn how to use concordancing on their own.

Understanding these relationships between the choices writers make about syntax and lexicon and the rhetorical intent of the paper is important for understanding the rhetorical purpose of the writer and the rhetorical context of the writing. Extensive studies on the role of rhetoric in academic writing have shown that academic texts are not simply a clear and logical presentation of facts or data, as had been argued for hundreds of years, but are all really a set of arguments wherein the writer tries to convince the reader that the research is significant, the data is accurate, the explanations are plausible, and the conclusions are important.

Research in the social construction of academic texts has shown that this "rhetorical turn" (Simons, 1990) involves writers making careful rhetorical choices designed to win the allegiance of the reader to the claims the writer has made (Bazerman, 1988; Gilbert & Mulkay, 1984; Latour, 1988; Latour & Woolgar, 1986; Myers, 1990). Hyland (2003b) states that genre-based instruction should increase the students' "explicit awareness (p. 22). of the language and conventions of "expert texts," or what has been called the "local knowledge" (Geertz, 1983) of the writing context. Hyland's (1998) study of hedging and Hunston's (2000) study of evaluation illustrate the importance of concordancing use to study word choice in these rhetorical decisions, reflecting what Hopper (1998) calls the interaction between the grammatical and rhetorical manifestations in a given piece of discourse.

To understand how grammar choices emerge from rhetorical contexts, Hopper argues that linguists have to study the regularities of language in these rhetorical contexts rather than concentrate only on isolated sentences. Rather than simply finding a program to correct mistakes or to tutor the student in learning discrete points, concordancing programs can help students develop an intuition about grammar, particularly with how grammar can be seen in actual rhetorical contexts instead of as artificially isolated sentences, what Johns (1994) refers to as "data-driven learning." Instead of learning rules, the learner can develop a *metadiscourse* about the language and how it can be used. Concordancing software does not provide users with "correct" or "incorrect" answers, and sometimes it provides no answer at all. Students might feel frustrated by this ambiguity, but simply obtaining answers is not necessarily the strength of concordancing. Concordancing is best used in developing the intuition of the user to make judgments about appropriate usage. As Frodesen and Holton (2003) argue, the "overt and systematic teaching of language forms can help students use their own intuition well" (p. 144). Hyland (2002a) suggests that it is important for students to understand how rhetorical features can vary across genres according to the different purposes writers have, their different assumptions about their audiences, and the different kinds of interactions they desire to have, which is a methodology that concordancing software can provide.

The explicit teaching of grammar and vocabulary as part of the genre-based approaches inevitably includes a discussion of the grammatical items that are appropriate within and across different forms of different genres. It is central, for example, for the teaching of genre to develop in students their knowledge of the language being used through the examination of expert texts (Hyland, 2003b). As Hyland (2003a) has said, genre pedagogies need to explain to students how to manipulate the lexico-grammatical patterns of usage for their own communicative purposes. In this way, the student can begin to gain an understanding of the relationship between grammar, lexicon, and rhetoric.

The Systemic View of Technology

This chapter has addressed a variety of individual technologies that could be useful in the composition classroom. However, in reality, technologies are usually used not in isolation but as part of collective systems. As Haas (1999) argues, these different technologies must be considered interconnected and integrated. A student may be able to write a paper on a computer, send it to peers or teachers over the network, discuss it using synchronous or asynchronous forms of discourse, use a concordancing program to help make decisions about grammar usage, and then post the paper on a personal web page or in a blog to gain a wider audience. As with other issues in the use of technologies, this integration brings additional challenges for both the teacher and student.

The use of technology in composition classrooms must also be integrated into the development of composition theories, as was discussed earlier. Every technology not only requires complimentary technologies but also complementary composition theories before successful implementation and use. The introduction of web page design required the development of tools that simplified the coding process.

As a result, the use of technologies must also be continually revised as the technology itself develops. This development can be seen in the effects of changes in screen layout, screen size, and the location and arrangement of computers. Computer hardware has changed as memory and processing speed have dramatically increased and monitors have become larger with better resolution. However, at times, change never came. One of the most notable examples has been the tremendous increase in the amount of paper still used in digital environments (Brown

& Duguid, 2000), which may indicate that switching between the printed page and the computer screen is not obsolete. Students who are not familiar with the computer may also find using paper to be preferable (Haas, 1996).

This process of systemic interaction can be illustrated by examining how a process, such as revision, can be affected by the interaction of these technologies by looking at the debate over whether teacher comments affect student writing and how the context of the comments can affect how the student uses them (Goldstein, 2004). As previously mentioned, the connectedness of computers and networks has had a dramatic effect on how students produce papers and how they interact with their potential readers. This debate has been a controversial issue in L2 writing since it has been difficult for the research to take into account all the factors that affect revision: whether the student uses the comments to revise, the nature of the comments themselves, and the context in which the revisions are taught—that is, how much classroom or tutorial time is used for discussing the grammatical points the student is being asked to revise.

The use of these technologies for commenting may affect older controversies regarding whether such teacher commenting is effective (Ferris, 1999, 2004; Truscott, 1996, 1999) since the debate has focused only on paper-and-pencil comments, and this now may need to be updated in response to the introduction of newer online approaches. Online commenting has long been thought to be a part of the social context of writing, both in education and in business. The second generation of computer programs designed specifically for writing classes, such as CommonSpace, featured ways for teachers to type comments in columns alongside the text. Commercial word processing programs like Microsoft Word would later develop their own comment functions that helped make programs like CommonSpace obsolete. Here too architectural changes to the program have affected how the program could be used.

In the earlier versions of Microsoft Word, the comments appeared on the screen when the cursor passed over the piece of text the comment was linked to, but when the paper was printed out, the comments appeared at the end of the text so the link was lost. In this architecture, it was much easier to edit a paper on the computer screen. Even in a face-to-face tutorial, the paper had to be opened on the computer screen if both parties wanted to see the comments. In the newer versions of Microsoft Word, the comments are placed in the right margin, so when the paper is printed out, the comments still appear in the margin with dotted lines connecting them to the text, making it much easier to work on the paper from a hard copy if so desired—which returns us to the question of whether to revise on paper or on screen.

Moreover, there is evidence that the nature of the comments change when new technologies are used. In using CommonSpace, for example, Bloch and Brutt-Griffler (2001) found that because the architecture required the reader to attach the comment to a specific piece of text, there was a greater tendency to make local rather than global comments; moreover, it was difficult to make comments that linked one part of the text to another part. This problem, however, was not absolute; as Bloch and Brutt-Griffler pointed out, it could be remedied by the way the software was implemented and how the readers were trained to use it. Readers could be encouraged to attach global comments to the writer's name or the title of the text, or if the texts were exchanged using attachments to email, the reader could make the global comments in the email message.

Newer technologies may further dramatically affect commenting. New types of computers have attempted to improve on entering information by hand, which some teachers may feel more comfortable doing. However, even the current software at this time is difficult to use. Verbal comments, which take up a large amount of space, may become more common with increases in broadband speed and storage space.

Other consequences of a systemic view of technology can be seen in how the students' drafts are exchanged. Computer networking has had some of its greatest impact on the logistics of sending papers between the teacher and the student. Prior to the development of computer networks, the writer still had to print out the paper and wait until the next class to turn it in. The reader still had to make comments by hand and perhaps wait until the next class to return the paper.

However, with the development of LANs and then the Internet, these processes changed. The result is that neither the reader nor the writer has to frantically rush to finish a paper before the class since the student can submit a paper the moment the writing is finished, and the teacher or peer reviewer can return it the moment the commenting is finished—which can create more opportunities for revision as well as more work for both teachers and students. This ability to reduce the time between when a paper is sent and returned could increase the number of drafts the writer could do, which, in turn, could affect the number and types of comments given on the paper.

The systemic view of the use of technologies in L2 composition will inevitably change not only how composition is taught but also how other debates within the field are being discussed. The need to see the use of technologies in such a way is another factor that teachers will have to deal with in choosing appropriate technologies and using them effectively. None of these systems comes prepackaged, so teachers need to be able to conceptualize how these technologies may interact and what consequences and problems may arise.

A Critical View of Technology

As discussed in Chapter 1, it is important to take a realistic and sometimes critical view of the use of technology to gain a perspective on its strengths and weaknesses. All of us have been negatively impacted by technology in some ways, whether by the bombardment of spam or the frustration of computer crashes. Many still do not have reliable access to the technology. The newspapers today are full of stories about the dangers of technology: children stalked in chat rooms, teenagers posting death threats in their blogs, or damaging email being sent to the wrong people. These issues have often been exaggerated; however, they reflect real fears that students, or sometimes their parents, have. While not as dramatic, problems are continually sprouting up with the use of technology in the composition class. One of the most interesting for composition teachers is the role technology can play in facilitating or preventing plagiarism. As with teacher commenting, discussions about plagiarism have been controversial, but many teachers see the Internet as exacerbating the problem.

Taking a critical view of technology requires looking at the consequences of using it and looking at how it impacts other practices.

Plagiarism is only one of a number of instances in how the Internet has affected the use of intellectual property in the classroom, which has caused a great deal of confusion over how teachers can use both print and online intellectual property. As can be seen in the well-publicized battles over downloading music from the Internet, working online has raised a number of highly contentious issues regarding what intellectual property is and whether online intellectual property should be treated in the same way as physical property (Woodmansee, 1994; Woodmansee & Jaszi, 1995; Lundsford & Ede, 1994). Many of these issues have spilled over into the composition classroom. We constantly hear teachers who may have downloaded music from the Internet think they can now cut and paste from the Internet. But the laws and rules regarding the use of intellectual property are often not well understood by both teachers and students. This confusion over the use of intellectual property requires teachers to have a deeper understanding of the legal issues regarding intellectual property and fair use—something few composition teachers are trained in. Technologies, such as the copying machine, have already had dramatic effects on how teachers view intellectual property. They can easily copy a few pages of a textbook, perhaps legally or not, to hand out to their students. However, the Internet has dramatically increased the number of legal and ethical battles that have arisen from how teachers develop materials. Issues regarding how students use the materials they download from the Internet can also apply to how teachers can use these same materials. For example, can teachers post materials on a website? How do they incorporate multimedia taken from the Internet? Can they create corpora or use online texts in the teaching of grammar? These questions are all affected by shifting legal interpretations of the nature of online intellectual property.

The legal issues surrounding the Internet as a source of information have become increasingly complex and contentious. Developers of corpora for concordancing programs have to consider whether they are violating copyright law when they cut and paste texts into a corpus or whether their own corpora can be copyrighted. In the United States, new laws such as the Digital Millennium Copyright Act (DMCA) can make it illegal to do electronically what may have been legal in print (Samuelson, 1999). While giving a magazine or newspaper to a friend is legal under what is called the doctrine of first use, giving someone a password to access the same magazine or newspaper online may not be legal. The use of popular plagiarism detection programs like Turnitin.com has raised legal questions about whether teachers can force students to place their intellectual property into a commercial database.

Technology has been a powerful force in shaping new attitudes toward intellectual property. While many have dismissed possible differences and argue that all forms of intellectual property should be treated the same, alternative concepts, such as "open-source" (Raymond, 1998) or "copyleft" ("What Is Copyleft," 1999; Barlow, 1993), have challenged how traditional principles of intertextuality, text attribution, and collaboration have been affected by the use of technology. Alternative views of copyright, such as the Creative Commons movement (http://creativecommons.org/), have changed how the ownership and distribution of intellectual property are viewed. How these new views on intellectual property will affect our views of plagiarism will be an interesting question.

In the battle over the moral implications of posting and downloading information, it has sometimes been forgotten that teachers have rights, which can vary in different countries, to use these materials. Nevertheless, how they use them, whether they can publicly display them or must limit access to them, are complex questions that teachers have to consider (e.g., "Copyright and Digital Media," 2005). It is therefore important that teachers become active participants in this debate not only to better understand their rights but to protect these rights from being infringed on.

There have been many warnings over the years that these technologies have failed to have the desired effects or worse, that they create conditions that might be detrimental to the learning process. Therefore it is not enough to justify a technology on the basis of its efficiency but rather by its affects on the educational process, which are often ambiguous.

As Feenberg (1999) has argued, these relationships are often hidden to users of technology who believe the technologies are simply neutral with regard to their effect on what they are being used for. Sproull and Kiesler (1993) argued that research into the use of technology has demonstrated a more complicated picture than was initially thought. These complications can be seen wherever technologies are used.

The ambiguous nature of the evaluation of the use of these technologies has always been the case and will always be the case in the future. As Feenberg (1999) argues, technology cannot be simply seen as a tool to accomplish one's objectives since the ultimate effects of such a "tool" can never be fully known. Likewise, he argues that choices about which, if any, technology is most appropriate must depend on how the users perceive not only the usefulness of a technology but also its relationship to interests and beliefs of the user.

The difficulties in understanding how a technology should be used are not new. There has always been difficulty in moving from an older technology to a newer one because of the time it takes to break away from the constraints of the earlier technologies. Therefore, the criticisms of technology cannot be simply dismissed as coming from neo-Luddites. However, the problem may not be inherent to the technology but to the way it is being implemented. In CALL, promising technologies such as artificial intelligence and virtual reality have yet to produce the kind of language learning environments its advocates have hoped for. Even when technologies appear to be successful, their practitioners are often unaware of how they may be affecting their pedagogy. Widely used programs like PowerPoint have been criticized for how they can force users into certain ways of presenting information (Tufte, 2003). It is crucial, therefore, that both research and teaching need to reflect this critical perspective.

While all pedagogies are constrained by social, political, and institutional factors, technology is not only affected by these constraints but also by whether teachers have access to computers, to the Internet, or to technical support. These issues have been central to the debate over the usage of technology: Is it worth the time, and especially the money, that implementing technologies requires? Selfe (1999) argues that teachers must pay attention to technology both in its micro usage in the classroom and its macro usage in furthering the social and economic goals of the society. She decries the dichotomy between those who support the use of technology in the classroom but do not pay critical attention to the issues it raises and those who oppose the use of technology and therefore believe they can ignore it. As a result, she argues that the composition community has not always given technology the necessarily focused attention needed to understand its complex social and cultural contexts.

This same discussion has taken place over the larger role of technology and society. Much has been made, for example, about the social affects of the introduction of technologies such as the Internet and cell phones, especially in the developing countries of Asia. Some of the affects have been positive, some negative (e.g., Negroponte, 1995; Rheingold, 2003).

Years ago, Negroponte argued that countries like China could solve their communication problem by skipping a generation of technology and jumping directly to the use of cell phones, something which has come to fruition, at least in urban areas. There have also been dramatic increases in access to the Internet in China, but, at the same time, the recent controversies over Yahoo® and Google™ blocking websites indicates that some things have not changed. Moreover, there are always questions about the cost and availability of access to these technologies that exist on a global level, which are similar to those on a local level. The answers to these questions are more complex than they once were because of the tremendous changes that are going on all over the world. L2 composition teachers and, especially those who are fluent in languages other than English, can make a great contribution to understanding the problems and consequences of these changes at a global level.

This chapter has provided a theoretical overview of the use of a variety of technologies in the L2 composition classrooms. The challenge to L2 composition teachers is that greater attention must be paid to the nature of each technology and how each is being implemented in the classroom. Researchers and teachers, however, are often overwhelmed with the constant introduction of new technologies, which is often a result of the frenetic pace at which new technologies are introduced.

One result of this dilemma is that teachers often must discover on their own how these technologies interact and then decide on their implementation, often without a great deal of research to support their decisions. The implications of these choices can be profound. Teachers need to be aware, as Kramarae (1988) warns, that technologies can provide new competencies to those who have mastered them but can increase the levels of oppression for those who do not. Students who enter ESL programs lacking not only the necessary writing skills but also the necessary technology skills may be placed in double jeopardy. At the same time, teachers and students who have these skills may find new and exciting ways for the technology to be used. In the end, as Richard Florida (2002) remarks, the ultimate success of a technology does not depend so much on the nature of the technology but on the creativity of its users, including both teachers and students.

L2 composition teachers, as well as students, can take over this creative role with the proper consideration of what technology can be used for, in what contexts these technologies are most effective, and how the appropriate implementation of the technology can affect the use of the technology. Hawisher et al. (1996) argue that the computers and writing community have been moved by a sincere desire for "better, more just, and more equitable writing classrooms," which can lead to "better, more just, and more equitable systems of education" (p. 2) and ultimately society. As Lessing argues, "Understanding technology should be an essential component of global citizenship" (cited in "What Is Technorealism?" 1998, para. 24).

Taking control of the research is an old theme in composition (North, 1987) and in CALL (Egbert & Hanson-Smith, 1999). To achieve whatever one's goals for the implementation of technology and respond to the challenges that using technology entails, teachers need to take control of their own research agenda through every stage of implementation from the design of spaces where the technology is used to the day-to-day classroom decisions (Selfe, 1992). They cannot rely on a few elite researchers to provide answers. Who better to make those observations than classroom teachers?

Reflection Questions

1. Think about your own writing. Many of our assumptions about writing are based on the concept of a social network. We share our ideas or our paper with others. This book was read by friends, associates, and editors before you. When you write, do you talk to other people or have them read your work? How has technology facilitated these relationships?

2. How do you read on the Internet? Do you click around, and do you read in the same way you read a print text? Do you prefer reading online or in print? What are the differences? How comfortable are you and your students with reading online? Many teachers do not have the experience with "visual literacy" that is becoming more and more valued on the Internet. How do you feel about your own visual literacy? How can you develop your comfort level with visual literacy?

3. In my courses I use some CMD for different purposes, such as listservs or blogs to discuss the content or issues related to the course. The students frequently use email to contact me about questions. How do you use CMD in your own life? How have you used CMD in your interactions with your students and teachers? What different forms of CMD do you use? How do they differ from each other? How do you think those differences can be applied to the classroom?

4. One of the points that the book makes is that you can use technology in the classroom to help students with writing in general or you can use the technology to help students learn about using the technology. Which of the technologies do you think the students should learn to use as part of the development of their computer literacy?

5. The use of concordancing software requires teachers to think about how they want to teach grammar. How do you teach grammar or think that grammar should be taught? Can you teach generalizable rules? Do all rules vary? Do you only teach grammar in context? Do you teach all items discretely or do you like to mix them up? Do you like to teach a lot of different items or do you teach a few items over and over, not bothering to discuss some? How do you think your students will respond to the types of learning facilitated by concordance software.

6. The book stresses the importance of taking a critical view of technology. Where do you think technology has been harmful in education? What kinds of activities would you rather do in the traditional way instead of trying to use a new technology?

7. One of things that sometimes bothers teachers about the use of CMD is that students send them email all the time and expect them to respond right away. Sometimes when you send an email, particularly when it is important, you wonder if it was received, especially if you haven't gotten an immediate reply. How do you feel about the demands of being in constant touch with your students or teachers or even friends and family? What do you think is an appropriate length of time to respond to an email? As a teacher, do you feel students have a right to get a response to their email right away? How long do you wait for a response when you send an email?

8. All teachers are impacted by intellectual property law. How do you feel about the use of intellectual property? Where do you obtain content for your classes? Do you download articles and hand them out to students? What do you think the restrictions are? What do you think your rights are? Visit the Berkman Center for Internet Law and Society *(http://cyber.law.harvard.edu/home/)* to find articles or listen to podcasts about intellectual property and think about what issues are impacting your teaching.

Chapter 3

Integrating the Computer and the Internet

This chapter discusses how the computer and the Internet can be integrated to create a tool or even an entire curriculum for an L2 composition course. The integration of these technologies in the classroom has long been one of the goals of designing technological environments for all purposes, including writing. One of the biggest commercial breakthroughs in software development was the integration of word processing, spreadsheets, and databases into one software package. With the development of the Internet, this goal of integration has progressed to the point of having a great effect on how technology is made available to the writer wherever and whenever it is needed, which has been referred to as J^3: "just enough, just in time, just for me."

Technology has become simpler to use, more available, and more personalized for the learner's special needs. Teachers can use these various technologies individually or as integrated units. Some of these technologies, like word processing, can be required or "pushed" to the students while others, like concordancing programs, can be "pulled" by the students from anywhere and at anytime they need them.

Integrating the Computer and the Internet

Understanding Student Computer Use

Creating an integrated environment for writing begins with an understanding of the primary users—the context, the students and the teachers. To assess this group of users requires knowing the skills, attitudes, and backgrounds they bring to the classroom. The technological literacy necessary to use technology results from being able to conceptualize how a variety of technologies are used inside and outside the classroom. This literacy can entail the ability to recognize that a certain technology might be useful in a particular context or to more specifically decide whether a listserv may be more appropriate than blogs or what kinds of assignments will produce what kinds of writing.

When ETS was designing early versions of computer-based testing, it considered a variety of technological skills, such as using ATM cards or a touch tone phone, in measuring technological competence (Eignor, Taylor, Kirsch, & Jamieson, 1998). Of the many ways to assess what students bring to the classroom, the easiest is either to ask them or to watch what they do—the problems, frustrations, and mistakes. This is how to check user testability. When we at Ohio State initially used questionnaires to evaluate the technological competence of the students entering our L2 composition program, we found great variation in their experiences. Thus, specific lessons had to be designed at the beginning of the course to address problematic areas, such as attaching files to email. Later assessments showed that every student knew how to do this, so these lessons could be nearly entirely eliminated.

As more complicated tasks were introduced, it was important to assess the students' backgrounds on specific tasks. When web page design was introduced into one of our composition courses, the students were surveyed about whether they knew how to create web pages, what experience they had in programming, and the computer tools they used. When we found that few of them had any background in designing web pages, a course could be designed that did not place too many technological demands on the students, even though some of these demands might have produced interesting results. By limiting the amount of technological background required, the amount of student resistance or frustration could be minimized while giving students with more experience the opportunity to use their skills.

The same need to assess the skills and attitudes applies to teachers. The expectations they have for using a technology can often affect their willingness to work through problems with it (Bloch & Brutt-Griffler, 2001). Palmquist, Kiefer, Hartvigsen, and Goodlew (1998) noticed a resistance by teachers who are forced to use technology but may not feel confident in using it. Teachers can also feel frustrated by software they do not understand or that has flaws. Unlike students who may have to use a technology and understand it because their teachers require them to, teachers may simply refuse to use it.

Teacher resistance to the possible domination of the technology can come in other forms. The growth of Wi-Fi, which allows the user to connect to the Internet without a fixed connection, illustrates just how something that can be liberating in one context can be confining in another. The ability to connect to the Internet through Wi-Fi means that students can access valuable information whenever they need it. Having students work online means that the teacher is tied to a home or office computer. On the other hand, laptops and Wi-Fi allow teachers to break away from these confines but can give them the feeling they can never escape from their work.

These concerns should not be simply dismissed. People who oppose the use of technology are often called neo-Luddites; however, this is unfair. The original Luddites understood that the introduction of technology was going to threaten their jobs and way of life. This ambiguity about technology that teachers often have began once the first computer premiered in the classroom. If teachers are interested in using the technology, it is critical that they are given training in not only when the technology can be used but also when it cannot or should not be used. Therefore, as technologies become more widespread and more complex, teachers will become more essential for their effective use.

Digital Writing and a Sense of Place

Teachers who use computers have always been concerned with the space in which learning takes place, whether it meant rearranging the chairs or decorating the classroom. The design of a technology learning space can and should influence how writing is going to be taught. Palmquist et al. (1998) argue that while a course could have the same goals in both online and face-to-face environments, teachers and students will have different teaching and learning strategies, attitudes, and interactions. In a computer lab, one of the most important factors is the arrangement of the computers. Each modification of this arrangement can change the nature of the writing experience. Numerous factors must be considered. Are students primarily using the computer at home, at a location outside of school, or in the school labs? If in isolation, where is the computer located? If at home, in which room? Who, if anyone, is around to help—a technical person or a spouse? What kind of Internet access, if any, is available: dial-up or high-speed broadband? Is the student working alone or with other students? Is there a classroom teacher present?

In more traditional computer labs, how the computer is arranged can determine the physical relationships among the students (Palmquist et al.). Arranging computers in rows may encourage more individualistic work; arranging them in pods may encourage more group work. Having a table nearby may encourage students to move between print and digital text, and change how they interact with their classmates. The latest issue to affect the design of computer spaces has been mobility, whether it refers to using a laptop to move around the room or using Wi-Fi to log in from inside or outside the classroom/lab. Newer technologies such as WiMax (Worldwide Interoperability for Microwave Access), which allows for a greater coverage than Wi-Fi, may further change the concept of space. Even cell phones and PDAs are being thought of as writing devices since these mobile devices can substitute for desktop computers to create a different type of learning environment that allows students to move around and interact with individuals or groups. If the teacher wants to talk with the entire class, the students can rearrange themselves for a lecture. More important, laptops and Wi-Fi extend the learning environment beyond the classroom/home to anywhere one can find access—other buildings, cybercafés, and coffee shops. However, as with every other technology, there are new questions and problems that arise, such as privacy and security that must be factored into any decision about their use.

Technology and the Writing Process

When personal computers first became widely available, teachers were fascinated by the ways in which the technology could influence the writing process. In one of the earliest studies on computer drafting, Daiute (1985) argued that the blinking cursor seemed to invite writers to produce more text and thus longer papers, something that was never borne out empirically. As with the introduction of many technologies, drafting an essay on a computer was not much different from drafting it on a typewriter. As the computer technology evolved and teachers and students began to reconceptualize the potential of the technology, the writing process began to change.

We discussed in Chapter 2 that the way teachers comment on student papers might be affected by how they integrate the available technologies. Technology clearly affects the commenting process, for example, if for no other reason than the ability to comment online remediates the problem of reading handwriting. Technology can clearly affect the reading and writing processes for both teachers and students in a number of ways. I have found that it is both easier and faster for me to type in comments on their electronic files, which the students can read without having to ask me what I wrote.

Moreover, the ability of students to send in papers at any time and for teachers and classmates to respond at any time has made having to rush through writing or grading papers on a fixed deadline obsolete. The use of comment functions like that in Microsoft Word allows users to retain their comments from one draft of a paper to another. By creating keyboard macros, which allow the user to enter a string of words by clicking on two or three keystrokes, the same comments can be inserted into the paper without having to type them over and over (see Figure 3.1). The student can either read the comment in the box or as pop-ups by moving the cursor over the comment. Each time a new comment is added, the list of comments is reformatted so that it is possible for teachers to insert a larger number of comments.

One interesting consequence of commenting online is that the writer can make comments or ask questions as easily as the reader can, which can create a dialogue between reader and writer. The comment function in programs like Microsoft Word allows the recipient of a comment to write a response, perhaps asking for a clarification on the original comment. However, not every student is comfortable reading comments on screen and may feel more comfortable printing out the paper and working from a hard copy.

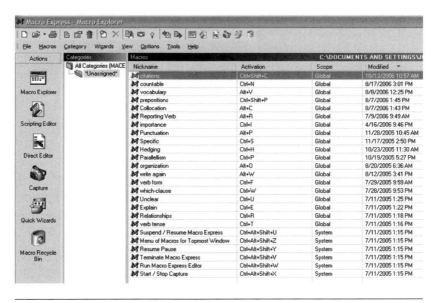

Figure 3.1. Programs like MacroExpress® *(www.macros.com)* allow users to easily make comments that can be inserted into the document using keystrokes. This program can save the reader time writing the same comments over and over again. These comments can be longer and more detailed than ones normally written by hand. Word-processing programs such as Microsoft Word and WordPerfect also have features for making macros; however, this kind of program can greatly simplify the process. Used with permission.

Traditional research in both teacher commenting and peer review may need to be rethought in an online context. Little is known about whether there are differences in how teachers or students make comments online as opposed to on a hard copy. Teachers sometimes make more micro-level comments online because they have to attach each comment to a specific piece of text and not to the paper as a whole (Bloch & Brutt-Griffler, 2001). However, this is another issue that can be addressed by training teachers on how to attach more general comments to the name or title of paper.

There are other areas where the use of online commenting can enhance the commenting process. Goldstein (2004), for example, discusses how teacher comments can affect the research process students use to find information or arguments to support their claims. Online commenting allows for inserting links directly into the comment that could guide the student toward articles and websites that might help in doing research.

Using the Internet to Extend the Composition Classroom

Online commenting is one of a number of ways that technology can extend the writing environment beyond the physical classroom space. It has long been the goal of software designers to extend the scope of a word-processing program to encompass additional goals that teachers might have for using computers. New conceptions about the Internet, which is sometimes referred to as Web 2.0 (O'Reilley, 2005), have affected how the integration of the Internet is seen. O'Reilley writes, "You can visualize Web 2.0 as a set of principles and practices that tie together a veritable solar system of sites that demonstrate some or all of those principles, at a varying distance from that core" ("What Is Web 2.0?" What Is Platform section, 2005). Traditionally, we have "pushed" technology to students, for example, by requiring them to use word processing or to send their papers via email.

However, the term *Web 2.0* reflects a conception of where pieces of technology exist that users can "pull" whenever they need to. The idea of Web 2.0 is that there are a large number of highly specialized websites that can be linked together, in this case, into a writing environment. If users want to design a blog, they can go to Blogger; if students want to make a podcast so that they can read what they want and add pictures or music to their texts, they can go to podOmatic *(www.podomatic.com)* to host the podcast; if they want to work with pictures, they can go to Flickr™ *(www.flickr.com);* if teachers want to share their bookmarks with their students or with other teachers, they can use a site like del.i.cio.us *(http://del. icio.us).* Teachers can exploit this way of thinking about the Internet in the same way to design modules that students can use whenever they need them, as will be discussed later. The importance of a "push-pull" Internet (Hagel & Brown, 2005, para. 122) to the composition classroom is based on the premise that the Internet is populated with objects that the student can access. The idea of connecting small pieces of information or specific learning materials has great potential for L2 composition teaching.

The Internet contains many useful websites that students can access. Since many topics are not adequately covered online or should be covered in less traditional ways, it is useful to supplement existing online materials with materials designed by students. All of these websites and objects can form a constellation of learning materials students can draw upon as needed. The phrase *small things, loosely joined* (Weinberger, 2003) provides a useful metaphor for conceptualizing how materials can be connected to provide resources for L2 composition courses.

Putting Class Materials Online

One way to show the linkage between various elements of a course is to put links to all the materials on a course website (see Figure 5.2). Today, many teachers use commercial course management systems, such as Blackboard *(www.blackboard. com)* or WebCT *(www.webct.com),* to display all the materials and websites in one place, but these programs are closed

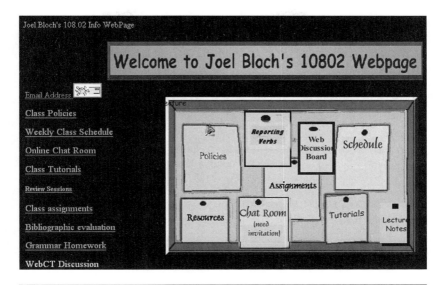

Figure 3.2. An early attempt to create a course website for a graduate course in L2 composition. Based on suggestion by Siegal (1996) for creating a metaphor to reflect the layout of information, I chose a bulletin board metaphor. Today, however, some people feel the use of such metaphors has been overdone.

systems and often expensive.[1] The website in Figure 3.2, on the other hand, contains materials that are open for other students and teachers to use. Today, wikis can also be easily used for class websites.

Web page design can be extremely time consuming for both teachers and students; however, it can also involve students in the construction of hypertext. With varying degrees of technical assistance, a design program such as FrontPage, a good book on web page design, and some experiences with coding, teachers can bypass the sometimes high cost and bureaucratic nature of these course management systems by designing their own class websites. There were web pages containing examples of materials from a variety of disciplines so that the students could analyze texts they might be more familiar with. The website is awkwardly designed by today's standard, but the

---

1. An alternative approach can be found in Moodle, which is a free course management system that uses an open source approach in its development.

idea of using the web to present a variety of authentic materials for students from different fields is still relevant to web page design today. For example, in the class, which had graduate students from a variety of departments, we would hand out an example of a text; however, we could not give them examples from each of their disciplines.

Integrating Outside Websites into the L2 Composition Classroom

A different approach to website design can be found in what are called learning objects. Learning objects are often thought of as being narrowly defined to address a specific issue. Dave Wiley (2001) uses the term *learning objects* as a metaphor for designing interrelated online materials. Though not specifically related to language learning, Merlot *(www.merlot.org)* has become one of the leading depositories of these materials. These kinds of specialty web-based objects, along with countless other pre-existing sites, can be accessed by learners at the time in their writing process when they need it, creating what has been called the "just-in-time" web. For example, links can be inserted into comments that help students access learning objects or websites related to the comment.

Online Plagiarism Resource Sites

- Bedford St. Martin's Technotes*: http://bedfordstmartins. com/technotes/techtiparchive/ttip060501.htm*
- CBB Plagiarism Resource Site: *http://leeds.bates. edu/cbb/index.php.*
- Plagiarism.Org.: *www.plagiarism.org/*
- Scholarly Communication Center: *www.lib.ncsu. edu/scc/tutorial/plagiarism/*
- San Jose State University: *http://tutorials.sjlibrary. org/plagiarism/*
- Acadia University: *http://library.acadiau.ca/tutorials/ plagiarism/*

- The University of Southern Mississippi: *www.lib. usm.edu/research/plag/plagiarismtutorial.php*
- Rutgers University: *www.scc.rutgers.edu/douglass/ sal/plagiarism/intro.html*
- The Plagiarism Resource Site: *http://plagiarism. phys.virginia.edu/home.html*
- University of Alberta: *www.library.ualberta.ca/ guides/plagiarism/*
- The Plagiarism Court: *www.fairfield.edu/x13870. xml*

Plagiarism is one issue that has been dealt with using such an approach. There are already many websites designed specifically for teaching about plagiarism that can be readily linked. These plagiarism resource sites were often designed by universities to acquaint the students with their policies regarding plagiarism. The sites offer a variety of handouts and other information about plagiarism, including interactive tutorials that present students with a series of scenarios relating to different aspects of plagiarism and ask them how they would respond.

One interesting example is at *http:/leeds.bates.edu/cbb/ index.php.* This website exemplifies how pedagogical assumptions can affect the architectural design. Since one assumption underlying the tutorial is that there is an uncontested and clearly articulated set of rules regarding plagiarism (cf., Howard, 1999), the tutorial is designed so that users cannot continue to the next question until they give the "correct" answer. Regardless of what one might think of this approach, it provokes interest. Teachers can use each website regardless of whether they agree with it. The students can take the tutorial, and their answers can be used in discussions on the nature of plagiarism and how it should be handled. If a teacher wants to present alternative views on plagiarism (e.g., Angélil-Carter, 2000; Howard, 1999), other similar tutorials can be designed to get students thinking about plagiarism in other ways, as exemplified in our website *(esl.osu.edu/staff/ bloch/plagiarism).*

Our website provided a number of scenarios that were designed to have students discuss or argue about whether an act should be considered plagiarism and how those acts should be treated.

In addition to having the students discuss issues relating to plagiarism, it's also necessary to help them develop strategies for dealing with plagiarism. For example, since we had already designed pen-and-paper exercises on paraphrasing and the use of reporting verbs, which were directly related to dealing with plagiarism, we posted these exercises online at Hot Potatoes™ *(http://hotpot.uvic.ca)*. Hot Potatoes™ can be used to create containing traditional types of interactive CALL exercises, such as cloze texts or fill-in-the-blanks, but it also has features that allow designers to integrate video or other multimedia functions.

Underlying the openness of the design of these websites is the concept of a *commons*. As mentioned earlier, the term was popularized by Eric Raymond (1998) as a way of thinking about information as being decentralized and accessible to everyone. The idea of a commons is that there are multiple, usually unregulated access points to the information. Sites like Merlot and Wikipedia, for example, are open sites where large amounts of information can be stored and easily accessed. Unlike traditional encyclopedias that have been repackaged in a digital environment, Wikipedia, for example, allows anyone who has registered to post entries and, more controversially, to edit the existing entries.

Another way of integrating outside websites into the classroom is through the use of online writing centers (OWLs), which are created by universities to provide their students with both information and help, but some portions are open to outsiders. These sites often function as online handbooks and provide interactive tutorials to involve students. With online commenting, the URLs to these sites can be directly inserted into the student's paper. Information on four OWLs is provided.

Although some information is password-protected, much of the information is open and therefore can be

NAME	URL	DESIGN	EVALUATION
Purdue's Online Writing Lab	*http://owl.english. purdue.edu/*	Contains a variety of handouts and links, including some specifically for L2 students.	Most of what is open to people outside the university are handouts and links to resources. Includes a specific section for L2 students.
Writing@CSU	*http://writing.colostate. edu/index.cfm*	Contains a variety of resources, tutorials, and demonstrations.	Much of it is designed specifically for Colorado State students, but some of the tutorials and demonstrations can be useful for L2 students.
Longman's mycomplab™	*www.ablongman.com/ mycomp/htdocs*	A commercial site with a variety of features that can guide students through the writing process; provides sample exercises, links, and essays; allows online peer review and commenting.	This site requires purchasing access to a generic version or a version tied to either an electronic or print textbook. Designed primarily for L1 composition students.
Bedford St. Martin's Re: Writing	*http://bcs. bedfordstmartins.com/ rewriting/*	A commercial site that provides writers with a variety of interactive exercises that deal with such topics as general forms of writing, research paper writing, visual rhetoric, making presentation slides, avoiding plagiarism, and grammar.	Students can use these exercises without a fee. The exercises are designed for L1 students but do not require a high reading level, so many are accessible to intermediate- and advanced-level L2 composition students.

easily linked and accessed by members of the class or by non-members. Students can use just one module on the website or jump from module to module.

I have only scratched the surface of how composition teachers can integrate all the available tools for creating a writing environment. There is no question that the integration of the great number of "loosely connected" learning tools and writing environments into the L2 composition classroom is one of the greatest challenges that L2 composition teachers face. This decentralization of learning, or what has been called "distributed cognition" (Salomon, Pea, Brown, & Heath, 1993), has given teachers and students the freedom to work locally to adapt the technology to their needs. Local computer networks and the Internet have helped teachers integrate various materials so students have access to them whenever they need them.

Siemens (2005, para. 31) urges teachers to utilize these materials to create their own environments, provide opportunities to work collaboratively with various and often contradictory sources of information, and take advantage of the skills students bring to the classroom. But teachers will also need to create materials themselves, just as they might in a traditional classroom, to address the issues and challenges inherent in their own teaching approaches. These "engineered" products can be integrated with the found products to create a vast network of materials that students can access.

Integrating Writing and Hypertext

We have already discussed a number of ways to take advantage of the primary benefit of the Internet—accessibility—but one way to integrate hypertext into the classroom is to have students design web pages.

In this section, I want to discuss the integration of web page design in a basic-level writing course. This is a more traditional approach but one that can have some interesting possibilities. Basic-level writing courses have often focused primarily on structural items such as syntax and paragraph organization.

Only after students have mastered these aspects of writing could they go on to write more meaningful texts. These texts were often themselves very short, perhaps one paragraph, or at best, the notorious five-paragraph essay (Atkinson & Ramanathan, 1995; Ramanathan & Atkinson, 1999).

The Internet can provide a variety of opportunities for using different forms of litreacy. On a web page, even one paragraph may constitute a perfectly authentic text, which can sometimes turn even mundane assignments into meaningful and publishable texts that not only help students better conceptualize their writing but also can foster their critical thinking about the nature of the Internet itself. A one-paragraph description written by a student to describe her home can with the use of links, images, colors, videos, and music and video be transformed into a fascinating web page. Even students who can write only a few sentences could turn them into an authentic piece of digital text. A Thai student, for example, transformed what had been a simple assignment about discussing his past, present, and future life into a multitextured page about his life with links to and images of various sites from Thailand, his university, and what he hoped to do in his future.[2]

Web pages primarily use a computer language called HTML, although more specialized kinds of web pages may use other languages. While some have thought that it is important for students to learn to write code or create their own images or video, many teachers have found that by simplifying the use of the technology they can accomplish their goals. One of the most important pedagogical issues for implementing web page design is the choice of tools and materials, which affects the amount of coding the students are expected to do. This kind of multimedia approach is most often found in upper-level writing courses where students have already mastered many of the writing skills or in professional writing courses where these skills are often prerequisites for obtaining a job. For ESL teachers who may rarely teach this kind of class,

2. See *esl.osu.edu/staff/1062002/joseph/lite.html.*

such devotion to hypertext and multimedia may be a luxury few of them can afford. The approach described here attempts to find some middle ground where students are given many opportunities to make programming decisions about linking and the visual component of their texts without having to learn the details of writing code.

Integrating hypertexts or other forms of multimodal writing requires some commitment of time and resources that could otherwise be spent concentrating on other aspects of the writing process. Even in this course, which was devoted to web page design, the design was still not the central focus of the course since only two days a week could be spent in a computer lab. Without such lab time, it may not have been possible to use this approach. Our initial assessment of the students indicated that they had little background in learning to use the kinds of sophisticated tools—Dreamweaver, Flash, or Photoshop—often used in such courses. Therefore, we decided to use simpler and more readily available tools, such as Netscape Composer or FrontPage, to design the web-page.

Even these simple tools can be controversial for teachers who believe that a student cannot really understand the construction of a web page without understanding how to write code. Knowing how to write code can help designers fix their own problems as well as better understand the underlying architecture of their own pages. Nevertheless, it was felt that web design offered a possible solution to some of the pedagogical concerns basic-level writing courses have raised. Since the course did not primarily focus on web page design, the goals were limited to:

1. Introduce students to the forms of writing they will need in their other writing courses.
2. Introduce basic forms of web page design, including page layout, color selection, navigation, the use of multimedia materials, and hyperlinking.

3. Ask students to evaluate the types of information and materials they found on the Internet.
4. Give the students the opportunity to publish their writing on the Internet.

Since we needed to evaluate individual writing, the students were required to work on individual web pages. However, because of the collaborative nature of web page design, they were also asked to work on collaborative projects of their choice. For each assignment, the students were asked to design a web page for publishing their writing, to choose a color combination and page design, and to add navigation and hypertext links as well as images.

Teaching about the Visual Nature of Hypertext

Designing web pages could be of great benefit for the students who already value visualization, for students whose L1 values different forms of rhetorical patterns that may better align with how text and images interact with each other, or for students whose home cultures are less print literacy–focused.

One goal of the course was for students to think about the need for visual images to help explain their texts. Visualization is not only a matter of choosing images and colors but of creating an entire visual motif that is related to the written text.

The course introduced the students to a rather simple approach to thinking about design, an approach referred to as "safe visual rhetoric." Since this was not a web page design class, only a limited amount of time could be devoted to developing web pages. Students were asked to create a basic grid using the table function (Siegal, 1996), choose from a limited palette of colors, and insert at least two to three images per page, which alternated with the text. Today, students have a much greater opportunity to use images, photos, flash animation, and videos. Regardless of what materials are used, the primary goal is still to create a connection between the visual design and the needs of the audience. Its purpose was to construct a design that might reflect one's own needs as both a creator and a consumer of information over the Internet.

The importance given to this multimedia literacy raises complex pedagogical questions for a class using web page design. To help the students think about these issues, they were asked to read and summarize a number of articles related to visual literacy. Writing about these issues was also an integral part of the reading and writing assignments in the class. The students were asked to consider the elements of effective website design, the use of colors and images, and the implications of intellectual property law for website design. We added another layer of writing to the course by asking them to reflect on different aspects of the design process. In this assignment, the students were asked to respond to an article on the use of color. In this example, one student wrote:

To make my website spectacular I applied different colors for each web page's background. I used three colors like blue, green, and pink. I utilized them to let my visitors know that my life is colorful and not boring. I want everybody who visits my website to feel free and happy, and I think those colors make them fresh and active.

While changing colors for each web page is not necessarily a traditional design approach, it seemed here to match the goals of the writer to help explain the meaning of her text.

Integrating the readings with the design process seemed to help students develop a critical awareness of what they were reading. One student discussed how reading an article on color helped her with the problem of choosing appropriate colors for her readers:

My website's background color is dark blue. At first, I wanted to use black as my background color because black shows knowledge and elegance. However, there are some negative meanings of black. In some cultures, black means death, evil, and sadness, and most people like happy colors. Therefore, I changed my mind and chose dark blue, which means peace and confidence.

The students had read about the cultural basis of color, and in this reflection, the student refers to the article as a framework for discussing her own choice of colors. Nevertheless, this part of the course was clearly the most difficult for the students because many felt their designs were not very good. They weren't prepared to be beginners at this because they have seen so many well-designed sites.

As discussed in Chapter 2, visual aspects of literacy are often marginalized in the schools, so many students and teachers lack experience in using it. As one student wrote about the design of her page:

I don't like my website much. I think it is not beautiful and interesting.

Another student felt that his problems with visual literacy were issues that could not be dealt with in the context of the class.

I have no idea about design concepts. From childhood, I have had no aesthetic point of view. . . .Because I have no idea for design concepts, I should spend time to learn basic scheme of graphics. But I spent lots of time in writing English homework and watching TV to learn English quickly.

His reflection is a good illustration of the frustration some students felt about thinking visually as well as about the goals of the course. Although the students were not graded on the quality of their design, this student still seems to resist the idea that the design element of the course should be an important goal of a writing class. The student's resistance is understandable given the difficulties visual design entails and the lack of support from the teacher. For the designer or the user, choosing a visual design requires translating one form of meaning into another (Kress, 1998), which, like any form of translation, is inherently problematic.

The student's resistance also illustrates the larger problem of how much technology should be required to use in a writing classroom. As Wickliffe and Yancey (2001) point out, it is naïve to think that students can develop a profound sense of visual literacy simply by choosing images to illustrate a text. Even their frustrations indicate that students are becoming aware of the connections between visual literacy and print literacy even if they are having difficulty understanding that relationship. As the frustrated student noted, "If I had more time, I would surf the Internet to catch the best way to construct my images." Despite his frustrations, he does seem to be aware of the important design issues he must confront when he is a consumer or producer of Internet content.

Teaching about the Composing Process Using Hypertext

While creating hypertexts requires a reconceptualization of many aspects of the writing process, there are also rhetorical issues regarding the composing process that cut across all types of writing. Since this course still had to fit into a traditional writing program, it is useful to focus on how hypertextual writing can be used to introduce the writer to some of these issues. In this section, I focus on three issues that are central to writing in any media: responding to the audience, creating rhetorical ethos, and evaluating sources.

Eportfolios and Digital Storytelling

The evolution of Internet architecture has created a variety of new ways that a writer can interact with an audience. There has been an evolution in how the Web is being used by students as not just a place for class assignments but for multimedia areas for creating and storing the artifacts and texts related to their work and their lives. Eportfolios can be used to collect and link a wide range of work a student does that cuts across the boundaries of classes and the institution itself.

Digital Storytelling can similarly link more personal artifacts—texts, song, images, videos—everything that is connected to the ongoing development of multiple forms of literacies we are engaged in using (Lambert, 2003). Digital storytelling can give a new dimension to the relationship between visual and written texts discussed in Chapter 4. Transforming a written text into an oral one, and then adding other forms of multimedia, opens up a variety of new possibilities for having students explore the nature of multimedia texts.

Responding to the Audience

The evolution of these writing assignments from class-based to web-based enhanced audience awareness from the assignment's visual and hypertextual nature. Web page designers consider how every factor—layout, color, or links—can affect not only how the user reads the text but how the reader evaluates it. Designing the appropriate number and kinds of links, as well as choosing images, a suitable layout, and a clear navigational pattern, require an increased focus on the audience. Readers of a web page can easily link to additional information; therefore, the designer has to carefully consider which additional information a reader might need or want, which in turn places responsibility on the writer for the quality of that information.[3] Therefore, web page designers must be able to judge the quality of the website and its appropriateness for the potential audience or audiences.

Understanding the nature of an audience is, of course, crucial for any form of writing. Many of the factors are the same, but some are unique for Internet readers. For example, a popular assignment in teaching web page design is to have the students design a web page for a group with which they are familiar or associated. Siegal (1996) writes that a website designer should understand an audience's personal background, such as gender, race, or culture, as well as the readers' personal interests and experiences with the Internet, all of which may affect how they use the site. As with other forms of writing, this audience can be well defined or it can be as Ong (1997) put it, "imaginary."

Nevertheless, audiences in cyberspace may not always be as "imaginary" as they often seem to be in traditional composition classes. Therefore, understanding the nature of an audience in cyberspace may entail factors different from the ones writers in composition classes encounter. As Rea and White (1999) argue, a web page without a focus on a specific audience will be less useful. Since considerations of an online audience can be different than for a print-based one (Smith, 2000), decisions regarding audience can be more complicated because there are more factors to consider, including the web page layout, the choice of colors and images, and the necessity to choose and evaluate other websites that the designer might want to link to.

Here one student designer wrote about considering the knowledge background of his audience. To do this, he first had to make a guess about how familiar the audience would be with his topic.

---

3. Sometimes commercial websites, such as newspapers, do not to put in links to other sites inside the text in order to avoid the moral or legal responsibility for the information on those sites.

> [My topic] is not familiar to all readers. I tried to enhance the understanding and attract readers by using a detailed explanation and beautiful pictures.

The audience in this case seems more like the imaginary audience that Ong discussed.

While we usually want to aid writers in their understanding of the text, sometimes it might be necessary to challenge them, perhaps as a means of having them think about the content in different ways. Readers can be challenged, for example, by the choice of the font or layout of a page. At other times, it is important to anticipate the kinds of problems readers may have in reading a web page. Readers may be viewing the page with different browsers, which can affect the layout, or different access speeds, which can affect the rate at which images are downloaded. There are numerous other technical concerns that a designer must address. As seen in this student's reflection, his imaginary audience has real concerns, both in terms of the nature of the content and the limitations of the technology:

> I wanted most readers know that there are many interesting things and wonderful cultures in Thailand. [However] I applied only 3 pictures in my introduction web page because I realized that if there are too many pictures, downloading my website will take so much time.

The design process here must also take into account technical issues that are usually not present when considering the audience for a print-based text. In this case, the writer considers the question of downloading, which is especially true when using dial-up services. For example, readers may not feel comfortable having to scroll down a page, so care must be taken as to how much text is on the front page.

Particularly when thinking about web page design in relationship to print-based texts, linking may still be the important aspect that a designer has to consider. All forms of writing involve some form of "linking," or what is often referred to as intertextuality. Since inserting links into a text requires an ability to predict readers' needs (Charney, 1994), it is important for the designer to make decisions about what texts to link to, which could be compared to the decisions an academic writer makes when deciding which texts to cite. One way to directly bring the audience into this process was through peer review sessions, which were used to help the designer decide what those needs were. The students/readers were asked to read each other's texts and indicate where they wanted more information. The designer could then add a link to respond to these requests.

In her reflection on designing her website, a student in the website design class discusses how she tried to make those connections for her audience while taking into consideration the concerns her audience might have for the amount of time it will take to view the website:

There are three processes I used to attract people's attention. First, I used many interesting pictures. Because there are many beautiful and brand new pictures on my web, readers can enjoy my web. These pictures excite readers because they can see the pictures at the first time they view the page. Second, I selected the links, which don't take too long to load. If the links take too long, readers may become tired. Furthermore, readers may dislike my website and not look at all my pages. Finally, I selected a good color. I used light pink as the primary color because most children like happy colors and adults like more conservative colors, so I chose a light color, which is more conservative.

The student seems to realize, as Landow (1997) argues, that hypertexts create a different kind of context for both reading and writing, which can depend on a number of non-print factors.

The considerations of an online audience are especially complicated when designing websites. Many of the factors overlap to what is considered important across all forms of writing. However, there are many factors that are considered unique. Web page design gave us a unique opportunity to have the students reflect on the complexity of responding to all these factors. As is the case with transferring any writing skills between one context and another, the process is not easy. However, as I have tried to show here, the consideration of audience in web page design raises a variety of issues for the students, who by reflecting on them, can gain great insight not only in how the design of websites can influence their own use of the Internet but also the importance of audience in all forms of writing.

Creating Rhetorical Ethos

Implementing web page design introduced our students to another rhetorical concept, that of *ethos,* that could help the students understand both their own use of the Internet and the role of authorship in their own writing or in this case the designer. Ethos refers to the image that the writer wants to project of himself or herself: Is the writer an intelligent person, a reliable resource, and/or a good person? In traditional rhetorical terms, the writer, one who may be unknown to the audience, must be able to construct or "invent" a reputation that gives trustworthiness to a creation (Crowley, 1994). For example, an academic writer may have to cite a range of appropriate texts or use a well-defined methodology to establish *ethos* in a paper (Latour, 1988).

The question of ethos has become more complicated on the Internet. The ability to take on multiple personas can make it difficult to judge who an author really is. While the absence of gatekeepers has been the most fundamental reason for the growing importance of the Internet as an information provider, the downside is that more responsibility has been shifted to the reader for evaluating the credibility of information on a website. As Belcher (2001) argues, the vast amount of information available to the reader, with no gatekeepers present to evaluate its quality or truthfulness, can make it difficult for the user to sort out what is useful or even what is truthful.

The freedom the Internet gives individuals to create alternative personae can have both positive and negative consequences. Cheung (2000) argues that the Internet encourages writers to present often contradictory views of themselves. This ability could be liberating for some writers but problematic for others. In this example, the student was concerned with how the choice of visual images could affect the readers' impression of him:

To make my readers to trust me, I needed a more thoughtful graphic design. To meet this criteria, I should have selected more conservative and topic related graphics.

The student recognizes how good visual design is related to the ethos of the writer in that good design helps foster a good impression. In these cases, we can see the exploration metaphor used by constructivists exemplified by how these students explore different concepts of themselves in the same way they had explored different concepts of their audiences and then tried to adjust their web page design to their audiences' needs. As with the consideration needed to deal with the questions of audience, the amount of effort it takes to negotiate all the factors that go into designing a website may help the designer understand how, in any writing context, the choices made can affect the credibility of both online and print texts.

Suggestions for Teaching Hypertext

- Keep web page design simple. We asked the students to start with a 3 × 2 table and alternate images and texts in each cell of the table. If the students wanted to create a more elaborate design, they were free to do so.
- Ask the students to use blogs or some other form of CMD to reflect on the issues they encountered in their design or to evaluate their classmates' websites or commercial websites like Turnitin.com which the students had discussed in their class on plagiarism. A discussion of this website can also raise important questions about both plagiarism and the use of intellectual property. These issues can be the basis for their evaluation of other websites as well as for initiating discussions of web page design.
- There are a number of simple and free authoring programs that students can use to design web pages and edit and store images. There are also sits such as Flickr™ to store and share images, podOmatic to share and store podcasts, as well as sites like YouTube for videos and pod safe music network *(http://music.podshow.com/)* for music.
- Lab time is essential for doing web page design. Teachers may have to spend a great deal of their class time in labs giving students the opportunity to design their web pages.
- The study of fake websites can help students both in their analysis of website design as well as raise their consciousness about fraud on the Internet. Sites like Bogus and Questionable Web Sites *(www.ualberta.ca/~rreichar/bogus.htm)* can be useful sites to evaluate since many of the questionable issues that can easily be demonstrated.

- A discussion of the relationship between visual and written texts no longer requires teachers to spend a great deal of time on web page design. Sites like Flickr™ are used to share photos, either among friends or with anyone on the Internet. Flickr™ has a function that allows for annotating the photos and another function for posting them to a blog (see Chapter 4). These kinds of sites can provide especially beginning-level writers a chance to integrate writing and visuals and then post what they have done to the Internet. Some blogger sites also easily allow inserting pictures into blogs.

Evaluating Websites as Source Texts

Web Page Evaluation

URLs

- What kind of web page is it? A business, a government, an organization, or a university?
- Are there any names in the URL you can recognize?

Author credibility

- Who is the designer of the page?
- What is the expertise of the designer?
- With what, if any, organization or group is the designer associated?
- What bias do you think this organization or group may have?
- How is the credibility of the designer expressed in the website?
- Can you contact the designer to ask questions or supply feedback?

Reliability of Information

- Who is the audience?
- Are the content and the links clearly described and suitable for the expected audience?
- What is the primary purpose of the site?
- When was the site published? Has the site been revised?
- How complete and accurate are the information and the links?
- Do you agree with the information you found on the site?
- Is the information presented in a balanced way or is it one sided?

Interface

- Does the site do things that could not be done in a print text?
- Do the graphics and art help you understand the information or do they make the layout more confusing to follow?
- Is the information easy to read? Is there too much or too little information on a page?

Navigating the page or site

- Can you find your way around and easily locate a page from any other page?
- How up to date are the links? Do all the links work?
- What kinds of information are linked to?
- Is it open to everyone on the Internet, or do some pages require fees?

Underlying the design and use of websites is the need to evaluate a site. Not only does the ability to evaluate websites help students become better producers and consumers of hypertexts, it raises issues about the credibility of the author and the information provided that are applicable to the evaluation of any text. However, the evaluation process is often more difficult on the Internet than it is with print texts. Without the traditional gatekeepers, there is no centralized and authoritative system to discern the credibility of the information. This lack of gatekeepers can be both liberating and problematic at the same time. The users of the Internet have developed what are called *reputation systems* to deal with the potential problems that have arisen in establishing trust on the Internet.

Reputation systems are a means by which the sheer mass of individuals on the Internet can share information about the credibility of information, whether it relates to shopping or doing research. Commercial sites like Amazon.com and Netflix allow their users to read unsolicited reviews of the books and movies before they buy or rent them. eBay® allows consumers and merchants to discuss their transactions so users of eBay® can obtain information from a greater number of people and become more informed about the opinions of both buyers and sellers than shoppers relying on people they know or may meet in a face-to-face context.

One of the most interesting examples of a reputation system has been Wikipedia. This site uses a wiki to allow users to publish information in an encyclopedia format, which can then be checked and posted by other users. This process allows information to be collaboratively checked in ways that make the Internet a giant "reputation system."[4]

---

4. An incident that started as a joke where someone was falsely accused on collaborating in the assassination of John F. Kennedy led Wikipedia to modify its openness and have people register before they could add information.

Using Wikis and Blogs for Peer Review

What makes Wikipedia unique is the opportunity to enter the site and change or correct what one thinks is incorrect. If others disagree with this change, they can then go in and make more changes. Applying this approach to a writing class might yield some interesting results both as a means of peer review and collaboration. Unlike traditional forms of peer review, wikis and blogs can allow an individual, a group, an entire class, or groups of classes located anywhere on the Internet to interact in the creation and editing of texts. Sites like Wikispaces *(www.wikispaces.com)* provide space for setting up wikis. These spaces are places where texts can be posted and edited or commented on.

While blogs are not designed for this kind of interaction in the way wikis are, they can be set up to allow for a similar form of peer review. Students can post their papers to the blogs, and then the other students can post comments in the same way one can post to any blogging post. We have found, in general, that simply having students read each other's writing, notice how they are approaching the assignments, and asking for clarification or more information is one of the best approaches to peer review.

However, even the best reputation systems are not infallible, as examples of manipulation on eBay® and the falsification of information on Wikipedia have shown. To participate in this virtual world, therefore, students need to be able to evaluate the usefulness of information they find on the Internet; therefore, as both consumers and producers of hypertext, they need to develop what Gee (2003) calls "metalevel thinking" (p. 50) about the relationship between general principles of writing and the needs of the specific domain for writing, which here is the Internet.

I have discussed the importance of this kind of metalevel thinking throughout this book since I have argued that technology can be used to both develop writing skills and develop an understanding of the type of the technology itself. A more controversial issue is whether this type of metalevel thinking can elevate the student's writing to a higher level of critical thinking than is often seen in the classroom. Gee (2003) argues that such thinking promotes active and critical learning, which can then be applied to other domains such as the writing process and the general use of the Internet. In our classes, the students were given a number of criteria for evaluating a website in order to foster this level of thinking. In a course that discussed plagiarism, for example, the students were asked to evaluate the Turnitin.com website and then use their evaluation as part of their assignment to write an argument about whether the university should purchase a license to use this site. For more information on web page evaluation, see *http://lib.nmsu. edu/instruction/evalcrit.html* or *http://www.lib.berkeley.edu/ TeachingLib/Guides/Internet/Evaluate.html.*

Reflection Questions and Projects

1. If money were no object, how would you design a space for using technology? What kinds of computers would you use – desktops or laptops? Would you have a dedicated lab or just wheel in a cart of laptops? How could you control the use of websites during the class? If your school or university were designing a new building, how would you design it so the students could best use their computers in the new building?

2. Think about designing a class website. What purposes would you have for a class website? What kinds of materials would you put on the website? What kinds of other websites would you like to link to?

3. Programs like Hot Potatoes™ are popular for designing online lessons. Go to Hot Potatoes™ and try to use the program to design a lesson. What are the goals for the lesson? Which of their programs can be used for designing your lesson? What kinds of materials do you want to use? Do you have any other oral or visual materials you would like to put on the site?

4. How would you teach hypertext? Think of a hypertext or website project for your students to do collectively. One popular way is to think of a group or organization that may need a website and have the students design one for that group. What are the goals for the site? What aspects of web page design would you teach? Which authoring system would you use?

5. When would you allow students to use a site like Wikipedia? Is it reliable or not? What does the controversy around Wikipedia tell you about ethos and audience on the Internet?

Chapter 4

Computer-Mediated Discourse in the L2 Composition Classroom

Choosing among Different Forms of CMD

While all forms of synchronous and asynchronous computed-mediated discourse (CMD) can facilitate some degree of interaction and discussion, each form has a different architecture and ambience so that each may be most appropriate in different pedagogical contexts, which have different purposes and outcomes. Hawisher (1994) states that the first question a teacher should ask when implementing CMD is, What's the purpose of its use?

Many factors affect the choice as to which form of CMD, if any, is appropriate for a given writing context. First is the choice regarding when to use an asynchronous form of CMD versus a synchronous form. The differences between asynchronous and synchronous forms of CMD can produce a great variety of interactions and forms of discourse. In his study of different uses of technology in online peer response, for instance, Honeycutt (2001) found that email facilitated a deeper processing of information than could be found in synchronous discourse, although he also argued that synchronous discourse could be useful for ongoing discussion or more general types of response without specific reference to the text. While this study is interesting for its comparison between synchronous and asynchronous uses in peer review, Honeycutt points out that the ease by which one can make references to the text using the comment feature in word processing programs may make email less useful, although its distinction in terms of depth of processing may still hold true.

Once a form of CMD is chosen, then great care must be taken in selecting the particulars of implementation. Because of the variety of factors involved in the implementation of a technology (see Chapter 2), what may have worked in a face-to-face class may not work in a hybrid or online course and vice versa. As a result, when focusing on the use of CMD as a way of forming groups, consideration must be given to both the size of the group and the composition of its participants. For example, small groups may not be as effective when using asynchronous forms since there might not be a sufficient amount of discourse generated to make for a meaningful conversation. On the other hand, a small group may be ideal for synchronous discourse since it could encourage all the students to participate and make following the threads of the conversation easier.

The use of CMD can also affect the perceptions of students regarding strong and weak skills, which previously may have been deduced only from oral discourse. Liu and Hansen (2002) found that mixing linguistically diverse students in group work could benefit students with weaker language skills but could also discourage the students with stronger language skills from believing that the students with weaker skills could help them. However, if this finding is placed in an online context, CMD could decrease the gap between the students with weaker and stronger language skills. For example, since asynchronous discourse allows the participant as much time as needed to think and compose a message, it may help the students with weaker language skills to respond in ways that are just as com-plex as those of students with stronger language skills. Thus, both students and teachers must be able to "think digitally" about the nature of the writing environment in order to take advantage of the potential of the technology.

There is always the question of whether CMD produces "better" writers, and there is some evidence to this effect. Benbunan-Fitch & Hiltz (1999) found that CMD may help writers in business classes create better reports and case studies, an outcome attributed to the greater visibility of the responses that can lead to more in-depth reflection on what has been written. But there may be other aspects of the technology that could negatively affect the writing process. The lack of face-to-face contact can affect interactions that depend on subtle cues needed for establishing relationships within a group. Arguello, Butler, Joyce, Kraut, Ling, and Wang (2006) found in a study of online communities that interactions can be affected by the types of language used. They point to the use of pronouns or references to one's self as features that affect whether questions receive responses and conclude that participants in an online community may need assistance in learning how to participate in these communities.

Benbunan-Fitch and Hiltz also noticed that some of the participants in their online groups had more difficulty coordinating the distribution of work, which led to dissatisfaction with the writing process. Similarly, since synchronous discourse places more emphasis on producing discourse quickly and on the participant's typing skills, it could also negatively affect students who cannot type quickly. Kern (1995) found that this combination of features makes synchronous discourse, especially when there are multiple threads being discussed, often confusing to follow. Synchronous discourse can, therefore, be more problematic when students are not fluent readers or writers.

Many of these issues can be remediated through careful decisions about the implementation of the technology. The difficulty for the teacher is in deciding between the many forms of CMD currently available on the Internet (see Chapter 2). This decision not only affects whether the activity is successful but also how the introduction of CMD will influence the writing process.

General Uses of CMD

- Using CMD offers opportunities to write both formally and informally. Students, therefore, should know when to write informally and when to write more formally. In their textbook for an academic writing class, Swales and Feak (2000) offer a number of examples for using email in academic contexts to make requests and send academic communications.
- Despite the attention given to netiquette, group norms are not universal and what may be acceptable in one group may not be appropriate in another group (Herring, 2001). Therefore, teachers and students need to set up some guidelines as to what is appropriate netiquette for that group. These guidelines should include choice of topic, concerns about language, forms of address, ways of responding, and penalties for violating the guidelines (for more information, see *www.albion.com/netiquette/netiquiz.html*).
- Flames, even those that may be well motivated or unintentional, are always a problem because they can cause some people to withdraw from the group. Factors such as culture or gender may affect how students interpret messages as flames. This problem is complicated in an L2 context where students do not always have control over their use of language, so that what appears to be a flame might not have been intended to be one.
- On the other hand, flames, as well as other types of inappropriate language use, such as the use of inappropriate forms of address or signatures, can be used for a class discussion on the conventions of online writing.
- While many teachers would agree that publishing online rather than writing only for the teacher and

fellow students can help students better understand the nature of audience, publishing for a wider audience involves certain considerations about who may read the online message and consequently what should be included and left out.

- While lurking, or not participating, is usually acceptable in an online community, participation in class-based online discussions is more of a necessity, which means students often need an incentive to participate. Although students may come together voluntarily to work on projects or discuss exams, teachers often need to give class credit to motivate participation in more general discussions. However, some feel that because of the greater pressure for producing language quickly, particularly in synchronous discussions, there needs to be greater tolerance for lurking since not everyone can produce language at the same rate.

Using Synchronous Discourse in the L2 Composition Classroom

The past few years have seen an increase in the use of oral discourse in chat rooms and with other forms of presentation software. Not only is CMD becoming more aural, it is also becoming more visual. Chat areas, which were once purely text based, now have the capacity for live discussions and visual demonstrations. Images have become easier and easier to insert, and even PowerPoint presentations, as controversial as they are (Tufte, 2003), can be viewed during the chat. Some spaces are designed visually either in 2-D or 3-D (Ingram, Hathorn, & Evans, 2000). Synchronous communication can be accomplished in a variety of spaces using text-based spaces. Although not as popular as they once were, MUDs (multiple-user dimension) and MOOs (multiple-user dimension, object-oriented) can be designed either by teachers or students so that they mimic some of the social attributes of physical spaces and produce many of the same social interactions (Curtis, cited in Reid, 1955). These spaces can include a variety of visual motifs that can contribute to the ambience of the text space. MOOs are often designed around metaphors that reflect the different types of interactions that occur inside them. Unlike the fantasy-based metaphors that sites such as Lingua MOO were built around, a site like Tapped In®, which is a MOO specifically designed for teachers, uses the metaphor of a faculty office building for the place where conversations take place. This office metaphor seems to create a less playful atmosphere for discussion, which many students may feel more comfortable with. Newer technologies can allow a visual feed, along with an audio feed, to be integrated into the text.

Some features in the architecture of a synchronous discourse environment influence the nature of the exchanges. For example, the Elluminate® environment has a lecture area where the speaker, or perhaps teacher, is the central focus. In a small chat area, the listeners can discuss the issues among themselves or raise questions for the speaker to respond to. (See Figure 4.1.)

The design of these spaces illustrates the impact of the unique features of the architecture on the nature of the inter-actions—something that has always been recognized in CMD. Pavel Curtis (2001), one of the earliest developers of MOOs, found that different MOOs have different personalities, elic-iting different effects on the participants. Every form of syn-chronous discourse engenders a different and distinct culture (Herring, 2001), altering the interaction and writing that will occur in that space.

Synchronous exchanges have been often seen as being more playful than other forms of discourse, perhaps because of the more ephemeral nature of the messages, the speed at which they are transmitted, and the potential for high levels of interactivity between reader and writer (Danet, Ruedenberg, & Rosenbaum-Tamari, 1998). There may be other architectural design elements as well. Holmevik (2004) believes their roots are in the fantasy role-playing games like Dungeons & Dragons and fantasy literature like *The Lord of the Rings*.

Some online communities, for example, have their own forms of saying *hello* and *goodbye*. Often this level of phatic,

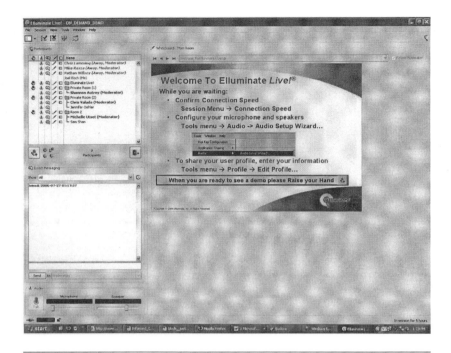

Figure 4.1. Elluminate® technology can be used to create an interactive, multimedia voice and data session. The box on the right side is a voiced lecture by the presenter, while the boxes on the left show the participants and provide an online chat room for listeners to ask questions or have discussions while the lecture is going on. In this space, listeners can also ask questions using an audio connection. For an archive of chats in Elluminate® related to the teaching of ESL, see the Bridges across Cyberspace archive at *www.wiaoc.org/*. (Used with permission.)

or social, discourse can delay the beginning of the actual topic of the conversation. Phatic communication plays an important role in all social interactions (Malinowski, 1947), including synchronous discourse (Bloch & Panferov, 2003). This type of communication may encourage more participation, which can be beneficial for the user's cognitive processing of the information (Herring, 1999). But for newcomers, these kinds of exchanges can be confusing or annoying, even causing the participants to sign off or decide not to return. Moreover, since users often do not use the same conventions as found in print language (Reid, 1995), some language teachers may worry about students picking up nontraditional language habits.

These usages can include nonstandard forms of capitalization and punctuation (Crystal, 2003), as well as nonstandard forms of spelling and syntax, which have become a major concern with the development of text messaging (Rheingold, 2003).

Designing or Choosing a Space for the Writing Classroom

Architectural features impact the pedagogical use of CMD. For instance, Tapped In® has features like a Whiteboard that allows someone to post a piece of text that will remain as the discussion text scrolls off the screen. This feature is useful for students who may read more slowly and cannot keep up with the often rapid exchange on the screen. A recorder creates a transcript of the exchange so that after the session is over, it can be emailed to anyone who wants to review it. Having a transcript from an online tutorial or review session allows the student to review what has been said at the time the student may need to revise a paper or prepare for an exam.

It goes without saying that different forms of synchronous discourse require varying degrees of training. Some spaces, such as Instant Messenger, require almost no training, whereas more complex chat rooms can require the user to download special software, go through a series of steps to access the chat room, and learn a series of commands in order to participate. Some MOOs allow the user to create their own environment—that is, they can design their own chat rooms by describing the objects they want in the rooms or the settings the exchanges will be in. For example, a student might design a coffee house with virtual coffee or an outside setting with animals nearby. Such contexts create a playful ambience that might help some writers but not others (Fanderclai, cited in Langham, 1993). Harris (1996) used this feature to study *Dante's Inferno,* asking students to create rooms where they could write about the different levels of Hell.

The newest type of spaces are virtual worlds such as Second Life® *(www.secondlife.com).* These 3-D virtual worlds share some of the features—and some of the problems—of multi-user games. Virtual worlds have long been thought of as a space conducive for language learning; however, until now, implementation has been difficult. Although their primary use is not for education, teachers in business schools (Terdiman, 2006) have been using them for a variety of educational purposes. They require high-speed broadband and a high-speed graphics card, which can limit who can use them. How they can be used in composition classes has not yet been explored, but with many students using these virtual worlds playing online games, it is inevitable that uses will be found.

The Nature of Synchronous Discourse in the L2 Composition Classroom

Warschauer (1999, 2000) has written extensively on the use of synchronous discourse in the classroom, offering a variety of ways it can be used with or without a teacher, in groups or one-on-one, and for a variety of purposes. I have used synchronous discourse as an "electronic tutorial" to replace the traditional face-to-face tutorial or class review session. In this session, much like is found in any face-to-face interaction, the conversation begins with a small amount of social communion.

yingdi [guest] arrives from nowhere.
yingdi [guest] says, "hello Dr. Bloch"

JoelB says, "hi yingdi, how are you"

yingdi [guest] asks, "good. how's your weekend?"

yingdi [guest] asks, "will a lot of people join this chat room today?"

JoelB says, "no, only you and Mr. Lee contacted me"[1]

---

1. These examples come from a transcript of the tutorial. Tapped In® provides a virtual "recorder" that can provide the owner of the room with a transcript of the discussion within a few minutes after the owner logs out.

What is interesting about these openings is how they differ from those often found in other MOO communities where the introductions can be more elaborated and stylized. In this example, Yingdi jumps right into the discussion, showing evidence of what Mynard (2003) referred to as the heightened ability for participants to set and prioritize goals within a MOO. Perhaps because these students only came to the MOO once, they did not use the often highly stylized and nonstandard forms, jargon, and slang that are sometimes found in MOO spaces.

Although we do not have data comparing this student's style in a face-to-face tutorial, here she is an active participant in raising questions for the instructor rather than simply relying on teacher comments, which is often the case in face-to-face tutorials. In this next unedited example (numbers added), after a brief introduction, the student asks a question about the topic of her paper, which concerns the wearing of mandatory school uniforms.

1. yingdi [guest] says, "ok. then I'll ask you some quick questions. Save time"

2. JoelB says, "that's okay - take your time"

3. yingdi [guest] says, "about the argument essay for final, does the length of the paragraphs need to be the same."

4. yingdi [guest] says, "becuase most of them are for dress-code."

5. JoelB says, "It's hard to say. generally, I would say so, but it depends on how you organize it"

6. JoelB says, "you may use up all the arguments if you are against the dress code"

7. yingdi [guest] says, "so, it's hard to find the agianst side. it's hard write the same length."

8. yingdi [guest] says, "I think I'll take for since there's hardly any agaist."

Here the format is a question/answer session similar to the face-to-face sessions. However, in face-to-face tutorials, the teacher typically dominates the exchange. In a study comparing face-to-face and online tutorials, Jones, Garralda, Li, and Lock (2006) found that the face-to-face tutorials were more hierarchical, with the tutor dominating the conversation. On the other hand, in the online tutorials, there was a greater equality in the exchanges. In the previous session described, the student initiates most of the questions with the teacher then answering them. Sproull and Kiesler (1991) have found that CMD seems to narrow the differences in status: "High-status" individuals (e.g., a teacher) may have less influence and a "low status" individual (e.g., student) may have more.

What is most interesting about this exchange is how the student engages in the revision process by attempting to reflect on positioning herself in the argument and the type and amount of evidence she needs for the counter-claim. This metacognitive awareness, reflected in her ability to verbalize her question, may be useful in developing her rhetorical awareness. At the same time, her discourse is utilitarian, focusing only on how to do the assignment without extending the discussion much beyond that. Romano (1993) found that this kind of exchange is typical when the potentially egalitarian narrative associated with CMD merges with the institutional constraints of the course. This metacognitive nature of the exchange may be heightened by recording the exchange so that both the teacher and student could reread it and reflect on its significance at a later time.

But problems exist. There is often a lack of cohesion, in part due to the difficulty in knowing when one participant can jump in and another one has finished. Note how in Lines 5–6, I try to respond to her question, but before I finish, she jumps in with Lines 7–8. This lack of cohesiveness can be confusing for English language learners in a one-on-one session but even more more so when there are more participants involved.

Moreover, not every session is as egalitarian as these examples. In the next example, the discussion is about the final exam and the role of the teacher is now more authoritative since he is the only who knows what the final exam will be about. The result is that the exchange seems to resemble the traditional student/teacher interaction. The teacher explains in detail the format of the exam (Lines 1–3), and the student makes sure he understands what the teacher means (Lines 5, 7–8). Note how even adding one more participant to the discussion complicated the exchange and interfered with the flow of the conversation. I am having an exchange with SRI_109 when Alex enters the chat.

1. JoelB says, "then the third issue—about confusion"

2. JoelB says, "there should be three well developed paragraphs"

3. JoelB says, "do the same thing on the exam"

4. alex [guest] says, "well i have a question"

5. SRI_109 [guest] says, "so you mean I should separate those issues into the different issues.."

6. JoelB says, "alex—feel free to jump in"

7. SRI_109 [guest] says, "then I would have so many paragraphs..."

8. SRI_109 [guest] asks, "is this ok?"

Not knowing whether the exchange with the first student was over, Alex jumps in (Line 4). Alex may not know how to enter into a conversation late since the conventional cues that a new participant can use are often absent. In a face-to-face conversation, Alex would have to wait until the first student finished speaking, but online, it can be difficult to gauge the flow of the conversation and type at the same time. As a result, Alex can interrupt without knowing for sure if he is interrupting the flow of the conversation.

To continue the conversation with the original student (Line 5), the moderator had to take a more active role in replacing the missing cues by signaling who should speak. In a face-to-face situation, the teacher may reprimand Alex for jumping in, but here the teacher allows Alex to ask his question even though he had interrupted the flow of the conversation. (In more graphically oriented chat rooms like Elluminate®, participants can click on icons to "raise their hands," thus avoiding this problem.)

Teachers must be aware of these types of issues and take a more active role in remediating them. In these situations, teachers need to rethink their traditional role in a tutorial to adapt to a new context. The instructor might want to take a less central role or even withdraw completely from the chat room, allowing students to first discuss the issues before coming to the teacher. Even if students initially entered the chat room to get help from the teacher, they may find some of the answers to their questions from other students.

These changes in implementation do not guarantee success since no technology is useful in all contexts and for all purposes. It is therefore the role of both the student and teacher to explore the possibilities of a technology, attempt to remediate its limitations, and then judge whether the technology is appropriate. Despite these limitations, the strength of these synchronous interactions can be seen in their ability to support the invention, planning, and revision strategies the students use in their writing processes. These examples offer evidence for the value of synchronous discourse in extending these invention and planning processes outside the constraints of the classroom. These dialogic interactions can provide a powerful heuristic for generating new ideas, but one that takes place in a different environment with different constraints. The examples indicate that the social interaction that occurs during these stages differs when compared to face-to-face interactions in tutorials and in the classroom.

Finally, it must be noted there has been much resistance over the years to substituting online communication for face-to-face communication, even when it may have been more convenient, and even potentially more useful for the students, to do so. Even strong advocates of the use of technology in composition classrooms have supported this resistance. As

Charles Moran (2005) has said, "We need to resist this techno-logically and culturally driven tendency to move away from face-to-face instruction, the writing-speaking connection, and oral communication in general" (p. 67). There has been a fear that the push for online courses has ignored some of pedagogical issues that have not been dealt with adequately in the development of online courses. These issues include the quality of online exchanges (e.g., Noble, 1998) as well as a variety of questions about the role of teachers and the own-ership of digital materials ("Copyright and Digital Media," 2005). Nevertheless, moving away from the limitations of face-to-face communication can have positive consequences for both teacher and student.

More Suggestions for Using Synchronous Interactions

- MOOs have a number of tools and commands that can be used to help deal with some of the problems that have been found (Schweller, 2001). Tools such as recorders can be used to make a transcript of a conversation to send to the students to review. Teachers can also use the transcripts to make sure all questions get answered, and perhaps after the session is over, respond to unanswered questions.
- Whiteboards or slide projectors can be set up in some chat areas beforehand to make available ques-tions or pieces of text the teacher wants the whole class to see.
- Teachers need to understand the nature of the room they are using for a MOO (Haynes, 2001). MOOs like Tapped In® give teachers a room that can be used anytime they want. Other MOOs may allow teachers to create their own rooms, so they can adapt them to reflect more personal tastes or specific course goals.

- Because of the unique problems in using synchronous discourse, students need to be carefully prepared to use chat rooms. Except in a purely online course, it is often useful to bring students together to a computer lab to have them practice using the chat rooms before the scheduled session.
- Synchronous discourse can be used for one-to-one or group work. When using it in a group setting, great care must be taken in setting up groups that can interact well together. Putting students into online groups requires some of the same considerations. Liu and Hansen (2002) discuss for creating face-to-face groups.
- Additional technical as well as linguistic capabilities also need to be considered. Typing ability, for example, can also affect the interaction of the group. Students with weaker typing abilities might be grouped in smaller groups than the students with better skills. Another possibility is to experiment with the homogeneity of the groups, mixing students from different backgrounds or with different language skills together.
- Because participants can pose questions or comments in rapid succession, students can frequently "interrupt" each other, something that may be considered rude in face-to-face contexts. Therefore, they need to be more aware of conventions that make it clear when they can enter a conversation.
- MOO sites like enCore *(http://lingua.utdallas. edu/encore)* provide free open-source software for designing MOOs and are free to clients logging in. Web-based sites like Tapped In® are not as flexible but can be simpler to use. Other types of spaces, like Alado Webcasts *(http://alado.tripod.com/index. html)* or Elluminate® combine video technology in order to webcast a lecture, provide a space for posting slides, and another space for the online audience to simultaneously have a discussion or ask questions.

- Mynard (2003) reported that students sometimes find it difficult to work independently and set their own discussion topics, which means they may require more or teacher involvement throughout her course. She also found that her students often had trouble transferring what they did in the chat room to their writing assignment. This problem may be helped by giving the students recorded transcripts that can be reviewed later.

Using Asynchronous Discourse in the L2 Composition Classroom

Despite the interest in synchronous discourse, asynchronous forms have been more popular in the L2 composition classroom. Students who feel uncomfortable in the more fast-paced world of chat rooms may perceive asynchronous discourse as more user friendly. Unlike in chat rooms where texts can scroll too quickly to be read, online groups appear much more concrete and better organized (Aycock & Buchignani, 1995). There are a number of types of asynchronous discourse, including email, Usenet groups, listservs, threaded discussions, and most recently blogs. Each type functions differently and therefore needs to be examined separately.

Synchronous versus Asynchronous

Differences between face-to-face and online communication necessitates making sure that all questions or comments have been responded to. Face-to-face conversations allow the use of a variety of strategies to ensure that there has been an appropriate response. However, because of the speed of the discourse in chat rooms and MOOs or the length of time between the posting and the reading of a message in asynchronous

formats, it is easy to have a question forgotten. Not having a question answered is one of the most frustrating
experiences online and can seriously affect a student's
willingness to participate in the discussion.

Synchronous and asynchronous forms of discourse
may be introduced at different points of the writing process. An online chat, for example, might be
scheduled before the first draft of a paper is due or,
as our examples showed, as a tutorial or a review
session. In traditional views of process (Olson, 1995)
approaches, where the invention phase primarily
occurred at a fixed time, usually before the drafting of
the paper began, this approach may be more appropriate since using synchronous discourse can require a
more structured form of scheduling. However, in the
current view of process writing that holds that these
different stages can occur at any time throughout the
writing process, a technology that allows for more
flexible scheduling may be more useful.

Using Email in the L2 Composition Classroom

Email is the most well-known form of asynchronous discourse.
Since its beginnings, CMD has been used to foster personal
interaction although that was not its original purpose. Kraut,
Mukhopadhyay, Szcypula, Kiesler, & Sherlis (1999) compare
the development of CMD to the development of the telephone
since neither was originally developed for social communication. They describe how ARPANET, which was the original
instantiation of the Internet developed by the U.S. Defense
Department in the late 1960s, quickly changed from its original
purpose of providing the military with a reliable data network
in case of nuclear attack to a place where academic researchers
could collaborate, trade notes, and even gossip.

Kraut et al. (1999) found that email is the most frequently
used application on the Internet and that the primary use of
email was to maintain relationships.

As with other forms of CMD, email can be used both as an instrument to support composition teaching and as a form of writing. The widespread familiarity of email has made it an important application in the teaching of language (Bloch, 2002; Li, 2000; Liaw, 1998; Warschauer, 1995; Velma, 1994). Swales & Feak (2000) argue for the direct teaching of email in the academic writing classroom, as it exemplifies what Swales (1990) calls an "occluded genre" that can be discussed in the same way as other genres of writing. The use of email in teacher/student relationships has also been studied (Bloch, 2002; Casanave, 2004; Warschauer, 1999). Bloch, for example, examined the various ways that students could use email to both create and negotiate relationships with their teacher. One popular use is to link classes whose students have different language backgrounds and/or ages (Boswood, 1997; Yagelski & Powley, 1996).

The linguistic and rhetorical impact of email, as well as how email can affect reader/writer relationships, has been discussed by Sproull & Kiesler (1991), Baron (1999), and Crystal (2001). As with other forms of online discourse, email allows writers to explore different aspects of their personality that they may not feel as comfortable expressing in face-to-face situations. In their study of a hearing-impaired Japanese student, for example, Casanave, McCormick, & Hiraki (1993) found that the student presented a much different and more authoritative self in his email than he did in the classroom.

I have argued that there is a relationship between how students write and the ability they have to write about whatever they wanted to (Bloch, 2004). In my study of a Chinese group constructing a response to an American television program that many people considered racist, I found that student writing in a second language contained a passion plus well-reasoned and logically constructed arguments more developed than what is often found in the L2 classroom. It may have been that the greater permanence and structure of the discourse seemed to help students with the social construction of their ideas, arguments, and refutations, which in the end results in a substantial body of knowledge that students can use as a source of ideas in their own writing.

From its beginnings, the Internet was a place where people could cluster together around their favorite interests. Some of the first spaces used for online writing were Usenet groups, which allowed individuals loosely bound by a common interest to communicate with each other. As with listservs and older forms of asynchronous discourse such as bulletin boards, Usenet groups reflect the original goal of the Internet to foster communication. Wikipedia defines a Usenet group as "a distributed Internet discussion system….Users read and post e-mail-like messages (called articles) to a number of distributed newsgroups, categories that resemble bulletin board systems in most respects. The medium is sustained among a large number of servers, which store and forward messages with one another." "Usenet," para. 1.

Usenet newsgroups were one of the earliest means for posting ideas and sharing information about a variety of academic and nonacademic interests, even for people who did not have access to ARPANET. Usenet groups were one of the first forms of CMD with an architecture that encouraged the formation of social groups, a function that has largely been replaced by other types of CMD. These groups allow people with similar interests, such as watching soap operas (Baym, 1995), or similar cultural backgrounds, such as being a Chinese ex-patriot (Bloch, 2004), to post messages to share with other subscribers to the site. In a fascinating study of Usenet groups where one member of the group was accused of murdering four of his colleagues, Aycock and Buchignani (1995) found that the Usenet fostered a social construction of the murder by all the members of the group, although few of them were personally acquainted with the murderer.

Although Usenet groups have had limited use in education, research has uncovered some interesting findings that are applicable. The concept of a Usenet group can still be found in threaded discussion boards, which are popular among teachers who use course management systems like WebCT. One of the most interesting findings is the passion with which individuals can write when they choose topics that are of great importance to them. I (2004) examined a Usenet group called social.cultural. China, which was primarily made up of Chinese-speaking participants. I examined an online discussion among these Chinese students about a television program on an American network charging that the Chinese government was sending spies to the United States. The television show had upset many participants in this group, which triggered a prolonged discussion about the show and how to respond to it. The participants in the Usenet group were able to use the architecture of email as a means of creating a new intertextual piece of discourse, utilizing what Moran (1995) calls "interface rhetoric" (19). In the example that follows, the participant used the respond feature of email message systems to interweave his own text with that of a letter received from the president of CBS News, the television channel that had aired the broadcast, in a way that creates a new text from the two. In the posting, the writer takes issue with the wording of the letter, especially the claim that there were many more potential spies than the one the show had reported on.

> >On May 19th, we reported the Chinese Ministry of State Security
> >has _recruited hundreds_[2] of ordinary Chinese citizens to steal U.S secrets.[3]
>
> Can CBS news tell the difference between "hundreds of" and
> planeloads of? Why did CBS report "planeloads of" instead of "hundreds of"? Can CBS tell
> the difference of dozens of and hundreds of?
>
> >military, technological, trade, and computer secrets.
> >This, according to the United States Defense Information Agency in
> > Washington.
>
> Is there a grammar mistakes here? or an incomplete sentence?
>
> >Between 1986 and 1993, one in eight of all illegal export
> >enforcement cases closed by US Commerce Department involved the
> >People's Republic of China. Security experts have told CBS News that many of the spy cases
> >uncovered are then hushed up and the
> >suspects deported, so _the problem may_ be even greater than we
> >reported.
>
> Doesn't the above statement show that CBS did not report correctly as they understood
> that the problem may be even greater than they reported.
> Shouldn't CBS have reported that the problem might be even greater than CBS was
> reporting. Should CBS report, not planeloads, but city load, provinceload, countryload?
> (cited in Bloch, 2004)

---

2. The author actually marked the texts with a series of carets ^^^^^^^^^^, which I have interpreted as being underlined for emphasis.

3. I have tried to preserve the format of the interchange here.

While the format the student uses in his email may not be standard for classroom-based writing, its dialogic nature shows the same rhetorical strategies that are important in the classroom: appropriating published texts for the students' own rhetorical concerns, critically evaluating these, interjecting their own ideas, and then creating a new text. The fact that this new text resembles a popular form of Chinese dialogue ("cross-talk" or "*xiang sheng*") illustrates how non-native English speakers can appropriate the Internet for their own uses. These types of texts force us to rethink how we define textuality and what we think of as standard forms, as well as what is considered plagiarism.

As this example also illustrates, asynchronous discourse also can provide a space for writers to work together to enact change in the society outside the Internet. The participants were able to use the media for their own political purposes. The students organized a committee to meet with Connie Chung, a prominent Chinese-American journalist who reported on the story and became the target of much of the participants' anger, and the president of the network news department to discuss their grievances.

Although the research was done outside the classroom, this research illustrates ways that CMD could be used in a classroom to create new types of relationships and new kinds of texts. The contrast between the type of writing found in Usenet groups and the more restrained nature of students often found in the classroom seems to illustrate the kinds of issues Turkle (1995) and others have raised about how writing online gives a freedom not always found in physical spaces to express these alternate selves, what Bargh, McKenna, & Fitzsimmons (2002) call the "true self" (34). This kind of online research demonstrates how CMD can empower students not only to write passionately about topics they care about but also to show them how their writing could even affect the policies they care about. Such research can also show teachers the importance of choosing assignments that have significance for the student and about which they have some "expertise." Finally, the research can demonstrate how this interaction between the determinism and the transparency of technology can affect classroom practice. Obviously not all the lessons learned from this research can be successfully integrated into the classroom, but the research on CMD demonstrates its potential for extending the writing process outside the classroom.

More common in the L2 composition classroom have been listservs, electronic mailing lists, which take advantage of the students' familiarity with email and its more interactive nature. In this example from a class listserv, the writer attempts to refute the claim that it is easier to cheat on exams in an online education course.

I read Ming-chun yu's[4] opinion about online education can't prevent cheating on exams. Actually, online education prevent cheating on exams... the online courses ask students to see some local teacher as proctor. Even some courses ask them to go to campus and take the exams.

Although this example exhibits the kinds of politeness strategies that many students often used in their criticisms of their classmates (e.g., Davis & Thiede, 2000), the writer engages the idea in ways we hoped could be used in the classroom.

Students also used the listserv to help them with their assignments at any time they felt they had a problem.

Is there somebody could help me to find other issue that I could write on my synthesis paper. "when is your class due for final paper? is that supposed to be this Friday or monday?

This query about the paper occurred toward the end of an assignment rather than at the prewriting stage that often occurs in the composition classroom or even using online chat rooms. Perhaps more important, the student is forced to direct his question to his classmates instead of relying only on the

---

4. The name has been changed.

teacher. Without the physical presence of the teacher, these questions must be directed to the other participants. In this way, the listserv can deemphasize the role of the teacher and make student/student interaction the primary focus.

The ease with which many students seemed to take critical positions when they wrote online made us hope they could express the same critical thinking in their print texts, something that was not always the case. Therefore, one goal was for them to write synchronically first and then transfer the writing directly into their paper with some rewriting because of the differences in the writing space. For example, the students were required to write an extensive evaluation of what they had read. They were encouraged to write this evaluation on their listserv or blog and then directly transfer what they had written into their papers. The students often used the same rhetorical forms with a greater development of ideas in their asynchronous form of discourse that they struggled with in their formal writing assignments, although they were not always able to transfer these rhetorical strategies to their classroom-based writing (Bloch & Crosby, 2005).

Inevitably, there is a question about whether these forms of CMD really help develop the thinking and writing skills of the students. Weasenforth, Biesenbach-Lucas, and Meloni (2002) found that the use of the listserv was successful in implementing a number of cognitive goals they wanted their students to demonstrate. For us, the ultimate goal of using this listserv was to generate ideas the students could use in their papers but not necessarily to improve the fluency of the students, which might be addressed in the classroom assignments. A listserv can be used to create a social context in which the students can discuss an issue on an ongoing basis and, at the same time, take some risks in arguing their positions and, ultimately, to transfer their ideas and to cite the ideas of their classmates directly into their papers. Unlike other uses of technology, the listserv served a more utilitarian approach, not as a form of writing itself but as a means to improve the process through which traditional print-based writing was created.

Using Email, Listservs, Threaded Discussions, and Usenet Newsgroups

- Students are often not afraid to send email; therefore, they can be given as many opportunities as possible for doing so, such as submitting papers online, to take full advantage of its potential.
- An ongoing concern, especially among users of listservs, is how much of the email to include in the reply. While some feel that including the message makes reading inconvenient, we have found that it is important for each email to refer back to the email being responded to so that everyone can follow the discussion. The fragmented nature of messages means that individual senders must "link" their messages to the ones they are responding to or "quote" a piece of that message (Herring, 2001).
- There are advantages and disadvantages to using listservs, Usenet groups, and threaded-message boards. Listservs, for example, may have a greater immediacy because the messages are deposited in the students' email. However, the messages could also pile up so that, as with any large amount of email, the student may simply want to delete them. Course management systems, such as WebCT or Blackboard, often require extra steps for logging in, which may discourage readers if they do not have any other reasons for checking in. Therefore, the instructor must be able to tailor the different roles of CMD to the form of architecture that underlies the course management systems.
- Different forms of asynchronous discourse can affect writing in terms of length, formality, and levels of interaction. We have found anecdotally that using threaded messages, as well as blogs, produced longer messages but less interactivity; therefore, students were required to post responses.

> • Teachers cannot always control for such factors, but they need to be aware that the quality and the quantity of participation may vary greatly among students and therefore adjust their implementation to make the Internet useful for all the students.

Blogging in the Composition Classroom

Recently, no form of CMD has been more discussed than blogs for their potential use in education (e.g., Farmer, 2005; Lowe & Williams, 2004; Richardson, 2006). As mentioned in Chapter 1, blogs are a form of asynchronous discourse that shares many of the characteristics of listservs, Usenet groups, or other forms of CMD, but that have their own unique qualities that make them suited for classroom use, such as:

- managing personal knowledge by organizing the writer's thoughts in reverse chronological order
- furthering public discussion both through responding or linking to others' blogs
- providing a space for social networking where people can find others with similar interests
- enhancing the circulation of information freely across communities (Paquet, 2002)

Podcasts and Vodcasts

Blogging can be an interesting way of introducing students to the possibilities for incorporating multiple modalities into the writing. While blogging, like other forms of CMD, is primarily a text-based medium, increasingly more importance has been given to visual and oral forms into the written texts. Video blogs, which are also called vodcasts (see *www.vodstock. com/make/how-to-make.php*), and oral blogs, called podcasts (see *www.apple.com/education/solutions/ podcasting*), represent new opportunities for integrating multimedia into the composition classroom. While writing is not a prerequisite for these types of blogs, written texts can be used as a basis for both podcasts and vodcasts. Students can be asked to write texts that can be integrated with music and an image, creating what is sometimes referred to as digital storytelling (see *http://storycenter.org*). As has been the case with text-based blogging, there have been a number of free websites springing up to host these new forms of blogs, for example, podOmatic *(www.podomatic.com)* and ClickCaster *(www.clickcaster.com)*.

For L2 composition teachers, blogs can be an important means for combining personal and academic writing in the same writing space. Unlike web pages, whose format is organized around some concept of "a page," the format of the blog allows for publishing short pieces that would not be appropriate for a web page (Hourihan, 2002). The architecture of a blog has made it more suitable for writing on a variety of different subjects that do not necessarily have any connection to each other. Blogging allows students to post a personal blog about what they have been doing over the weekend and then, beneath it, another post discussing the issues raised in the classroom.

Why Blog?

- Blogs are much easier to set up and maintain than traditional kinds of websites.
- Blogging is becoming an important form of writing, which may encourage students to write more.
- They have an open architecture, which allows the writing to be more easily shared.
- They provide students an unlimited amount of space where they can write outside class.

- They can be used to introduce other aspects of hypertext such as linking and images.
- Compared to email lists, they are more permanent and therefore could be used in a variety of ways.
- They can allow students' work to be read and commented on by people inside and outside the class.
- They can be set up either individually or with a group, giving students a variety of concepts of authorship and allowing teachers to take different approaches to using them.

Setting Up Blogs for a Composition Class

Blogging Services	**Blogging Add-ons**
• Blogger *(www.blogger.com)*	• Flickr™ (adds images) *(www.flickr.com)*
• mo'time™ *(www.motime.com)*	• Bloglines (aggregates blogs) *(www.bloglines.com)*
• Edublogs *(www.edublogs.org)*	• Haloscan (commenting and trackback) *(www.haloscan.com)*
• Tabulas *(www.tabulas.com)*	• Technorati™ (searches for blogs) *(www.technorati.com)*
• vox.com *(www.vox.com)*	

From a technical standpoint, blogs are like web pages; both are created using a computer code such as HTML or XML and are hosted on a server or host computer or can be integrated into a variety of course management systems. One blog can be set up for the entire class, a number of blogs for smaller groups, or one for each student. This decision may have an important effect on the students' writing, but there has been little research in this area (see Farmer, 2006). The creator of the blog can choose a template for the design of the blog and a URL so the blog can be viewed on the Internet. A hosting service usually gives the user a space for composing the blog before posting it.

Privacy Issues

Many new technologies have blurred the distinction between what is public and what is private. Phone calls that were once held in private booths now take place in public places. What are the consequences of these changes? Blogging, perhaps more than other technologies, raises such questions about privacy in the classroom. Bloggers often feel freer to discuss personal matters in their blogs than they would in other writing contexts. Students need to be reminded that anyone can read what they write, so they have to be careful about what they say. Privacy is a critical issue when using blogs with younger children. Tabulas *(www.tabulas. com)* asks if you want to prevent Internet search. Some services like mo'time™ allow you to create password protection to guard against unwanted readers, although passwords may undermine the open nature of blogs. Blogger and Vox™ allow administrators to limit who can view blogs. Blogs can also be hosted on one's own servers, which can be protected, although completely blocking outside access undermines some of the advantages of blogging. Teachers can also control who is allowed to post or comment to the blog in order to protect against spamming. While these measures do not guarantee privacy, they are one way of trying to ensure outsiders cannot spam or post unwanted messages.

Many of the blog sites can greatly simplify the process of creating a web page as well as the basic functions of hypertext such as inserting links. The screen is a writing space that has the look and feel of most word processing programs. When the writer is finished with the blog, he or she can click on the "publish post" button, and the posting will appear both beneath the writing space and on the blog website.

From elementary school to graduate school, teachers are experimenting with blogs in their classrooms. To understand how to use blogging in a classroom, it is important to know the possible uses for blogging and then match the goals of the course. One of the main purposes of blogging is to allow writers to publish personal online diaries. These types of blogs can foster the idea of community even though the community may be loosely connected and short lived. This blog, for example, was written by a Korean hearing- and speaking-impaired student who could only communicate with her teacher and classmates through a computer.

My name is ***. I am deaf and from Korea. I became deaf at age of 3 years due to fever. I can speak and lipread Korean but can't speak and lipread English. Also, I can sign Korean Sign Language. I know American Sign Language but I am not good at ASL. When I lived in Korea, many people thought that I can hear because I can speak very well in Korean. In fact, I have communicated with other people not through lipread (sight) but through hearing.

I have learned Korean speaking from my mother and sister. Then I went to regular school from kindergarten to high school but the school for deaf. Because I was born very small rural and there are no schools for the deaf. The more importantly, my mother wanted me to be strong people through competing with hearing friends and she believed that I had enough potential ability much as competing as them.

Blogging provided a unique opportunity for the student to communicate with her classmates at a point when we were struggling to integrate her into the classroom discussion. Her attempt here to communicate with her classmates was especially powerful for her instructor since she had previously confided a sense of isolation from the other students.

For many of the students, blogging provided an important means of expressing themselves in whatever form of literacy they felt most comfortable with, something that is not always possible in an academic writing class. The students could write about their lives without a concern about grammatical errors. In this blog, for example, a Somali immigrant is wrestling both with her writing and her adjustment to college.

I don't think I have a lot things to say but I would like to share with my class mate what I am feeling right now. We all now that this is out first year in real world that means college or University, even thougt some of us just transfer from another college however the majority of studnt is new. the reson I would like to talk about this is I am being so good around her. the first month we start school was so straces full for me, but I relize that I couldn't do any singe thing if i am being strass full on every step i step or on every sorcamistances I do I was not satsfy on my work and happy most of the time when I came to school I couldn't enjoy my time that i spen in here but I don't know why. The reson of this I hurt my self people keep asking me why am i losing a lot of wait. Please don't light at me i have been exercing every day this last summer to lose wait but I didn't. Is there any one who had the same problem i have been though ? Don't be really straces full do your work. try your best as long as you try you will get it back.

Thnks for your pacent.

There are still some L2 teachers who struggle with the question of whether they should be concerned with grammatical correctness in blogs. Although there were a number of spelling and grammar errors in this blog, the student created a great deal of text, which offers a new perspective on her writing ability than had previously been seen in her classroom-based writing; there she struggled to create even a paragraph. Blogging offers composition students the ability to both write and read at their own pace and at any time during the writing process, not just at the time set up by the teacher.

One of the most important reasons to use blogs, as well as listservs, has been to provide a writing space where students could discuss the issues they were writing about in the classroom. In this class blog, for example, the student discusses his ideas for an argumentative paper regarding what universities should do about plagiarism.

Teachers in 106 classes teach students about plagiarisms. They should not give punishment to students if the students commit plagiarism, because the students do not understand what the plagiarism is. However, they have to tell the students when the students commit the plagiarism, because the students have to know what is recognized as plagiarism. It is important because the plagiarism in the other class can give the students severe punishments. Position of Rose[5] at Marita case can be suitable to the teachers in 106 classes, because Rose is most sympathetic to the plagiarism. However, Rose gave her light punishment, rewriting paper. So, teachers in 106 class should be kinder than Rose; that is, there is no punishment in 106 classes.

---

5. This reference is to Mike Rose's book *Lives on the Boundary*.

The students here could use the blogs for expressing their opinions and joining in an ongoing discussion, just as blogs are used outside of class. The writer is able here to address specific policies regarding how instances of plagiarism should be dealt with, developing arguments to support his position, and cite other sources to back him up. Mortensen and Walker (2002) have said that weblogs are usually more briefly developed than the more developed forms of argumentation found in an academic article. Yet, they can still be used to discuss the same issues and use the same writing strategies in a more accessible way than in more formally written articles (Bloch & Crosby, 2005).

One issue that Krause (2005) has raised is the extent to which blogging can foster the dialogic quality of discourse. The nature of such discourse in the L2 classroom, particularly when it involves critiquing another classmate, has been of great concern (Carson & Nelson, 1999; Ramanathan & Atkinson, 1999). As the next blog illustrates, the writer can use this space to take an opposing position over the issue of whether teachers should warn their students that they are using online detection software to find out if the student had plagiarized a paper, which was an issue already discussed in class. In this example, the students were asked to take a critical view of another student's blog, which was a rhetorical strategy they were expected to incorporate into their research papers.

Fusako's argument is oppsite to my argument. Fusako says that teacher have to announce to students to using plagiarism detection website previous, but my opinion is not. I think that teacher have right to control their students and can give punishment and point out the error

---

We have consistently seen this type of critical exchange in other forms of asynchronous discourse (Bloch, 2004; Bloch & Panferov, 2003) where Sproull and Kiesler (1991) argued that the distance between reader and writer allows for greater risk-taking in the kinds of criticisms one can make.

This process of constructing knowledge, as was illustrated in the blogs about plagiarism, contains a number of the elements of the social process by which academic knowledge is first created, discussed, written down, and later published and discussed again. The ease by which text can be published and commented on allows students to gain first-hand experience in how knowledge is socially constructed. As Siemens (2002) argues, blogging allows knowledge to be acquired and shaped as a social process, which results in the logarithmic increase in the amount of knowledge available: "I say something, you comment on it, I evaluate it, comment and present a new perspective; you then take it to the next level and the process repeats until a concept has been thoroughly explored (online)." Participating in this process can be valuable for students who, as Haas (1996) has found, see texts as being objective and static and not as part of a dynamic process of knowledge production.

Unlike oral forms of discussion, the written nature of blogs can be exploited by having students use them as texts that they cite in their own papers or that can be cited by other students. Using blogs in this way is another way of making blogging a more dialogic experience, but more important, having students cite each other's text can give the students a more in-depth understanding of the textuality of their own writing and place a greater value on their classmates' voices. The ability to publish their ideas as texts, as well as to take responsibility for what they say, may help students see themselves more as authors. As Canagarajah (1999) has argued, students must be able to value their own voices in both their L1 and L2. Blanton (1999) likewise has stressed the importance of students valuing their own voices and ideas and connecting them to the voices of others.

In the classroom, many of our students, especially our immigrant students, have had a great deal of trouble conceptualizing the role of texts in academic writing. These students have little experience with either writing academic texts or using them much beyond using an encyclopedia (e.g., Rose, 1989) or a textbook as a source for finding information that could simply be copied or paraphrased into their texts.

Blogging provides a tool to try to solve both to the problem of having students produce their own texts using a variety of rhetorical strategies and then integrating them with the texts of other students in constructing their ideas. Students can write blogs in a number of styles and registers and then publish them to the Internet. The blogs can in turn be used by other students to develop their own texts. In this way, the students gain a sense of the textuality of their own writing and the intertextuality that results from citing other students' blogs and seeing their own blogs cited by their classmates. However, as with any tool, there is no guarantee of success.

As we've discussed throughout this book with various technologies, it's the architecture of blogging that makes it more suitable for the writing classroom. Mortensen and Walker (2002) argue that because blogs are instantaneously posted in a reverse chronological order, they encourage "spontaneous, timely and concise expression of thoughts" (p. 268) that can be linked with other writings in other blogs. Although blogs are often more informally written, they share some of the qualities of print literacy, which may result from their greater degree of permanence than other forms of online discourse have (Miles, cited in Mortensen & Walker). Because of these qualities, blogging may have a greater potential for use in composition courses that focus on academic writing.

The problem with this kind of approach, as Gee (1996) argues, is whether the student can transfer knowledge from one form of discourse to another. Gee (1996) argues that the ability to move from acquiring, which is subconscious, to learning, which is conscious, requires the student to develop a certain level of meta-knowledge about the task, which can help the transfer process from the blogs to the print text. Gee (1996) also argues that for students to succeed in their academic work, it is critical for them to go beyond their primary discourses and for teachers to provide scaffolding for their attempts to do so. In our classes, we treated blogging as a form of text, but it was also hoped that blogging could be a form of scaffolding to bridge this divide between primary and secondary forms of discourse.

In this blog, for example, which was written after a class discussion on plagiarism, one student confessed about his own past experiences plagiarizing.

Yes, frankly I plagiarized so many time in my former school which located in West Virginia. When I had a homework or research paper, sometimes I plagiarized. I am not different to Ally[6], Marita and Jamal [people and characters we had discussed in class]. Sometimes, I plagiarized by cut and pasted the paper like Haley and sometimes I listed the internet sources or magazines to my research paper like Marita. Moreover, I just turned in somebody's paper to the professor by changing original name to my name like Jamal[7].

This blog raises a variety of issues that are central to what I have been discussing here about the nature of CMD. On the one hand, the blogs seem to encourage this kind of openness, which can be valuable both as a means of expression and a way for the students to share their experiences. On the other hand, it may be naive to discuss things that one may regret making public in the future. This is a highly problematic area that highlights the necessity of not just thinking about how to use blogs as a tool but also about how to discuss them as a writing type or genre.

Another form of reflection that can be incorporated in the blogs is to have students share the problems they are having with their classroom assignments. This kind of reflective writing has long been common to help students understand the nature

---

6. Not her real name.
7. The students had read stories about two students—Haley (Heaton, 2003) and Marita (Rose, 1989)—who were caught plagiarizing. Jamal is a fictionalized character from a movie called *Finding Forrestor*.

of their writing, and blogging makes these reflections public, which allows these problems to be shared and discussed. In this next blog, a Somali student discusses the problems he has with writing a synthesis paper, which required the student to compare the ideas in their own blogs, the blogs of their classmates, and the texts they had been reading and then reflect about the issues regarding attitudes toward plagiarism.

The first day when professor Cate the synthesis paper I thought myself it will be easy to do. Because my mind told me, we already discuss about the articles and the video that we watch. That should be easy to do that is what I said to myself.

Here the problem that I find out when went home. I thought I deeply understood what the paper about, but I didn't and I was wrong. Synthesis paper is not like the other essay I did before. The synthesis paper was to write about all three students who plagiarism and compare all three of on one paper. I never wrote this kind of paper before. First of all, I had problem on my introduction. I didn't where to start because I had the idea but couldn't express on the paper.

This student had a good idea about what the writing task was but clearly struggled to transfer what he had written in the blogs to a classroom assignment. The blog allowed him to share with classmates and teachers his own metadiscourse about his problems, a step that Gee (1996) argues can be important in helping resolve these problems.

Blogging is an interesting example of how the architecture of a technology and the social contexts in which they exist interact to affect the pedagogical problem the teachers are facing. Blogging is simple enough to be used by students with little background in technology to share their ideas about whatever topics they think are important. Thus, when faced with the question of what technology could help create on ongoing conversation as well as potential texts to be cited, blogging was thought to be the most logical choice. In our course, for example, plagiarism has been an interesting topic to blog about since decisions about what constituted plagiarism and how it should be dealt with typically excluded students. The blogs allowed the students to voice opinions about an issue that could have a tremendous effect on their lives and careers. As Herring (2001) argues, however, the proliferation of any form of discourse on the Internet does not guarantee a democratic discourse if there is not an even playing field so that everyone can participate. Nevertheless, the proliferation of blogging has created wide-ranging discussions from all sides of the social and political spectrum.

Suggestions for Using Blogs

- Set up a class blog and use the questions raised at the end of Chapter 1 as assignments. Ask students to write as much as they can about each question and have them comment or write another blog to one of their classmate's blogs.
- Use blogging as a means of introducing hypertext. The ease by which blogging technology can be used to create personal web pages, with both links and images, makes them a useful way to introduce students to writing online and integrating texts and images. However, in comparison with using traditional kinds of web pages (see Chapter 3), blogging may not give students as deep an understanding of the issues surrounding hypertext. On the one hand, the results usually will be much simpler versions of web pages than can be created in a web page design course; on the other hand, blogs can be much more dynamic and are much easier to create since they require less specialized technology and little knowledge of HTML code (Lowe & Williams, 2004).

- Use blogs, either written by the students or from ones you have read in the blogosphere, as texts for classroom reading and discussion, just as you would use print texts. Farmer (2005) argues that blogs should be used as task-driven elements in a class. Blogs can be used in different ways depending on the pedagogical goals of the classroom, such as for discussing personal issues and class issues or for creating interactions among both class members and non-members. For example, we found blogs to be more useful for our goal of creating texts since they were more permanent than messages posted to a listserv and more easily accessible than messages posted to our threaded discussion board. By having students read and then cite their classmates' blogs in their own writing, we hoped to remediate the relative lack of interactivity that Krause (2005) mentioned (see page 161).

- Have students post about issues or personal experiences they might feel uncomfortable discussing in a classroom. Catera and Emigh (2005) suggest using blogs as a means of helping students comprehend the texts they are reading by having them write about it. In this way, quiet students can more easily participate in the classroom discussion. Teachers can check on student comprehension and find interesting points they want to follow up on in class.

- Discuss controversial blogging sites, such as *myspace. com*, to raise issues that students need to be aware of when they blog. One of the controversies regarding blogging is posting ideas or images that one may regret later if family or future employers should read them. Group blogs may mitigate this problem by burying the writing among a group of other writers.

- Experiment with individual blogs and class blogs. Individual blogs may be more useful if one goal is to teach students about blogging. If there is a concern about security features, for example, it may be better to have every student set up their own blogs, so they can learn how to set the features of the blog that affect its security. Blogging sites contain various ways of controlling for comments. Some allow you to choose who can comment as a way of controlling for spam and flames. Having each student set the levels of security for the comments can help them understand how they can protect themselves.
- Have students become acquainted with the blogosphere by searching for interesting blogs. Students can be introduced to the blogosphere through sites like Technorati™ *(www.technorati.com)* or Feedster™ *(www.feedster.com),* which catalogue blogs and allow users to do searches. Students can search for interesting blogs that they can write summaries about, evaluate, or just share. Have students aggregate their favorite blogs. Teachers and students can use aggregation sites like Bloglines.com to be notified when anyone posts to a blog or to make it easier to track all the blogs that one is following. Aggregating blogs can help students understand how information on the Internet becomes joined together.
- Have students take some pictures and post them to a blog. Websites like Flickr™ allow users to post and share pictures, annotate them, and post them.
- Blogs are not only for students but for teachers as well. Teachers can discuss their own classes, share ideas with other teachers, or collaborate together in group or team blogs *(http://evo05.blogspot.com/).* This approach can be useful in teacher training programs to link experienced and inexperienced teachers or in group programs so that all the teachers can keep up on what is going on in the other sections of the course.

Remediating Problems with the Use of CMD in the Classroom

As argued in Chapter 1, problems with a technology do not have to be seen as intrinsic to that technology but can result from how the technology is implemented. Changes in the implementation can address some of these problems. For example, our enthusiasm for using CMD was not always matched by the students. Post-class surveys of our use of CMD have consistently shown that the students were divided in their opinions of whether CMD was useful for their writing. As previously mentioned, students had little interest in using synchronous discourse to replace face-to-face interactions. These findings were consistent with some of the constraints Hammond (1999) has enumerated about student attitudes:

- concern regarding whether they had the time to post and read other postings
- concern regarding whether they had enough access and technological skills
- how committed they were to the discussion
- the extent to which the forum encouraged communication
- the degree to which the course supported online learning

A lack of participation can be a critical factor in the success of any list. On the listserv, students may have felt slighted when their postings were not responded to in a timely manner or at all. This lack of response necessitated more intervention from the instructors than was normally expected to make sure all the students' questions were answered.

The lack of participation has raised issues of whether to make postings compulsory. Our response to the problem of participation was to increase the credit for postings so that the students had more incentive to become more involved in the discussion. A second change was to require the students to respond more often to the other postings and give them credit for responding.

A lack of interaction can be a major issue in how effective the use of CMD can be. For instance, when using a WebCT discussion board, we found that the students were writing more but interacting less than on a listserv. A similar difference was noticed with the blogs. While there are often mechanisms for creating interactions, such as the comment feature on blog sites, student interactions on the blogs often seemed more perfunctory and less engaged than on the listserv. Having the students cite each other's postings was one way we have tried to deal with this problem of interaction.

As was previously discussed, one of the most troubling problems associated with computer-mediated discourse is the presence of flaming, (e.g., Sproull & Kiesler, 1991). Sproull and Kiesler show that the same kind of distance between the reader/writer, which we found to be an aid to critical thinking, could also be abused in ways that could have a detrimental effect on the functioning of the group. Although there have been very few instances of flaming in any of our uses of CMD, the ones that occurred, whether they were intended to be flames or not, caused a great deal of disruption to the list. In this example, the student appears to be upset about a previous posting and verbally attacks the sender.

That's really show how sensitive you are. Well...I don't want to get

it into personal and i have just simply responded my opinion to you,

not teasing you! I am welcome everone exchanging the idea with me

if they think I might be wrong. However not some kind of emotional

words!!!!

Even one such incident can impact the usefulness of the listserv where the message was posted for both teachers and students to read. However, even flames can have a useful pedagogical purpose for discussing both the use of the Internet and the kinds of language that may offend people. There were other incidents, however, that had a nastier tone, such as this one where the same student posted the same message to the listserv he had already sent to the course coordinator complaining about his teacher.

I am really angry! But nothing related on the article anymore. Not Only do I complain [name deleted] teaching approch, but also some of my classmates have this concern! As you know, now, it is the sixth or seventh week that we've already been! I really do not have any idea what she did for us. She has multiple standards that bad she picks on me can be the Good on the others. However, I thinks she is wasting my MONEY (which is from my very hardworking mother) and time (I am not a lazy student). She is the worst instructor. What she think that she is? She is cocky and nothing can do for student.

In this case, what once was a private issue became known to many members of his class and other classes as well. Here, the factors that can make email a useful tool in the classroom could also combine to cause a variety of classroom problems. Instead of being a private issue between teacher and student or perhaps among a small number of classmates, the issue became known to every member of the listserv. Other students then joined in, either in opposition or support. Even the architecture of the email, which allows the message to appear in the reply so that the thread can be easily followed, contributed to the perpetuation of the problem. However minimal the number of flames are, there is an inevitability of flaming because of the cultural diversity of the participants and the variety of norms they bring to the discussion (Smith, 1999). Students may lack the control of language necessary to precisely express their feelings, which can cause misunderstandings that can be easily clarified.

Despite the importance of free speech and the free flow of information in cyberspace, these types of incidents can undermine the usefulness of using CMD. To control such incidents, some form of administrative control may have to be implemented (Dibble, 1998; Reid, 1999). Mediating these conflicts was easier in an environment where the architecture of the listserv limited who could join the list and forced participants to identify themselves through their email addresses, factors which, on the other hand, could limit the ability of the participants to express themselves freely (Rheingold, 1993). In the end, managing this trade-off necessitated creating a number of rules for both what could be discussed online and what format their messages should be in.

Roles for Teachers in CMD

- Different forms of CMD require different degrees of teacher intervention. Teachers may need to do little if anything to have students use email. The more opportunities students have to use email, the more chances they will have to use different types of email
- Listservs, discussion lists, and blogs all involve varying amounts of time to set up and technical expertise. In some cases, teachers may find it necessary to give regular and compulsory assignments, but in other cases, they may not. For example, we could never make online tutorials mandatory since there was so much student resistance.
- There is often much greater variation in how much participation is useful. In online tutorials, clearly the instructor is going to make a large percentage of the contributions. However, in a class listserv or a blog, there seems to be less need to intervene except when problems arise.
- The use of CMD requires greater attention by the teacher to the issues of access faced by the students. The use of synchronous discourse can require that the student be able to access the Internet often and at any

time as well as have a stable Internet connection that they can use for longer periods of time. Students without a computer or laptop may be at a disadvantage in these situations. Before implementing CMD, teachers should survey students to find out what kind of access and what types of Internet connections they have.

- Many teachers and students want online discussions to stay on topic. Controlling the direction of the discussion is one of the more controversial issues in using CMD. Johnson-Eiola & Selber (1996) recommend not allowing participants to go too far off topic into dangerous or controversial topics, although sometimes such divergences can be useful in terms of developing interaction in the group.

- Teachers or moderators have to strike a balance between allowing students to feel comfortable expressing themselves and guarding against divergences that may upset the unity of the group.

- One way to form this community is to allow students to discuss topics that may be personal or may be considered off topic. The teacher or moderator in a group is often the one who has to draw the line as to what is an appropriate topic, but it can be important that participants have a clear idea about what should be discussed.

- Most of the research indicates that CMD should focus on content and not on grammatical correctness. It may not be necessary for students to worry about grammatical correctness when writing online. However, for teachers who want to integrate CMD into the teaching of grammar, there are a number of ways to do this without detracting from the integrity of the discourse. Although we tried not to focus on grammatical correctness, we did find that when students tried to paraphrase the discourse of the other students, they sometimes had to attend to grammatical problems in the postings.

As a writing environment, CMD is not necessarily a radical concept. Using the framework for multiple forms of literacy found in the pre-Internet work of Heath (1983) and Scribner and Cole (1981), CMD can be viewed as simply a technologically enhanced site for multiple forms of literacy. However, it could also be seen more radically as a space for fostering alternate forms of literacy. Regardless of how CMD is viewed as a writing environment, its tremendous popularity both inside and outside the classroom reflects the use of technology as a communication medium for supporting human learning and creating online communities (Feenberg, 2003). While fundamental differences exist between CMD and face-to-face communication, CMD does not exist apart from other spaces for social interactions (Jones, 1997) in the classroom or in society, so what occurs in cyberspace can be both supported and constrained by these other contexts.

Research has shown a tremendous increase in the amount of reading and writing done online, especially by young people using a range of newer technologies such as blogs (e.g., Rainie, 2005) and instant messaging (Shiu & Lenhardt, 2004). While blogs are becoming more and more popular in the L2 composition classroom, some of these technologies have not, and perhaps may never be, fully implemented. The ability to write in both virtual and physical environments is valuable for the L2 student because each of them can allow the student to use different forms of the language. Students who may be uncomfortable with formal academic forms of writing may feel more comfortable with the vernacular forms of literacy that are often found in CMD.

On the other hand, some students who have seen using CMD as a waste of time may not have seen any value in using it, which can be a justifiable position to take. Just as the acquisition of print literacy does not guarantee the type of social advancement that is often promised (Graff, 1987), learning how to communicate over the Internet may not benefit everyone equally. In their study of the use of the Internet, Kraut et al. (2002) questioned whether some groups benefit more from the use of the Internet. This group includes those who already have strong social support networks, such as friends, family, or colleagues, who can use the technology to create stronger or more frequent connections. Another group that Kraut et al. found to benefit from the use of the Internet is the "social compensation" (p. 58) group, consisting of those for whom the acquisition of technological literacy may compensate for a lack of social support.

While CMD does not necessarily facilitate the radical agenda found in pedagogical approaches favored by advocates of critical literacy, it does provide the writer with a means of engaging readers in a dialectical relationship with different forms of discourse. Even with the more formal forms of CMD, its implementation can foster this dialogic nature of knowledge development. However, these types of social communities do not necessarily develop or function on their own; they often need individuals, such as teachers or perhaps a few students, to make decisions about who can participate and what can be posted. There is a limitation in the generalizations that can be made between classroom-based and non–classroom based uses of CMD. The use of CMD in the classroom is not necessarily an "authentic" language experience since the participants may not be there voluntarily and they may not be writing about things in which they are interested. CMD seems to be most effective when students see a purpose for its use. As Katz (2002) argues, the strength and longevity of e-communities like The WELL™, which is one of the oldest social communities on the Internet, can be attributed to the ability of the moderators to discourage hostility and keep conversations on the topics that were generally acceptable. Unlike the participants in The WELL™ who all had joined voluntarily, some students in the course had chosen not to participate in the community and may be uninteresting or feel uncomfortable with the topics.

Teachers need to be aware of these social issues when they evaluate whether the use of CMD is appropriate and how to modify the implementation to reflect the specific needs of the students. An awareness of these issues helps avoid reliance on the utopian narratives of technology usage often heard (Hawisher & Selfe, 1991b; Romano, 1993; Takayoshi, 2000). Hawisher & Selfe (1991b) and Takayoshi (2000) suggest that teachers and researchers should not only give positive narratives but discuss their failures too, which is something we have tried to do here, if only as part of the process of revising the implementation of the technology.

The need for caution is necessary because the nature of CMD or its future development is not clearly understood (Johanyak, 1997). Both researchers and teachers often bounce from one technology to another, which has often resulted in chaotic introductions of technologies as a new one is being touted before the old ones are understood. As we have suggested throughout this book, it is incumbent on teachers to continually evaluate their own uses of these technologies to discover the advantages each form of CMD might offer and what problems might occur.

Reflection Questions and Projects

1. Join a listserv. You might want to join TESL-L *(www. hunter.cuny.edu/~tesl-l/)*. You can join their general list or one of the branches like the technology list or the jobs list. Think about the purposes of the list and the kinds of messages that are posted. What kinds of answers do the questioners receive? How is the list managed?

2. Explore different blogsites by yourself or with other teachers to see how different sites can be used in different ways. Different types of blogging sites can create different types of blogging communities and interactions among their participants. For example, some blog sites, such as Edublogs have been designed specifically for teachers. Does this make a difference? Therefore, teachers need to experiment with different sites to see which one best fits the goals of the course. Some sites are easier, for example, to post to; or other sites may allow images to be posted without knowing how to code them.

3. Create a blog. Go to a blog hosting site and set up your own blog. You can write about your experiences teaching or just your personal life. Search for other blogs by ESL/EFL teachers that you can link to. Go to Technorati™ and search for ESL blogs and see what you get. Search for blogs about anything you are interested in. Use an aggregator like Bloglines to capture feeds from these blogs. Keep an eye out for the TESOL online electronic village for courses on working online.

4. Open up an account at Flickr™. Post and annotate your own photos to share with friends, family, or the whole world. How can this be integrated into the writing classroom?

5. Write a script for a podcast—a lecture, a story, or anything you feel like talking about. Use a free software program like Audacity® *(http://audacity.sourceforge. net/)* to record it. Think about how you would use this in a writing classroom. Some teachers have thought you can replace all lectures with podcasts. What do you think?

Chapter 5

Corpus Linguistics in the L2 Classroom

      While concordance programs have been around a long time, their usefulness in the composition classroom has dramatically increased recently because of changes in how the programs can be accessed, in the choices of types or genres of language that can be studied, and in the way the program interface can be modified to reflect specific uses in the classroom. The change in access has been accelerated by three developments. The first has been the emergence of small, inexpensive programs like MonoConc 2.2 and WordSmith, which teachers can purchase to develop their own concordance-based materials from the corpora that the teachers themselves can create. The second has been evolution web-based programs, such as Collins Cobuild or The Compleat Lexical Tutor, which can be used by teachers or students to query lexical or grammatical items for in the classroom or for their own personal use (see box) although, as will be discussed, these interfaces can vary greatly in user-friendliness (Ari, 2006). The third factor has been how these websites have been designed to allow users to choose among a variety of sources to choose the types of language the user wants to study (see Figure 5.1).

Goals for Using Concordance Programs

Concordance programs have numerous features that enable students and teachers to explore various aspects of language use (Leech, 1997). For example, Leech argues that training

MICASE Concordance Search   Browse | Main

Search with Context	Speaker and Speech Event Attributes
Type a word or phrase to search for in the first box. The wildcard character * may be used at the end (but not the beginning) of a search word to represent zero or more characters (e.g. typing in *walk** will give you *walk, walks, walked,* and *walking*). In the context box, you may add an optional word or phrase to find in a specified proximity to the search word[s].	Each of the selection boxes on the left represents a speech event attribute category. Each on the right represents a speaker attribute category. You may specify any number of values from each category to make your browse more specific.

Word or Phrase: [   ]

Context Word or Phrase: [   ]

Within [   ] words
- ○ To the left
- ○ To the right
- ◉ To the left or right

Speech Event Type:
All
Advising Session
Colloquium

Academic Division:
All
Biological and Health Sciences
Humanities and Arts

Academic Discipline:
All
Advising
Afroamerican and African Studies

Participant Level:
All
Junior Undergraduates
Senior Undergraduates

Primary Discourse Mode:
All
Monologic/Lecture
Panel

Gender:
All
Male
Female

Age Range:
All
17-23
24-30

Academic Pos Role:
All
Junior Undergraduate
Senior Undergraduate

Native Speaker Status:
All
Native speaker, American English
Native speaker, Other English

First Language:
All
Arabic
Armenian

Choose Result Settings

Select up to 2 speaker attributes to appear in the results display
- ☐ Gender   ☐ Age Group
- ☐ Academic Role   ☐ Native-Speaker Status

[Submit Search]   [Reset Form]

Figure 5.1. In the MICASE interface, the user is given a number of parameters to choose from before entering a query.

students to work with these programs will aid them in learning about language and learning to study language. Leech suggests that a simple way to do this is to provide students with a hard copy of sentences on a lexical or grammatical item that was created from a query of the program. Alternatively, in their textbook, Thurston and Candlin (2002) introduce L2 composition students to the use of concordances by providing print-outs of corpus searches to discuss the meanings of specific words and concepts and then integrating these searches with a more traditional set of grammar exercises. This approach can help students to make inferences about syntactic or lexical usages (Hewings & Hewings, 2002), so they can become more independent users.

Concordance programs can allow students to explore issues they feel are important. Lee and Swales (2006) report on a course that focused extensively on using concordances with a focus on academic writing. The course not only asked students to write weekly assignments using various corpora but also asked them to compile their own corpora from their writings. They suggest having students compile their own corpora of both student and published writings as a way to deal with specific classroom concerns, such as grammatical differences

> ### Concordance Websites
>
> - British National Corpus *(www.natcorp.ox.ac.uk)*
> - Collins Cobuild *(www.collins.co.uk/Corpus/CorpusSearch.aspx)*
> - The Compleat Lexical Tutor *(www.lextutor.ca/)*
> - International Corpus of English *(www.ucl.ac.uk/english-usage/ice/avail.htm)*
> - Linguistic Data Consortium *(www.ldc.upenn.edu)*
> - VIEW *(http://corpus.byu.edu/BNC)*
> - Virtual Language Centre *(www.edict.com.hk/concordance/)*

across genres (e.g., Hyland, 2002d). Once students learn how to make inferences from the data, they can enter vocabulary items or lexical strings into the concordance program and receive a set of sentences from which they can induce the usage or meaning of the word. Sudents may need a fair amount of practice using these sentences before using the program itself.

Teaching Vocabulary and Grammar Using Concordance Programs

One of the most valuable uses of concordance programs is responding to the lexical or grammar questions students often raise. Schmitt (2000) suggests ways to use concordance programs for vocabulary learning, such as the direct teaching of vocabulary, collocations, and linguistic strings and lexical chunks (e.g., Pawley & Syder, 1983). Lee and Swales (2006) asked students to look at lexical items, such as *affect/effect*, that are problematic for students. In this example, a question had arisen about the usage of *that* and *which,* an issue that has come up because of how Microsoft Word marks the use of *which* as an error if it's not preceded by a comma (see Figure 5.2).

THAT—*that* **is only used here to modify the nouns that precede it.**

1. Tees's criticisms, however, in no way detract from a highly readable and at times thrilling account of a career **[[that]]** most would consider responsible for how we study human evolution today.

2. They have woven them together to create a complex tapestry **[[that]]** reflects the actual interdependence of the different levels of language study.

3. It was only Fowke's premature death **[[that]]** brought Alfred Waterhouse into the project and shifted the style to the Romanesque.

WHICH—*which* **is used either when the information is unnecessary to the meaning of the sentence or to modify an entire phrase.**

4. Unlike trees of populations, **[[which]]** only have biological meaning when populations bifurcate with little subsequent migration, alleles in any population, regardless of the population's demographic complexity, will have a genealogy that can be inferred and interpreted.

5. This capacity, **[[which]]** is language, allows us to communicate an infinite number of concepts to each other.

6. Thus Reagan was able to initiate Star Wars, **[[which]]** he did in a March 1983 speech written and supported by his science advisor George Keyworth.

Figure 5.2. An example of using materials generated from a concordance program to differentiate between the usage of *that* and *which*.

An important implication of concordances is the greater need to focus on the variation of meaning across different contexts. Tognini-Belloni (2001) argues that it can effectively demonstrate how words that may appear to be synonymous, in fact, may actually vary in different contexts. Lee and Swales (2006), for example, looked at variations in usages across different genres and forms of language (oral/written) by asking students to query the same form, such as differences in the use of tense using different corpora.

The initial impetus for using a concordance in language learning classrooms was to provide students with examples of authentic sentences to analyze (Francis, 1993). Unlike in traditional grammar textbooks that use invented examples often focusing only on the specific item being discussed, a concordance can provide a large number of examples of the target items that can be embedded with a variety of other co-occurring items. Concordance software can provide students with large and varied examples of authentic uses of vocabulary items or syntactic forms such as a hedging device or a reporting verb in a rich context. This can help the user decide about the appropriateness of each example, which may not be possible when using traditional grammar texts or dictionaries. However, the user must play an active role in making appropriate decisions, which Johns (1994) refers to as data-driven learning.

Our research into the use of reporting verbs has indicated that the use of words like *mention*, which is used by many students as a standard way of reporting claims, can vary depending on whether it is used to report one's own claims or someone else's. Our corpus study of student papers, which is often referred to as a learner corpus (Granger, 2003), showed that our students almost always used *mention* in an objective way, as a substitute for *state* or *write*. However, in our corpora of academic research and review papers, which was developed using academic writing from *Science* magazine, *mention* was used in a positive way only when discussing one's own ideas and when discussing others' claims, but it was frequently used negatively when repeating others' claims. By presenting students with examples of these different uses, as suggested by Ellis (2002b), our goal is for students to gain an "awareness" of grammar by helping them

> 1. Although other virus infections are **mentioned,** particularly hepatitis B virus infection, there remains a danger that conclusions from HIV-1 infection are assumed to be generally true for all viruses.
>
> 2. The author **mentions** that children like to read fantasy books, so it may seem more interesting for them to try to solve a fantasy problem rather than a real-life one.
>
> 3. Since her debut just three years ago, Dolly has been **mentioned** in over 4,000 news articles.
>
> 4. I have only space and time to **mention** rudiments.

Figure 5.3. An example of using a concordance program to discuss vocabulary items perhaps not used appropriately by students.

"develop explicit knowledge" (p. 32) of the relationship between a particular lexical item and its rhetorical purpose. For helping students gain this awareness, the universalist approaches to grammar teaching traditionally found in grammar textbooks do not work well because the emphasis has shifted to studying the "local knowledge" of language. Textbooks often present an autonomous view of grammar, which separates the grammatical item from the rhetorical context. Even the use of "authentic sentences," cannot always capture the sometimes nuanced differences in usage since this approach is still based on the material writer's intuition, which may not be the same as actual practice.

In Figure 5.3, the sentences found from a query of the word *mention* demonstrate that there can be a great variation in the rhetorical intent of the word. In Example 1, the author seems to use the word *mention* in the dependent clause as a negative evaluation of the claim—that the claim in the main clause is over generalized. Had other viruses been discussed in more depth, the writer may have recognized that the conclusions from HIV-1 infection are not generalizable. In Example 2, on the other hand, the claim seems to be evaluated more positively, but the resulting conclusion about children solving fantasy problems is seen to be a very weak claim since not much evidence was presented. On the other hand, there are times when simply mentioning something is enough. In Example 3 *mention* is used in a more positive way but only to make a very general claim. Of course, when reporting one's own claims, which would always be expected to be positively evaluated, as in Example 4, the use of *mention* is simply used to report a fact.

Concordancing can be used with a variety of pedagogies. If the goal of the composition course is to develop a student's intuition about rhetoric, it is crucial that language is taught within that same rhetorical framework. In these examples, *mention* is not simply a vocabulary item but part of a rhetorical approach to making evaluations and interjecting the students' own ideas into their discussion of the prior research. Providing such authentic examples can encourage the development of the students' meta-language about the grammatical and lexical use, its variation across texts, and how it compares to the students' L1 (Thompson, 2001). Giving students this context to explore possible meanings and usages, as in the example of the use of *mention,* can illustrate how the meaning of a word may vary, depending on the context, which allows for, in Hopper's (1998) terms, a better demonstration of the relationship between grammar and rhetoric.

These approaches to grammar teaching also require new roles for both the teacher and student to play, which can be supported by a technology such as the concordance program. As I have shown in these examples, there may be more ambiguity to what a word means or what is the correct grammatical form, which can be frustrating for both teachers and students. Students also need to be able to take more control of their learning (Lee & Swales, 2006). In this next example (Figure 5.4), our students had to guess what preposition was used with these nouns and then check with the concordance programs to see if their guess was given in the examples.

However, the use of concordance programs can be disconcerting for both teachers and students. Concordance programs do not give correct or incorrect answers, as is typically the case in grammar textbooks. Without a fixed set of rules to follow and a textbook to rely on, the students must be able to learn to find their own examples of the grammatical and lexical items that they need to know (see Figures 5.4 and 5.5). As Thompson (2001) has argued, the purpose of using corpora is to get

1. **Methodology** (of doing fermentation research)

2. **Research** (of the production of beets)

3. **Information** (for registering for classes)

4. **Explanation** (of how enzymes break down)

5. **Criteria** (for entering the food science graduate school)

Figure 5.4. The boldfaced words were identified from student papers as being problematic for the collocation between the noun and the preposition. The students were then given a list of these words and asked to generate phrases (an example of which is given in parenthesis) and asked to enter a string in Collins Cobuild (e.g., methodology + IN) and then try to guess from the results whether their choice was correct. Collins Cobuild, as do other programs, allows users to enter strings that contain a syntactic code such as IN for preposition, a lexical item, and a number indicating the range of the items.

1. **Research + IN**	Research __ OSU
2. **Criteria + IN**	Research __ biology
3. **Experience + IN**	Criteria __ research
4. **Comparison + IN**	Experience __ doing research
5. **Approach + NN**	Experience __ tools
	Experience __ being in America
	Comparison __ others
	Comparison __ two restaurants
	Approach __ science

Figure 5.5. In the right column are examples of prototype strings developed by advanced-level composition students (Jack Rouzer, personal communication, 2005). The prototype strings could then be used for developing materials for discussing prepositions in a lower-level composition class.

students not to rely on simple and sometimes unhelpful sets of rules but to construct a possible answer based on the available evidence, test hypotheses, and make generalizations (Leech, 1997), which in constructivist learning traditions, allows the learner to be a more active participant in the learning process (e.g., von Glaserfield, 1995), especially in the acquisition of grammar (Ellis, 2002b).

While grammar texts typically present sentences constructed to show specific grammatical items, these items may not occur in such an isolated fashion in naturally occurring sentences. More important, isolated sentences in grammar textbooks rarely explain how the choice of a grammatical item interacts with the rhetorical intent of the text. Using a concordance may be one of the best ways for students to observe this communicative process (Aston, 2000). But can all students benefit? Do higher-level students benefit more than lower-level students? Do students who have a strong basis in grammatical rules learn better than those who have picked up grammar outside the classroom? Data-driven learning requires a fair amount of intuition to deduce the patterns from a set to examples—that is, to decide which examples are or are not relevant and then be able to intuit the pattern. A concordance requires the users to make deductions about the uses from the data that can often be variable and ambiguous, which can be confusing for both teachers and students even while, as Hyland (2003b) points out, the students are searching for the regularities of a pattern across a wide variety of texts.

The argument that Hopper (1988) advances about how appropriate grammatical choices emerge out of context can mean that grammatical forms can only be learned in conjunction with other grammatical forms and the specific nature of the rhetorical context can make grammar teaching and learning extremely complicated. Explanations of usage often are accompanied by the expression "it depends" on what is meant or the context in which the syntactic or lexical item is used. This ambiguity may be frustrating for students who learned grammar and vocabulary from textbooks and dictionaries that present these items in a consistent way. This process of making hypotheses as a means of raising the consciousness of the students (Hunston, 2000) may be difficult for students who have not yet mastered basic forms or who have learned grammar in a different way. It would seem that the higher-level students who might have a sophisticated background in grammar would have an advantage; however, there is little research on this topic. The studies by Yoon & Hirvela (2004) and Lee & Swales (2006) both focused on the use of concordancing software with advanced-level doctoral students. Less is known about the use of concordancing with students who have different levels of writing ability or other degrees of experience with the genres being studied.

It could also be argued that concordancing may be most useful for students who prefer unstructured, discovery-oriented learning or lack formal training in grammar in order to help them build a representation of the purpose of choosing grammatical forms without necessarily the need for knowing the appropriate terminology (Ferris, 1999). There are technical factors as well that could affect the use of the program. Using a concordance program can force users to think about the use of these items in a way that is much different from the approach usually found in traditional grammar books. This approach assumes that we do not learn vocabulary or grammar rules by learning categories or definitions but that we learn from examples. The learner must be able to sort out the good examples from the bad ones. As Schmitt (2000) points out, concordance software can provide students with large and varied examples of authentic uses of vocabulary items or syntactic forms such as a hedging device or a reporting verb in a rich context, which can help the user make decisions about the appropriateness of each example (e.g., Hyland, 1998). The user must play an active role in this process, what Johns (1994) refers to as data-driven learning. Unlike traditional grammar textbooks that use invented examples often only focusing on the specific item being discussed, a concordance provides examples of target items embedded in a variety of other co-occurring items that textbook writers may find difficult to come up with on their own.

Implementing Concordance Programs in the Composition Classroom

The migration to the Internet, which has had two major consequences on how they can be used in composition classroom. First, users can easily access large online corpora such as Collins Cobuild, VIEW, or The Compleat Lexical Tutor from any computer site. Collins Cobuild made itself universally accessible by employing a dual pricing level, which is common on the Internet, whereby a limited use of the program was available for free and full usage could be licensed for a yearly fee. The other two programs are free and open to everyone. Second, the Internet provides online access so the sites can be used anywhere at the exact moment the user needs them. This form of "just-in-time" learning allows users to access the program at the precise moment they need help (e.g., Milton, 2000), which has become an important factor for facilitating the use of concordance programs by non-linguists. As has been discussed throughout this book, this question about how concordancing can be used is not only a pedagogical one, but, as Milton (1997) has shown in his development of concordance-based software, it is also a technological question with how the software is implemented and how it is designed and perhaps redesigned.

Further technological changes have facilitated the design of corpora so that individuals can develop them for their own specific purposes. Stand-alone programs like MonoConc 2.2 (Barlow, 2003) and WordSmith (Reppen, 2001) are disk-based and therefore may be better suited to teachers for developing course materials or placement in a lab. Additional programs, such as taggers, can be used to label items in the corpus according to their category (Biber, Conrad, & Reppen, 1998), which allows users to search by syntactic form (see *http://devoted. to/corpora* for examples). Their biggest advantage is that they allow developers to create smaller but more specific corpora according to their own specifications that can be used for well-defined purposes. If one wanted to study the introductions of scholarly articles, for example, a corpus of introductions could be created. Henry & Roseberry (2001), for example, examined specific text types such as letters of application and introductions to speakers as a means of obtaining detailed materials for demonstrating how specific communicative purposes are addressed. Thompson and Tribble (2001) used this approach to find variations in how citations were used across these different sections of a text.

Stand-alone programs allow teachers to create their own corpora. Perhaps the simplest way of creating a corpus is to cut and paste texts copied from the Internet into a large text file, which allows the creator to choose precisely which texts or parts of texts to examine.[1] As discussed in Chapter 2, cutting and pasting texts raises a question of intellectual property rights. As with many issues regarding the use of intellectual property, applying existing laws and court decisions does not readily clarify the issue. Kennedy (1998) suggests that permission be requested from the publishers of the text, although the legal issues for personal and noncommercial use are not clear.[2]

Corpora for composition classes can come from published texts or student papers, which is referred to as a learner's corpus, although the latter is probably more suitable for studying the kinds of strategies and errors learners make (Leech, 1997). While designing one's own corpus may seem to be a simple matter of cutting and pasting, it raises a number of theoretical and practical questions regarding the use of intellectual property that have never been clearly answered. The complexity of the legal issues regarding cutting and pasting from the Internet places teachers in the difficult position of having to know what can be legally done and what cannot. The ability to develop and possibly share these corpora inexpensively and easily depends on preserving a balance between the rights of owners to control intellectual property and the rights of the fair use of that information. Legal issues often revolve around whether

---

1. The status of copyright issues regarding creating one's own corpus can change if it is used for commercial purposes.

2. For our own use, we asked the publisher for permission but never received an answer.

the user of the property is gaining any monetary value or the owner of the property is losing any. However, there have been no court cases to date regarding the creation of corpora, and therefore the question of whether it is legal to do so can only be answered with a maybe.

Moral issues, particularly with regard to the use of student texts, are more complicated, although these issues can be dealt with by obtaining student consent forms. Recent laws making the copying of password-protected intellectual property illegal have never been applied to developing a corpus, and therefore there are no precedents to help a teacher know whether creating such a corpus is legal. New developments in such seemingly unrelated areas as encryption programs, which can regulate the flow of information, may make the development of such corpora more complicated. One thing teachers might keep in mind is how they would feel if their work was used as part of a corpora without their knowledge. In some cases, they may not mind, but in others, it could be a problem for them.

The discussion of intellectual property and corpora illustrates how technology, when mixed with pedagogy such as the teaching of grammar, can be embedded into larger social and political contexts. Issues such as the design of corpora are examples of how the direction of new copyright laws may affect the development of new ideas relating to technology (Lessing, 2001).[3] The ability for individual teachers to take control of the technology, through web-based interfaces and inexpensive concordance programs, is an example of what Lessing (2001) has called the tremendous boost given to innovation that has resulted from the free flow of information across the Internet. Giant corpora, such as the one contained in Collins Cobuild, are highly controlled both in terms of its access and usability. In Lessing's terms, such programs have absolute control over the way the programs are accessed and the nature of its content. Other approaches, such as the use of stand-alone programs like MonoConc 2.2, can give teachers greater control over the use

---

3. The fair use of information from the Internet is complex and is not uniform across the world. Many countries have laws regarding fair use, but the details can greatly vary. For a more in-depth discussion, see Brown and Duguid (2000).

of this technology but may not have the depth of coverage or the technological advantages of Collins Cobuild. It is therefore important that teachers understand the ramifications of how a topic that might seem as esoteric as intellectual property law can affect their teaching practices.

The Nature of Concordance Program Interfaces

Along with these social and political issues that affect the use of a technology, there are also technical issues that need to be considered. A user interface is the part of a system exposed to users and includes menus, screen design, and keyboard commands—all of which create the way a user interacts with the computer (see Wikipedia). In general, the system can be any kind of system with which a user may interact, such as a computer system. Interfaces, like other forms of technology, are never neutral. As Selfe and Selfe (1994) argue, interfaces, as with metaphors in general (e.g., Lakoff & Johnson, 1980), can impose a framework that controls how the technology is seen. They give the example of how the "desktop" interface, with its file folders and neatly laid out icons on a desk, facilitated the idea of computing as a business tool, which had important economic consequences.

The growth of web-based concordance programs highlights how different interfaces can affect how the site can be used. Programs such as Collins Cobuild provide a dynamic interface that allows users to enter lexical items or grammatical strings and then receive a web page containing sample sentences using those items. To receive these sentences, the user has to use a series of codes for each query. These codes, which may be intuitive for a linguist, can seem confusing for a student or even a teacher with little or no linguistic background.

Other concordance programs provide different types of interfaces, as can be found in programs like VIEW and The Compleat Lexical Tutor. One of the chief functions of the interface design is to allow users to choose from different corpora. The Compleat Lexical Tutor also provides the user with a series of functions that may seem daunting to the nonexpert. The Virtual Language Centre allows the users to choose from a variety of different corpora. There are no codes that the user has to learn, but without the codes, the user is restricted in the types of items that can be queried. The Virtual Language Centre also contains an interface that can be used to query vocabulary items. Like Collins Cobuild, it contains a program that will calculate the statistical analysis of the results, which can help users judge the relative frequency of an occurrence; however, the statistical feature is more complicated than the one in Collins Cobuild, which may discourage many users from trying it. Unlike Collins Cobuild, on the other hand, the lack of codes means that the user may be more restricted in searching for syntactic forms. Therefore, there is a trade-off in the different architectures that concordance programs can use.

A much different approach to interface design can be seen in *MICASE,* which contains a rhetorically based interface that allows the user to specify up to ten factors for each word or phrase that is searched, such as the type of speaker, the type of speech, and the location of the speech, as a way to limit the search (Simpson, Briggs, Ovens, & Swales, 2002). Although primarily designed for research in spoken English, the interface gives the user the ability to search the same corpora repeatedly by using different criteria to make rhetorical as well as linguistic choices. The choices of the parameters for using the program are written in plain English so that, while the user may need some theoretical background to understand the choices, the choices themselves are easily understood and do not require learning a code, as does Collins Cobuild.

The differences in interface design are necessary to understand how to use concordance programs and which type of students may benefit the most. All these differences have important pedagogical considerations. The complexity of factors inherent in the design of a concordance program means that the implementation is critically important. The importance of the implementation of a technology is based on the premise that no technology is static, and therefore no technology can be evaluated outside of the context in which it is used.

Technologies such as concordance programs may only be of limited use in certain contexts, such as finding out whether a given word or form is incorrect, so teachers and students have a sense for which types of problems a concordance is useful and for which type it is not.

The fact that concordance programs were initially designed for experts in linguistics or applied linguistics raises questions about whether they can be used for non-experts in the composition classroom. Yoon and Hirvela (2004), for example, found a number of problems that students have with using concordance programs. The most salient issue was the amount of time and effort it took to analyze the data received from any given query. Often there are too many sentences that may not be relevant to what the student is searching for, which can make it difficult to focus on the most useful data.

Remediating the Concordance Program

One of the best lessons that can be learned from the long tradition of CALL research is the importance of redesigning software to fit the pedagogical goals and the backgrounds of the users. Here I discuss how we designed a concordance program to fit a narrowly defined pedagogical problem to be used with a specific group of students.

In Chapter 3, I discussed an approach to the design of *learning objects,* which are websites best used for narrowly defined pedagogical goals and for an equally narrowly defined type of learner. In this case, the pedagogical goal was to teach the use of reporting verbs in academic writing to graduate students from a variety of fields in the university. Many, but not all, of them had strong backgrounds in grammar but little if any background in using concordance software. My concern with using concordance programs was that these students could be overwhelmed by the number of sample sentences they could receive for each query, which would make the process of sorting them out cumbersome.

Based on my analysis of the learning environment, I created three goals for the design of the program:

- a corpus based on academic writing that contained both formal research papers and evaluative papers, which corresponded to their assignments for the class
- an interface that presented them with a limited number of parameters to constrain the query, which were based on the decisions a writer must make when choosing a reporting verb
- a dynamic design for the website that would present users with only a limited number of hits for each query

The Design of Corpora

The first step in the design of this learning object was to create a corpus. One of the advantages of disk-based concordance programs, such as MonoConc 2.2, is that it easily allows querying of homemade corpora. With the availability of online corpora, many feel it is unnecessary to build one's own corpus, especially when considering the amount of effort involved. However, many of the most popular concordance programs use corpora developed from books, magazines, or newspapers containing more informal registers of language. Designing one's own corpus can give the users—both teachers and students—the ability to control for the types of language that the teacher wants to focus on and the contexts in which these language forms are used.

There are a number of critical factors to consider in designing one's own corpora. One is the types of assignments, such as a critical review or a research paper. Tribble (2002) describes the design of relatively small, highly specialized corpora that could be used for these purposes. He distinguishes between an "exemplar" corpus, which is directly related to the writing task, and an "analogue" corpus, which contains texts similar to the writing task. This distinction is a useful means of thinking about how closely I need to match the corpus with the classroom assignments. For example, for an assignment on writing a critical review, I developed an analogue corpus of reviews of various types of review articles since I could not find a set of articles directly related to the assignment. I could access this corpora using MonoConc 2.2 to create materials for teaching grammar that were related to their assignment for teaching.

This approach allowed me to look at items directly related to writing a critical evaluation as well as to explore possible variations that can occur within this type of writing. We had identified a teaching problem in how the students were using reporting verbs: Students do not always understand the variations in the uses of reporting verbs so they sometimes randomly substitute one for another, often only for stylistic but not rhetorical purposes. A dictionary was not always a solution to this problem since it often provides only a minimum of information that may not be helpful for making the appropriate decisions. It was felt that a concordance could provide students with a richer environment for learning about the syntactic and semantic information necessary to make better choices in their use of reporting verbs. Research on reporting verbs has shown that to make appropriate choices of reporting verbs, it is necessary to understand often subtle distinctions that are not always clearly expressed in dictionaries (see discussion of *mention* on pages 182–183).

The ability to create highly specialized corpora allows them to be tailored to the specific needs of the course. We identified a number of factors related to the course that needed to be considered in the design of the corpora:

- the types of writing assignments in the course
- the rhetorical goals of the course
- how the concordance program will be used
- the goals for grammar teaching in the course
- the types of language to be used
- the language ability of the users
- the academic background of the users

Based on these factors, there were several criteria to consider in the design of a corpus. The types of writing assignments determined the types of articles put into the corpus. The representativeness of the texts and the types of language they employed needed to reflect the fields in which our students were studying and their reading level. Since the students were our most advanced, the majority of them were studying in the physical sciences or engineering, we used *Science,* an academic journal that predominately published papers from a variety of fields.

These factors also influence the size of the corpus. A corpus can run from a few thousand words to millions of words. Large corpora, such as used in Collins Cobuild, have pedagogical value for general language issues but do not allow for the closer examination of genres or text types that more specialized corpora can. Focusing on a particular genre or type of language or a grammatical or lexical form may require a corpus with fewer words. As Ellis (2002a) argues, it is not always necessary to teach every grammar item but rather to focus on issues that students have problems with, an approach that a concordance can facilitate with its frequency counts.

Redesigning the User Interface

As the design of the MICASE shows, interfaces can be changed to fit the goals for the use of the program. Therefore, our interface needed to reflect the goal of helping students to understand the use of reporting verbs in an academic research paper. Instructional design theory describes the relationship between instruction and context and how methods of instruction can be broken into simpler components (Reiguluth, 1999). In this paradigm, an object can be created for one context, but another user can connect it to other objects to extend its function. According to Wiley (2001), this design requires that the object can be easily found and accessed.

Concordance programs are usually designed for searching a possibly "infinite" number of syntactic and lexical items. Our goal here, however, was to have students use the program for one specific grammatical form. We wanted them to be able to access the corpus using a group of syntactic and rhetorical criteria that have been identified as relating to the choice of reporting verbs in academic text. Finally, the interface was designed to be used by students while they are preparing their assignments, so the program had to be accessible from anywhere. The sample sentences generated from the use of MonoConc 2.2 had to be put into a database program (Microsoft Excel), along with a set of criteria to query them. The interface, therefore, had to allow this process to be carried from the Internet instead of using the database program.

There were three major problems that the interface needed to respond to:

- the architecture of the concordance program and the corpora
- the manner in which the corpora could be accessed
- the ability of users to access the concordancing site

Each goal had to be taken into consideration in the design of the program and its interface. The interface needed to be accessed through a number of different modes. For example, as discussed in Chapter 2, it could be accessed through a course website or after inserting its URL into a comment on the student's paper. Other tutorials could also easily be linked to this object.

The interface was designed so the students could access a sample of sentences according to a set of criteria they discussed for choosing a reporting verb (see Figure 5.6). One way to achieve this was to put the data from the concordance program in a database that students could query to obtain a more focused sample of sentences based on the criteria they had. MICASE, for example, uses a dynamic web-based interface that allows the users to make choices for a set of criteria and then receive a web page containing a sample of sentences based on these criteria. In our design, a final column was inserted that contained annotations about a grammatical topic that had been discussed in class, such as how tense was being used. See also Figure 5.7.

A variety of materials was developed to train the students to use the website. Another website was developed using

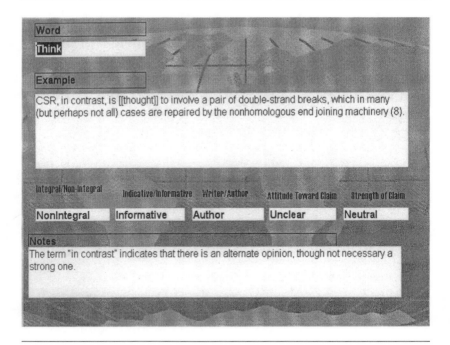

Figure 5.6. Based on research on the use of reporting verbs (e.g., Thompson & Ye, 1991), five criteria were chosen for querying the database. A sample query from the database gives the word, example sentence, the categories the user selected, and notes about the sentence.

Hot Potatoes™ to introduce them to the criteria they had to choose from (see Figure 5.8).

To practice using the interface, the students were given a set of sentences with missing reporting verbs and asked to first guess about the missing verb (see Figure 5.9). Then they could check their guesses using the program. Their answers could later be discussed in class, not as right or wrong, but as a general discussion on the use of reporting verbs.

The design of this website was not intended to be the definitive way of adapting a concordance to the particular needs of a classroom. Instead, its purpose was to illustrate the kinds of decisions made in this process. There were still major problems with the design. The evaluation of its use by our students showed that they had an understanding of some of the sentences from the corpora, a problem consistent with what

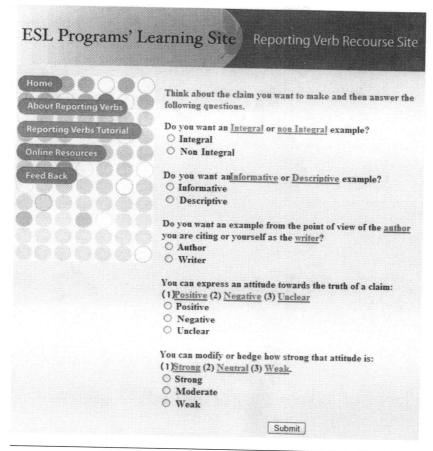

Figure 5.7. This interface allows the user to choose between searching for a specific word, which will yield 20 samples sentences, or searching by concept, which asked the user to first choose from a list of possible choices in five separate categories (see *www.digitalunion.osu.edu/ eslbloch/Search_by_Concept.php*).

Yoon and Hirvela (2004) found. By trying to make the corpora relevant for some students, it became too difficult for those in other fields. As with all the concordance programs and websites discussed in this chapter, there were inevitable trade-offs that had to be made. The discussion of this program illustrates the complex interactions among pedagogical, technological, and even legal issues. The most recent version of this program can be accessed at *www.digitalunion.osu.edu/eslbloch/*.

Using Reporting Verbs in Academic Writing

Identifying Reporting Verbs

One way of avoiding plagiarism is to identify the author of the text you are citing. When you put the name of the author or the claims of the author in the text, you need to also use a reporting verb. Reporting verbs allow you to insert your own opinion about the claim you are citing. The purpose of this exercise is to help you understand how reporting verbs are used.

To choose the appropriate reporting verb, you need to make decisions about how you want to use them and your attitude toward the claim. In this exercise, you will identify three aspects

1. Indicative/ 2. Informative
3. Fact/ 4. Opinion
5. Agree/6.Disagree/7.Don't know

For each of the three groups, choose one correct answer.

Show all questions

1/10 ⇒

People like Plantinga and Johnson [[claim]] the high ground without earning it, and so they seldom hold it long.

A. [?] 1.indicative

B. [?] 2.informative

C. [?] 1.fact

D. [?] 2.opinion

E. [?] 1.Agree

F. [?] 2.Disagree

G. [?] 3.don't know

Figure 5.8. This exercise, designed using Hot Potatoes™, introduced users to the categories they needed for the Reporting Verb learning object.

1. The author _____ that students _____ can get good grades by copying the work from the Internet, but he _____ it will cause them a big trouble.

2. The teacher _____ copying a sentence from the internet without putting the author name is stealing.

3. Mrs. Lodge _____ that the punishment is too hard and the student needs not a punishment but education for that.

4. Heaton _____ a girl, named Haley Lodge who faced on a big problem because she put off writing a paper until the last day.

5. Heaton _____ that thanks to advancing technology and the use of the Internet, our youth today with the click of a mouse can find an answer to all their academic problems on the Internet.

Figure 5.9. In this exercise the students are asked to guess the appropriate reporting verbs and then check their guesses using the program.

Suggestions for Using a Concordance

- A concordance can be useful not just to demonstrate the meaning of a word but also to show the syntactic forms that go along with it. Depending on how grammar is integrated in the composition classroom, concordance programs can be used in a number of ways for grammar instruction. Students can use concordance data to construct strings of words, to find examples of collocations, or to make judgments concerning the correctness of sentences.
- Another way of exploiting data-driven learning is to have students test their hypotheses about the appropriateness of a piece of discourse. For example, we ask students to guess about how to revise a piece of text, and then the student can use the program to test the hypothesis.
- The interface between the corpus and the user is crucial for how the program is to be used. Teachers need to decide whether the goal is to have students learn to use the concordance program, to get the answer to their questions, or some combination of both goals. The design of the interface depends on how the question is answered.
- Certain aspects of the statistical analysis of data, such as the frequency counts, may be useful in the composition classroom since this allows for a more focused approach to teaching grammatical and lexical items. In our work with teaching reporting verbs, we have used frequency data to choose the most commonly used reporting verbs in our corpora. Students can also study collocations using frequency data to judge the probability that certain words can occur together.

> - A concordance program may not be useful for every syntactic or lexical problem a student may encounter, so sometimes it may be simpler to have students use a dictionary instead. Other problems may not be appropriate for a concordance. Determining which problems can be addressed and which cannot is often a matter of trial and error.

The use of concordance programs in the last 25 years has been dominated by the research of applied and theoretical linguists who have been studying the nature of language. Researchers like Tim Johns *(www.eisu.bham.ca.uk/johnstf/index.html)* have attempted to link traditional approaches to CALL and concordancing. However, the distance remains great. Leech (1997) has described this process as a "trickle down" (p. 2) approach from research to teaching; however, the "trickling" is not always smooth, which is a good example of the problematic nature of moving a technology from one context to another.

The growing importance of using concordances in composition classes was not necessarily a result of an inherent fascination with the technology but more likely the result of a paradigm shift in the approaches to teaching grammar and vocabulary, just as the use of other technologies developed at the same time as changes in other aspects of how composition was being taught. The implementation of concordance software, as with any other technologies, is an ongoing process of evaluation and revision. The concordance is not always a simple technology to use; it can require the extensive training of the users and a commitment of the teachers to its use, evaluation, and redesign.

Reflection Questions and Projects

1. What kinds of uses do you think concordancing is particularly good for? What kinds of assignments do you think won't work well? How do these differences relate to how you teach grammar in your composition class?

2. Look at the different concordance websites that you can find, some of which have been mentioned in this book. Based on how you teach grammar, which of the websites are particularly useful and which are not? What does this exercise tell you about how the old question about the relationship of form and function relate to the design of concordance programs?

3. Look at the statistical data that some concordance programs give. Do you find such data useful? Does it help you make decisions about what to teach? Can students use it to decide which lexical item or syntactic form is best to use?

4. It seems that some teachers who want students to be independent users of concordance programs have to spend a lot of class time using them. How much class time do you feel you can spend? How would you justify spending this amount of time?

5. Do existing concordance sites provide the kinds of texts you want to use to search? What kinds of texts would you choose to include in a corpus? How would you create such a corpus? Do you think intellectual property law would limit your ability to create the kind of corpus you want?

6. Check out the demo of WordSmith. Do you feel that program is worth buying? What kinds of things could you do with it that you cannot do with a web-based program?

7. Do you think concordance programs can replace dictionaries? Could you make an argument that students should use concordance sites instead of dictionaries? When might one be better, and when might the other be better?

Chapter 6
A Final Word

There is a joke that a technology can be defined as anything that was invented after you were born. For my mother, refrigerators, washing machines, and dryers were all technologies. I remember "booting up" our first television and waiting anxiously to see if it would come on with the same apprehension and frustration as when I boot up my computer. To gain perspective on the role of technology today in the teaching of writing, it is important to remember that at some time in history, a block of clay, a tortoise shell, and a piece of paper were all radical technologies that had as profound an effect on literacy as the computer and the Internet do today. We have all experienced to some degree how our literacies have changed. I remember how my first electronic typewriter changed how I wrote a high school term paper and how the personal computer enabled me to write a dissertation.

Therefore, the questions that have been asked about using a technology in an L2 composition classroom today are not always new or abstract ones. As mentioned in Chapter 1, with the implementation of a technology there are always losses and costs, as well as gains. The fact that technology is challenging how we teach composition is not new either. Technology has always challenged the status quo in this way. In John Markoff's (2005) intriguing history of Silicon Valley, he describes, in terms that may be surprising to some, how many of the technologies used today were created by people who were immersed in the American drug and counterculture of the 1960s and saw technology challenging the dominant social order of the time. This view of technology continues today. Warschauer's (1999) study of how Hawaiian students used the Internet to try to preserve their native language is one such example. My own study of the use of the Internet by Chinese students to challenge what they perceived to be racism is another. New technologies can produce new opportunities. Filipinos using text messaging to organize demonstrations against their government is such an example. The importance of the blogosphere in challenging the social order may be the most widespread example of individuals using the Internet to try to effect social change.

The use of technology has been both liberating and frustrating in every phase of our lives. We no longer have to rush to pick up a ringing telephone or come home in time to catch our favorite TV show, but today we are bombarded by cell phones, text messaging, instant messaging, and the perceived need to keep up with the 24/7 availability of an infinite amount of information on the Internet. New demands are also being placed on the teacher to be able to fix things that do not work, to train students in using technologies that are continually changing, to keep up with the technologies their students are using, and to understand new literacies and new technologies they were never trained to understand. When we introduce a new technology into the classroom, we demand that students have the necessary computer skills, ready access to computers, and reliable access to the Internet. We demand they have patience with technologies that do not work as they should, with files that seemingly disappear, with servers that are down when they want to do their homework, or when they mysteriously get cut off from the Internet and lose their work.

For teachers to understand technology, they have to keep up with not only the literature every other composition teacher has to keep up with but also with the often dramatic changes occurring in the world of technology. To write this book, for example, I drew on years of teaching and researching composition and the use of technology. However, I also had to immerse myself in reading books and articles and listening to lectures and discussions that cover every area of technology. The Internet itself has become a vast source of information for teachers interested in technology. I spent hours listening to online lectures and podcasts by people who have dedicated their lives to the development of new technologies (e.g., EdTechTalk), which might seem irrelevant to teaching composition but helped me conceptualize the nature of these technologies and how they could be used (e.g., *www.itconversations.com*). As I have argued throughout this book, conceptualizing the use of different technologies across a wide variety of contexts is an important part of knowing how to implement them. Teachers must always be making decisions about which technology is appropriate for a given literacy context and how to change the design or use of a technology for that context.

These challenges also can become exciting opportunities for teachers. These technologies are in constant flux, and sometimes these changes bring with them the solutions to the problems. The growth of free blog sites, for example, has reduced the resources needed to have students publish their writing online. Political changes can have effects as well, whether it is the commitment of countries like Korea to increasing their bandwidth or the constant controversy in China over what can be published or read online. These changes can lead to pedagogical changes as well, as has been seen in how the Internet has affected the growth of the importance of the visual dimension of writing. The development of inexpensive and easy-to-make podcasts may have a similar effect on integrating an oral dimension into the writing classroom.

How successful the use of these technologies will be depends to a large extent on a teacher's ability to respond to the challenges inherent in choosing and implementing them. One way of doing this is through constant study. The ability of a teacher to be a lifelong learner requires a great deal of support from people who have technical backgrounds and know how to use the technology in the classroom. This support can come from colleagues, friends, and spouses, all of whom I have relied on extensively in my work.

One of the most important areas of support, of course, can come from the students. As previously mentioned, I have had an especially long struggle with the increased importance given to visual information and how it applies to composition teaching since I do not have a high degree of visual literacy. Despite my difficulties, this lack of understanding also led to important opportunities to involve students in the learning process. In one case, a graphic design student who hated writing became my unofficial assistant with helping the other students with their designs. While his involvement did not fundamentally change his attitude toward writing, he came away from the class with a new perspective on the relationship between visual and written texts.

For this student, the technology was liberating. It is almost inevitable that some students know more than their teachers. Across every field of teaching, technologically enhanced classrooms may be one of the truly student-centered language learning experiences. Hawisher and Selfe (2004) argue that when implementing a technology in a writing classroom, it is important that the multiple literacies—technological as well as print—students bring to the classroom be valued. Canagarajah (1999) argued that the multiple literacies students bring to the classroom be valued in a similar way. To achieve this goal in a technologically enhanced classroom, the technology needs to be integrated with composition pedagogy. As discussed in the section on blogging, for example, this technology can be used as a means of having students create different kinds of texts using different forms of literacy, including those that have been excluded from the classroom in the past.

New technologies are continually being developed. In some cases these new technologies have greatly enhanced how composition teaching is viewed. The growing importance of digital media, for example, has caused composition theorists to reconsider not only what is being taught, but also more basic questions about how different types of information can be best delivered (Lunsford, 2006). Information creators are no longer limited to written text to deliver their ideas but must now make decisions about which technology—a written one, an oral one, or a visual one—is most suitable for achieving their goals. The result has been that new kinds of writing spaces and new kinds of texts are continually being developed.

The future, however, is always impossible to predict. What kinds of users will students become? What kinds of new technologies will develop? Will enough teachers be able to use these technologies to make contributions to the development of new pedagogies? The complexity of these possibilities places further burdens on teachers in designing curricula to meet these changing needs. Therefore, teachers will require more and more ongoing support from both technical staff, students, and other teachers.

As with every other form of social networking today, this support can also come from groups online. Websites like EdTechTalk, Tapped In®, and LearningTimes™ *(http://www. learningtimes.net/)* offer real time and archived discussions of issues related to the use of technology in education. These discussions are not necessarily about composition or ESL but can help teachers frame solutions to many of the problems that they must face in the composition classroom. Support can also come from online groups like Webheads *(http://webheads. info/)*, or listservs like TECHRHET *(www.interversity.org/lists/ techrhet/subscribe.html)*, conferences like Calico or Computers and Writing, journals like *Computers and Composition,* and the continuing education courses that organizations like TESOL support in its online Electronic Village *(http://webpages.csus. edu/~hansonsm/announce.html)*.

Perhaps the most important result of being a lifelong learner is that teachers can become aware of how the use of a technology is affecting their teaching. One of the central issues that has been debated among teachers who use technology is the extent to which these technologies change what the teacher is doing in the classroom. Are teachers simply extending what they already do when using these technologies, or are they doing something different than they would have done in the conventional classroom? This book has argued that each technology, both in isolation and integrated together, will always affect teaching pedagogy in some ways. The key element in the amount of change is the nature of how these technologies are implemented.

The consequences of technological change cannot always be anticipated. There is no one issue for which this change has been more true than the question of the digital divide. Forty years ago the digital divide centered on the ability to use technology; today the focus is on access to the Internet. Any form of the digital divide is an issue that every teacher is or should be concerned with. However, how changes in the technology will affect this divide cannot always be predicted. Smaller countries, such as South Korea, have taken the lead in broadband penetration. At the same time, the divide will persist as long as social and economic disparities persist. The same is true of the divide between men and women.

For a variety of reasons, sometimes these smaller, developing countries take the lead. It has been reported that the Philippines has one of the highest usages of technology by women (Hafkin, 2006). The emergence of new technologies has in other cases made computer technology more appealing to women. On the other hand, social and economic disparities between the genders can cause the debate to persist. Women who have to work and take care of a family will inevitably have less time to be on the Internet than men. There are other possible divides, such as the differences in the ability of people in different countries to work around government attempts at censorship or simply to create alternative sources of information. There are no simple solutions to this problem. Teachers using these technologies can often be caught between the goals for using the technologies and the political, social, and economic realities they cannot control.

Today Negroponte (1995) is pushing his concept of a "$100" computer that does not need electricity *(http://laptop.media. mit.edu)*. He hopes the computer can be distributed to children throughout the world. While there is controversy over the value of such a computer, his vision of providing greater access to areas that could previously not afford it reflects a concern for how the promise of a technology is linked to the economies of that technology, as well as the condition of the infrastructure. Along with the dramatic development in free and inexpensive software on the Internet, these changes in the infrasctructure will undoubtably affect how technology will be used in language learning around the world.

Mobility may also become of greater importance than anyone has previously thought. In countries such as China, the ability to link to the Internet through cell phones can greatly increase the spread of technologies from the cities to the countryside (Mackinnon, 2005). Just as cell phones have allowed people to communicate whenever they need to, the growing importance of Wi-Fi has allowed users to access the Internet "just-in-time." The development of new technologies such as Wi-Max, which greatly increase the distances a computer user can roam and still stay online, could impact how we conceptualize the writing classroom. Cell phones, PDAs, and text messaging are all technologies that have not been thought of much in terms of the teaching of composition even though they may be of great importance to the students. However, their growing popularity means that eventually they will be examined for their potential for use in the composition classroom. The battle between Google™ and book publishers over digital publishing signals the beginning of a new way that information is accessed. Video games are being looked at as new learning environments (Gee, 2003). The significance of these trends in technology for L2 composition teaching is unclear.

One of the goals of this book has been to provide teachers with a theoretical background that will help them deal with the unanticipated consequences that result from the implementation of existing technologies and undoubtedly even more so from the introduction of new technologies. As Hawisher & Selfe (2004) argue, what is meant by computer literacy today has resulted from a varied array of technological changes, and what will be meant by computer literacy in the future will depend on both the technologies we know today and others not yet imagined.

Any teacher thinking about using technology is faced with a dilemma. The history of technology, especially over the last fifty years, has taught us many things about the potential and the failure of using technology in all areas of education. It is certainly true that these continuing changes have produced new technologies and have provided new tools and new contexts for writing. There are new technologies continually coming down the road that may be useful as tools for helping us teach composition or new ways of thinking about texts and books. This fascination with the new can be dangerous as well. Carbone warns teachers against "trying to understand only the latest thing to ooze from the broadband" (as cited in Hart-Davidson & Krause, 2004, p. 149). Teachers often feel the pressure to move from an older technology to a new technology before the older one is understood. Researchers often abandon studying these older technologies for the newer ones, and the result is that teachers can find little help with these older technologies. History also teaches us that it is not necessarily the technologies but the quality of the theories that underlie how they are implemented that will ultimately determine how well the technology is used, which is why teachers cannot separate their understanding of technology from their understanding of their approach to teaching composition.

Many of the earliest programs that were meant to help with process writing are obsolete today, not just because newer technologies have been developed but the theories underlying process writing have changed as well. There have been changes in the ease of creating multimedia texts, as exemplified by the growing popularity of podcasts and video blogs, which can change how both the visual and the oral can be integrated with writing.[1] These changes, however, do not necessarily make older technologies obsolete. There are still older technologies, such as word processing or computer networking, which are still relevant, and, as Carbone argues, still need to be studied but perhaps from a new perspective.

One of the first things we noticed more than ten years ago when we began to survey the attitudes our international students had concerning technology was, for the most part, how optimistic they were about the potential of technology in their education and their lives in general (Bloch, 1997). Today, many of the countries our students come from have surpassed the United States in various aspects of the use of technology. The approach used in this book has been to present teachers with a wide variety of technologies from which they can choose and a variety of ways they can connect these technologies to

---

1. For examples of video blogs in ESL, see You Tube *(www.youtube.com)* and type ESL in the search engine.

the kinds of methods they are using or may want to and the problems with these methods they are facing.

The decisions that need to be made in implementing this wide variety of technologies are not always easy. For every teacher, the question of accessibility and the burdens the use of technology can place on the student must be carefully weighed as part of the implementation process. However, even if the accessibility issue is solved, there is the issue of deciding which technology to choose. Throughout our society, the introduction of new technologies has raised new personal and pedagogical questions, whether they are the question of privacy on websites like myspace.com or the potential for the Internet to make plagiarism easier because of the ease of downloading papers.

This tension between the potential for using technology and the challenges for teachers can be seen throughout this book, particularly the choice of which technology is most appropriate. The continual introduction of new technologies can make the choices even more complicated. While newer technologies may seem to have more potential for solving certain problems than older ones do, the older ones can still be effective. In Chapter 3, for example, I presented a discussion on using web page design in an L2 composition course, which is a technology I no longer use but one I still feel has great potential.

At the same time, I know that in the world of Web 2.0, there has been a shift away from using web pages, which have been seen as reflecting an older view of the Internet (sometimes referred to as Web 1.0), to more interactive writing environments such as Drupal *(http://drupal.org)* or wikis, which allow users a greater degree of participation in publishing their own ideas. However, for both teachers and students, these new technologies may not be as accessible, or even as valuable, for creating writing environments for an L2 composition classroom. Thus, by advocating for the use of both old and new technologies, this book lies at the intersection of Web 1.0 and Web 2.0.

One thing is certain: All these new technologies will have a tremendous effect on teachers, even those who may not want to use it in their classes. This importance does not mean that teachers need to be locked into feeling they have to use technology. There is a time when teachers need to turn off the computer in the classroom just as there is sometimes a need to talk to someone in person instead of sending email or using an Internet messenger. Nevertheless, the Internet has created an environment that can empower teachers with the ability to connect with others sharing similar concerns so that every teacher readily can take advantage of the "collective intelligence" of the profession.

Technologies inevitably change what the teacher does in the classroom. Are teachers simply extending what they already do when using these technologies, or are they doing something different than they would have done in the conventional classroom? This book has argued that each technology, both in isolation and integrated together, will always affect teaching pedagogy in some ways. The key element in the amount of change is the nature of how these technologies are implemented.

By the time you read this book, there may be new and exciting uses for some of the technologies, both the technologies that have been discussed and ones barely mentioned. There may also be new technologies that have not even developed yet or put on the market. How does a teacher deal with this constantly changing landscape? There is another saying that the way to predict the future is to invent it. Few teachers may have the ability to invent new technologies, but every teacher can invent how those technologies are used. The primary purpose of books like this one is to help teachers take control of the use of the technologies in their classrooms so they too can participate in how their future and the future of their students will be invented.

Reflection Questions

1. What would you like to see if you could "invent the future?" What kinds of technologies would you like to see developed? What would you like to do with them?

2. I mentioned that by the time you read this book, some of what I had discussed may be obsolete, there may be new uses for some of the technologies, and new technologies that we haven't even imagined yet will be developed. What has changed since the book was written? Let me know at *bloch10@yahoo.com.*

3. What role do you think that these new forms of Internet texts have in the classroom? Would you give them as much value as traditional print texts?

4. What do you think of some of the controversies regarding the uses of Internet materials? What do you think of the use of Wikipedia in research writing? Has the growth of Internet materials changed your attitudes toward plagiarism?

5. What do you think should be the role of visual and oral materials in the composition classroom? What role should images, photographs, or movies have? What about podcasts or other types of audio files?

References

Agre, P. E. (2001). Changing places: Contexts of awareness in computing. *Human-Computer Interaction, 16,* 177–192.

Anderson, C. (2006). *The long tail: Why the future of business is selling less of more.* New York: Hyperion.

Angélil-Carter, S. (2000). *Stolen language? Plagiarism in writing.* Harlow, UK: Longman.

Arguello, J., Butler, B., Joyce, E., Kraut, R., Ling, K. S., & Wang, X. (2006). Talk to me: Foundations for successful individual-group interactions in online communities. In *CHI 2006: Proceedings of the ACM Conference on Human Factors in Computing Systems.* New York: ACM Press. Retrieved November 2, 2006, from http://delivery.acm.org/10.1145/1130000/1124 916/p959-arguello.pdf?key1=1124916&key2=2900842611&coll=portal& dl=ACM&CFID=5051795&CFTOKEN=23145484

Ari, O. (2006). Review of three software programs designed to identify lexical bundles. *Language Learning & Technology, 10,* 30–37. Retrieved January 4, 2006, from http://llt.msu.edu/vol10num1/review3/default.html

Arnheim, R. (1969). *Visual Thinking.* Berkeley: University of California Press.

Aston, G. (2000). Corpora and language teaching. In L. Burnard & T. McEnery (Eds.), *Rethinking language pedagogy from a corpus perspective* (pp. 7–17). Frankfurt, Germany: Peter Lang.

Atkinson, D. (2003a). L2 writing in the post-process era: Introduction. *Journal of Second Language Writing, 12,* 3–15.

———. (2003b). Writing and culture in the post-process era. *Journal of Second Language Writing, 12,* 49–63.

Atkinson, D., & Ramanathan, V. (1995). Cultures of writing: An ethnographic comparison of L1 and L2 university writing/language programs. *TESOL Quarterly, 29,* 539–568.

Aycock, A., & Buchignani, N. (1995). The e-mail murders: Reflections on "dead" letters. In S. G. Jones (Ed.), *Cyberspace: Computer-mediated communication community* (pp. 184-231). Thousand Oaks, CA: Sage.

Bander, R. (1978). *American English rhetoric.* New York: Holt, Rinehart, and Winston.

Bargh, J. A., McKenna, K. Y. A., & Fitzsimmons, G. M. (2002). Can you see the real me? Activation and expression of the "true self" on the Internet. *Journal of Social Issues, 58,* 33–48.

Barlow, J. P. (1993.) The economy of ideas. Retrieved August 11, 2004, from http://www.eff.org/~barlow/EconomyOfIdeas.html

Barlow, M. (2003). MonoConc 2.2 [computer software]. Houston, TX: Athelstan.

Baron, D. (1999). From pencils to pixels: The stages of literacy technologies. In G. E. Hawisher & C. L. Selfe (Eds.), *Passions, pedagogies, and 21*st *century technologies* (pp. 15–33). Urbana, IL: NCTE.

Bartholomae, D. (1985). Inventing the university. In M. Rose (Ed.), *When a writer can't write: Studies in writer's block and other composing processes* (pp. 134–165). New York: Guilford Press.

———. (1987). Writing on the margins: The concept of literacy in higher education. In T. Enos (Ed.), *A sourcebook for basic writing teachers* (pp. 66–83). New York: Random House.

Barton, D., & Hamilton, M. (2000). Literacy practices. In D. Barton, M. Hamilton, & R. Ivanič (Eds.), *Situated literacies: Reading and writing in context* (pp. 7–15). London: Routledge.

Barton, D., Hamilton, M., & Ivanič, R. (2000). *Situated literacies: Reading and writing in context.* London: Routledge.

Batson, T. (1993). The origins of ENFI. In B. Bruce, J. K. Peyton, & T. Batson (Eds.), *Network-based classrooms: Promises and realities* (pp. 87–112). Cambridge, UK: Cambridge University Press.

Baym, N. K. (1995). The emergence of community in computer-mediated communication. In S. G. Jones (Ed.), *Cyberspace: Computer-mediated communication and community* (pp. 138–163). Thousand Oaks, CA: Sage.

Bazerman, C. (1988). *Shaping written knowledge: The genre and activity of the experimental article in science.* Madison: University of Wisconsin Press.

Belcher, D. (2001). Cyberdiscourse: Evolving notions of authorship and the teaching of writing. In M. Hewings (Ed.), *Academic writing in context* (pp. 140–149). Birmingham, UK: University of Birmingham Press.

Belotti, V., & Edwards, K. (2001). Intelligibility and accountability: Human considerations in context-aware systems. *Human-Computer Interaction, 16,* 193–221.

Benbunan-Fitch, R., & Hiltz, S. R. (1999). Education applications of CMCS: Solving case studies through asynchronous learning networks. *Journal of Computer-Mediated Communication, 4.* Retrieved February 4, 2004, from http://www.ascusc.org/jcmc/vol4/issue3/benunan-ftich.html

Benkler, Y. (2006). *The wealth of networks: How social production transforms markets and freedom.* New Haven, CT: Yale University Press.

Berlin, J. A. (1982). Contemporary composition: The major pedagogical theories. *College English, 44,* 765–777.

———. (1990). Postmodernism, politics, and histories of rhetoric. *Pre/Text, 11,* 169–185.

Berners-Lee, T. (2000). *Weaving the Web: The original design and ultimate destiny of the World Wide Web.* New York: HarperCollins.

———. (2004). Interview with Christopher Lydon. Retrieved January 13, 2004, from Weblogs at the Harvard Law website: http://blogs.law.harvard.edu/lydon/

Biber, D., Conrad, S., & Reppen, R. (1998). *Corpus linguistics: Investigating language structure and use.* Cambridge, UK: Cambridge University Press.

Birkerts, S. (1995). *The Gutenberg elegies: The fate of reading in an electronic age.* New York: Ballantine Books.

Bizzell, P. (1982). College composition: Initiation into the academic discourse community. *Curriculum Inquiry, 12,* 191–207.

———. (1986). What happens when basic writers come to college? *College Composition and Communication, 37,* 294–301.

Blanton, L. L. (1999). Classroom instruction and language minority students: On teaching to smarter readers and writers. In L. Harklau, K. M. Losey, & M. Siegal (Eds.), *Generation 1.5 meets college composition* (pp. 119–142). Mahwah, NJ: Lawrence Erlbaum.

———. (2005) Student, interrupted: A tale of two would-be writers. *Journal of Second Language Writing, 14,* 105–121.

Bloch, J. (1997, May). *Where students are coming from: A survey of computer use among entering ESL students.* Paper presented at the 13th Computers and Writing Conference, Honolulu, HI.

———. (2001). Plagiarism and the ESL student: From printed to electronic texts. In D. Belcher & A. Hirvela (Eds.), *Linking literacies: Perspectives on L2 reading-writing connections* (pp. 209–228). Ann Arbor: University of Michigan Press.

———. (2002). Student/teacher interaction via email: The social context of Internet discourse. *Journal of Second Language Writing, 11,* 117–134.

———. (2003). Creating materials for teaching evaluation in academic writing: Using letters to the editor in L2 composition courses. *English for Specific Purposes, 22,* 347–364.

———. (2004a). Second language cyber rhetoric: A study of Chinese L2 writers in an online usenet group. *Language Learning and Technology, 8,* 66–82.

———. (2004b, March–April). *Blogging in the L2 composition classroom.* Paper presented at 38th the International TESOL Convention, Long Beach, CA.

———. (2006, March). *Cyberchase: The search for intercultural rhetoric on the Internet.* Paper presented at the 40th International TESOL Convention, Tampa, FL.

Bloch, J., & Brutt-Griffler, J. (2001). Implementing CommonSpace in the ESL composition classroom. In D. Belcher and A. Hirvela (Eds.), *Linking literacies: Perspectives on L2 reading-writing connections* (pp. 309–334). Ann Arbor: University of Michigan Press.

Bloch, J., & Crosby, C. (2005, June). Weblogs and academic writing development: One student's conceptualization of plagiarism. *Proceedings from EATAW 2005: Teaching Writing On Line and Face to Face.* Athens, Greece.

———. (2006). Creating a space for virtual democracy. *The Essential Teacher, 3*(3), 38–41.

Bloch, J., & Panferov, S. (2003, May). *Asynchronous discourse in an L2 composition class: Expanding the boundaries.* Paper presented at the Conference on Computers and Writing, West Lafayette, IN.

Blood, R. (2000). Weblogs: A history and perspective. Retrieved January 26, 2004, from http://www.rebeccablood.net/essays/weblog_history.html

Blum, R. V., & Cohen, M. E. (1984). WANDAH: Writing-aid and author's helper. In W. Wresch (Ed.), *The computer in composition instruction: A writer's tool* (pp. 154–173). Urbana, IL: NCTE.

Bolter, J. D. (1991). *The writing space: The computer, hypertext, and the history of writing.* Mahwah, NJ: Lawrence Erlbaum.

———. (2001). *Writing space: Computers, hypertext, and the remediation of print.* Mahwah, N.J: Lawrence Erlbaum.

Bolter, J. D., & Grusin, R. (1999). *Remediation: Understanding new media.* Cambridge: MIT Press.

Boswood, T. (Ed). (1997). *New ways of using computers in language teaching.* Washington, DC: TESOL.

Bourdieu, P. (1997). Forms of capital. In H. Halsey (Ed.), *Education: Culture, economy, and society* (pp. 46–58). New York: Oxford University Press.

Boyle, J. (1996). *Shamans, software, & spleens: Law and the construction of the information society.* Cambridge, MA: Harvard University Press.

Braine, G, (1997). Beyond word processing: Networked computers in ESL writing classes. *Computers and Composition, 14,* 45–58.

———. (2001). A study of English as a foreign language (EFL) writers on a local-area network (LAN) and in traditional classes. *Computers and Composition, 18,* 275–292.

Brown, J. S. (2002). Growing up digital: How the Web changes work, education, and the ways people learn. *USDLA Journal, 16.* Retrieved July 7, 2003, from http://www.usdla.org/html/journal/FEB02_Issue/article01.html

Brown, J. S., & Duguid, P. (2000). *The social life of information.* Boston: Harvard Business School Press.

Bruckman, A. (2001). Finding one's own in cyberspace. In C. Haynes & J. R. Holemevik (Eds.), *High wired: On the design, use, and theory of educational MOOs* (pp. 15–24). Ann Arbor: University of Michigan Press.

Bruffee, K. A. (1983). Writing and reading as collaborative or social acts. In J. N. Hayes, P. A. Roth, J. R. Ramsey, & R. D. Foulke (Eds.), *The writer's mind: Writing as a mode of thinking* (pp. 159–170). Urbana, IL: NCTE.

Bruton, M. (2006). Turnitin's response to recent posts discussing proper pedagogy. Kairosnews. Retrieved October 24, 2006, from http://kairosnews.org/turnitins-response-to-recent-posts-discu

Bu, W. (2004, April). *Youth participation and the digital divide in China.* Paper presented at China's Digital Future, Berkeley, CA. Retrieved December 11, 2004, from http://journalism.berkeley.edu/conf/chinadf/schedule.html

Burns, H. (1984). Recollections of first-generation computer-assisted prewriting. In W. Wresch (Ed.), *The computer in composition instruction: A writer's tool* (pp. 15–33). Urbana, IL: NCTE.

Burstein, J. (2003). The E-rater® scoring engine: Automated essay scoring with natural language processing. In M. D. Shermis & J. Burstein (Eds.), *Automated essay scoring: A cross-disciplinary perspective* (pp. 113–121). Mahwah, NJ: Lawrence Erlbaum.

Bush, V. (1945). As we may think. *The Atlantic Monthly, 176.* Retrieved January 19, 2004, from http://www.theatlantic.com/unbound/flashbks/computer/bushf.htm

Canagarajah, A. S. (2006). Toward a writing pedagogy of shuttling between languages: Learning from multilingual writers. *College English, 58,* 589–604.

Canagarajah, S. (1999). *Resisting linguistic imperialism in English teaching.* Oxford, UK: Oxford University Press.

Carson, J. G., & Nelson, G. L. (1999). Chinese students' perceptions of ESL peer response group interaction. *Journal of Second Language Writing, 5,* 1–19.

Casanave, C. P. (2004). *Controversies in second language writing: Dilemmas and decisions in research and instruction.* Ann Arbor: University of Michigan Press.

Casanave, C. P., McCormick, A. J., & Hiraki, S. (1993). Conversations by e-mail: A study of the interactive writing experiences of a Japanese deaf student and two English teachers. *SFC Journal of Language and Communication, 2,* 145–175.

Castells, M. (2001). *The Internet galaxy: Reflections on the Internet, business, and society.* Oxford, UK: Oxford University Press.

Catera, E., & Emigh, R. (2005). Blogs, the virtual soapbox. *Essential Teacher, 2,* 46–49.

Chapelle, C. (2000). Is networked-based learning CALL? In M. Warschauer & R. Kern (Eds.), *Network-based language teaching: Concepts and practice* (pp. 204–228). Cambridge, UK: Cambridge University Press.

Chapelle, C. A. (2001). *Computer applications to second language acquisition: Foundations for teaching, testing, and research.* Cambridge, UK: Cambridge University Press.

Charney, D. (1994). The effect of hypertext on processes of reading and writing. In C. L. Selfe & S. Hilligoss (Eds.), *Literacy and computers: The complications of teaching and learning with technology* (pp. 238–263). New York: MLA.

Cheung, C. (2000). A home on the web: Presentations of self on personal web pages. In D. Gauntlett (Ed.), *Web.studies: Rewiring media studies for the digital age* (pp. 43–51). London: Arnold.

Chun, D. M., & Plass, J. L. (2000). Networked multimedia environments for second language acquisition. In M. Warschauer & R. Kern (Eds.), *Network-based language teaching: Concepts and practice* (pp. 151–170). Cambridge, UK: Cambridge University Press.

Cobb, T. (1997). Is there any measurable learning from hands-on concordancing? *System, 25,* 301–315.

Coles, W. E. (1978). *The plural I: The teaching of writing.* New York: Holt, Rinehart, and Winston.

Connor, U. (2004). Intercultural rhetoric research: Beyond texts. *Journal of English for Academic Purposes, 3,* 291–304.

Copyright and digital media in the post-Napster world. (2005). GartnerG2 and the Berkman Center for Internet Law at Harvard University. Retrieved May 28, 2006, from http://cyber.law.harvard.edu/media/files/wp2005.pdf

Crews, K. D. (2001). The law of fair use and the illusion of fair-use guidelines. *Ohio State Law Journal, 62,* 599–702.

Crosby, C. (2004, September–October). *Hypertext and the reading/writing connection.* Paper presented at the Symposium on Second Language Writing, West Lafayette, IN.

Crowley, S. (1994). *Ancient rhetorics for contemporary students.* New York: Macmillan.

Crystal, D. (2001). *Language and the Internet.* Cambridge, UK: Cambridge University Press.

Cuban, L. (2001). *Oversold and underused: Computers in the classroom.* Cambridge, MA: Harvard University Press.

Curtis, P. (2001). Not just a game: How LamdaMOO came to exist and what it did not get back to me. In C. Haynes & J. R. Holemevik (Eds.), *High wired: On the design, use, and theory of educational MOOs* (pp. 25–42). Ann Arbor: University of Michigan Press.

Daiute, C. (1985). *Writing and computers.* Reading, MA: Addison-Wesley.

Danet, B., Ruedenberg, L., & Rosenbaum-Tamari, Y. (1998). Hmmm...Where's that smoke coming from? Writing, play, and performance on Internet relay chat. In F. Sudweeks, M. Maclaughlin, & S. Rafaeli (Eds.), *Network and netplay: Virtual groups on the Internet* (pp. 41–76). Menlo Park, CA: AAAI Press.

Davis, B., & Thiede, R. (2000). Writing into change: Style shifting in asynchronous electronic discourse. In M. Warschauer & R. Kern (Eds.), *Network-based language teaching: Concepts and practice* (pp. 87–120). Cambridge, UK: Cambridge University Press.

Day, J. T. (1988). Writer's Workbench: A useful aid, but not a cure-all. *Computers and Composition, 6,* 63–78.

Dean, C., Hochman, W., Hood, C., & McEachern, R. (2004). Fashioning the emperor's new clothes: Emerging pedagogy and practices of turning wireless laptops into classroom literacy stations @SouthernCT.edu, *Kairos, 9.1.* Retrieved February 28, 2005, from http://english.ttu.edu/kairos/9.1/binder2html?coverweb/hochman_et_al/intro.html

de Pourbaix, R. (2000). Emergent literacy: Practices in an electronic community. In D. Barton, M. Hamilton, & R. Ivanič (Eds.), *Situated literacies: Reading and writing in context* (pp. 125–148). London: Routledge.

Dibble, J. (1998). *My tiny life: Crime and passion in a virtual world.* New York: Henry Holt.

Doctorow, C., Dornfest, R., Johnson, J. S., Powers, S., Trott, B., & Trott, M. G. (2002). *Essential blogging.* Sebastopol, CA: O'Reilly.

Dreyfus, H. L. (2001). *On the Internet.* London: Routledge.

Eco, U. (1996, November 12). *From Internet to Gutenberg.* Retrieved November 4, 2006, from http://www.hf.ntnu.no/anv/Finnbo/tekster/Eco/Internet.htm

Egbert, J. (2005, November). *The end of CALL and how to achieve it.* Paper presented at the Webheads in Action Online Convergence. Accessed December 18, 2005, from Open Source for Educators website: http://www.opensource.idv.tw/moodle/file.php/20/Egbert/TheEndofCALLandHowtoAchieveIt.pdf

Egbert, J., & Hanson-Smith, E. (1999). *CALL environments: Research, practice, and critical issues.* Washington, DC: TESOL.

Eignor, D., Taylor, C., Kirsch, I., & Jamieson, J. (1998). *Development of a scale for assessing the level of computer familiarity of TOEFL examinees.* Princeton, NJ: Educational Testing Service. Retrieved November 6, 2005, from http://www.ets.org/portal/site/ets/menuitem.c988ba0e5dd572bada20bc47c3921509/?vgnextoid=7577457727df4010VgnVCM10000022f95190RCRD&vgnextchannel=d35ed898c84f4010VgnVCM10000022f95190RCRD

Eisenstein, E. (1979). *The printing press as an agent of change: Communications and cultural transformations in early modern Europe.* Cambridge, UK: Cambridge University Press.

Elbow, P. (1981). *Writing with power: Techniques for mastering the writing process.* New York: Oxford University Press.

Ellis, R. (2002a). The place of grammar instruction in the second/foreign language curriculum. In E. Hinkle & S. Fotos (Eds.), *New perspectives on grammar teaching in second language classrooms* (pp. 17–34). Mahwah, NJ: Lawrence Erlbaum.

———. (2002b). Methodological options is grammar teaching materials. In E. Hinkle & S. Fotos (Eds.), *New perspectives on grammar teaching in second language classrooms* (pp. 155–180). Mahwah, NJ: Lawrence Erlbaum.

Emig, J. (1978). Hand, eye, brain: Some "basics" in the writing process. In C. R. Cooper & L. Odell (Eds.), *Research on composing: Points of departure.* Urbana, IL: NCTE.

Emig, J. A. (1971). The composing process of twelfth graders. *NCTE Research Report* (13). Urbana, IL: NCTE.

Enos, R. (1988). *The literate mode of Cicero's legal rhetoric.* Carbondale: Southern Illinois University Press.

Faigley, L. (1986). Competing theories of process: A critique and a proposal. *College English, 48,* 527–542.

———. (1992). *Fragments of rationality: Postmodernity and the subject of composition.* Pittsburgh: University of Pittsburgh Press.

Fallows, D. (2005). How men and women use the Internet. Retrieved October 28, 2006, from http://www.pewinternet.org/pdfs/PIP_Women_and_Men_online.pdf

Fanderclai, T. L. (1995). MUDs in education: New environments, new pedagogies. *Computer-Mediated Communication Magazine, 2.* Retrieved January 8, 2004, from http://www.ibiblio.org/cmc/mag/1995/jan/fanderclai.html

Farmer, J. (2004). Communication dynamics: Discussion boards, weblogs, and the developments of communities of inquiry in online learning environments. In R. Atkinson, C. McBeah, D. Jonas-Dwyer, & R. Phillips (Eds.), *Beyond the Comfort Zone: Proceedings of the 21 ASCILITE Conference.* Retrieved January 29, 2005, from http://www.ascilite.org.au/conferences/perth04/procs/pdf/farmer.pdf

———. (2005) How you SHOULD use blogs in education. Retrieved September 5, 2005, from the Blogsavvy website: http://blogsavvy.net/how-you-should-use-blogs-in-education

———. (2006). Group blogs. Retrieved June 3, 2006, from the Incorporated Subversion website: http://incsub.org/blog/2006/group-blogs

Fay, A. (2006). Impact of laptop computers on students' academic lives. Retrieved November 29, 2006, from http://www.cmu.edu/teaching/LaptopStudyReport-2006.pdf

Feenberg, A. (1999). *Questioning technology.* London: Routledge.

———. (2002). *Transforming technology: A critical theory revisited.* New York: Oxford University Press.

———. (2003). Modernity theory and technological studies: Reflections on bridging the gap. In T. J. Misa, P. May, & A. Feenberg (Eds.), *Modernity and technology* (pp. 73–104). Cambridge: MIT Press.

Felix, U. (1999). Web-based language learning: A window to the authentic world. In. R. Debski & M. Levy (Eds.), *WORLDCALL: Global perspectives on computer-assisted language learning* (pp. 5–98). Lisse, the Netherlands: Swets & Zeilinger.

Ferris, D. R. (1999). One size does not fit all: Response and revision issues for immigrant students. In L. Harklau, K. M. Losey, & M. Siegal (Eds.), *Generation 1.5 meets college composition* (pp. 143–155). Mahwah, NJ: Lawrence Erlbaum.

———. (2004). The "grammar correction" debate in L2 writing: Where are we, and where do we go from here? (And what do we do in the meantime …?). *Journal of Second Language Writing, 13,* 49–62.

Florida, R. (2002). *The rise of the creative class and how it's transforming work, leisure, community, and everyday life.* New York: Basic Books.

Flower, L. S., & Hayes, J. R. (1981). A cognitive process theory of writing. *College Composition and Communication, 32,* 365–387.

Francis, G. (1993). A corpus driven approach to grammar. In M. Baker, G. Francis, & E. Tognini-Bonelli (Eds.), *Text and technology: In honour of John Sinclair* (pp. 137–156). Amsterdam: John Benjamins.

Frodesen, J., & Holten, C. (2003). Grammar and the ESL classroom. In B. Kroll (Ed.), *Exploring the dynamics of second language writing* (pp. 141–161). Cambridge, UK: Cambridge University Press.

Gaskell, D., & Cobb, T. (2004). Can learners use concordance feedback for writing errors? *System, 32,* 301–319.

Gee, J. P. (1996). *Social linguistics and literacies: Ideology in discourses.* London: Taylor & Francis.

———. (2003). *What video games have to teach us about learning and literacy.* New York: Palgrave MacMillan.

Geertz, C. (1983). *Local knowledge.* New York: Basic Books.

Gilbert, N. J., & Mulkay, M. (1984). *Opening Pandora's box.* Cambridge, UK: Cambridge University Press.

Giles, J. (2005). Internet encyclopedias go head to head. *Nature, 438,* 900–901.

Gilmour, D. (2004). *We the media.* Retrieved January 15, 2005, from the O'Reilly website: http://www.oreilly.com/catalog/webmedia/book/index.csp

Goldstein, L. M. (2004). Questions and answers about teacher written commentary and student revision: Teachers and students working together. *Journal of Second Language Writing, 13,* 63–80.

Goody, J. (1977). *The domestication of the savage mind.* New York: Cambridge University Press.

Graff, H. J. (1987). *The legacies of literacy: Continuities and contradictions in western culture and society.* Bloomington: Indiana University Press.

Granger, S. (2003). Error-tagged learner corpora and CALL: A promising synergy. *CALICO, 20,* 465–480.

Grohol, J. H. (2002). Psychology of blogs (weblogs): Everything old is new again. Retrieved January 9, 2004, from Dr. John Grohol's Psych Central website: http://psychcentral.com/blogs/blog_new.htm

Gurak, L., Antonijevic, S., Johnson, L., Ratliff, C., & Reyman, J. (2004). Introduction: Weblogs, rhetoric, community, and culture. Retrieved July 5, 2004, from the Into the Blogosphere website: http://blog.lib.umn.edu/blogosphere/introduction.html/

Haas, C. (1989). Does the medium make a difference? Two studies of writing with pen and paper and with computers. *Human-Computer Interactions, 4,* 169–189.

———. (1996). *Writing technology: Studies on the materiality of literacy.* Mahwah, NJ: Lawrence Erlbaum.

———. (1999). On the relationship between old and new technologies. *Computers and Composition, 16,* 209–228.

Haas, C., & Neuwirth, C. M. (1994). Writing the technology that writes us: Research on literacy and the shape of technology. In C. L. Selfe & S. Hillgross (Eds.), *Literacy and computers: The complications of teaching and learning with technology* (pp. 319–335). New York: MLA.

Hafkin, N. (2006). *Empowering women in a knowledge society.* Lecture presented at the Berkman Center for Internet and Society, Harvard University, Cambridge, MA. Retrieved December 1, 2006, from http://blogs.law.harvard.edu/mediaberkman/2006/11/28/empowering-women-in-a-knowledge-society/

Hagel, J., & Brown, J. S. (2005). From push to pull—Emerging models for mobilizing resources. Retrieved January 1, 2006, from http://www.johnseelybrown.com/pushmepullyou4.72.pdf

Hammond, M. (1999). Issues associated with participation in online forums: The case of the communicative learner. *Education and Information Technologies, 4,* 353–367.

Harklau, L. (2002). The role of writing in classroom second language acquisition. *Journal of Second Language Writing, 11,* 329–350.

———. (2003). L2 writing by "Generation 1.5 students": Recent research and pedagogical trends. *Journal of Second Language Writing, 12,* 153–156.

Harris, L. (1996). Using MOOs to teach composition and literature. *Kairos, 1*. Retrieved February 5, 2004, from http://English.ttu.edu/kairos/1.2/binder2.html/?coverweb/Harris/content.html

Hart-Davidson, B., & Krause, S. (2004). Re: The future of computers and writing: A multivocal textumentary. *Computers and Composition, 21*, 147–160.

Harwood, N. (2006). (In)appropriate personal pronoun use in political science: A qualitative study and a proposed heuristic for future research. *Written Communication, 23*, 424–450.

Hawisher, G. (1994). Blinding insights: Classification schemes and software for literacy instruction. In C. L. Selfe & S. Hilligoss (Eds.), *Literacy and computers: The complications of teaching and learning with technology* (pp. 37–55). New York: MLA.

Hawisher, G. E., LeBlanc, P., Moran, C., & Selfe, C. L. (1996). *Computers and the teaching of writing in American higher education, 1979–1994: A history.* Norwood, NJ: Ablex.

Hawisher, G. E., & Selfe, C. L. (1991a). *Evolving perspectives on computers and composition studies: Questions for the 1990s.* Urbana, IL: NCTE.

———. (1991b). The rhetoric of technology and electronic writing. *College Composition and Communication, 42*, 55–65.

———. (1999). *Global literacies and the World Wide Web.* London: Routledge.

———. (2004). Becoming literate in the information age: Cultural ecologies and the literacies of technology. *College Composition and Communication, 55*, 642–691.

Hayes, J. R., & Flower, L. S. (1980). Identifying the organization of writing processes. In L.W. Gregg & E. R. Steinberg (Eds.), *Cognitive processes of writing* (pp. 3–30). Mahwah, NJ: Lawrence Erlbaum.

Haynes, C. (2001). Help! There's a MOO in this class. In C. Haynes & J. R. Holemevik (Eds.), *High wired: On the design, use, and theory of educational MOOs* (pp. 161–176). Ann Arbor: University of Michigan Press.

Heath, S. B. (1983). *Ways with words: Language, life, and work in communities and classrooms.* New York: Cambridge University Press.

Henry, A., & Roseberry, R. L. (2001). Using a small corpus to obtain data for teaching a genre. In M. Ghadessy, A. Henry, & R. L. Roseberry (Eds.), *Small corpus studies and ELT* (pp. 93–133). Amsterdam: John Benjamins.

Henry, G. M., & Zerwekh, R. A. (1994). Human factors in CALL software design: Examples from the creation of multimedia dictionary software for Thai and Indonesian. In F. Borchardt & E. Johnson (Eds.), *Proceedings from the CALICO '94 Annual Symposium* (pp. 120–123). Durham, NC: CALICO.

Herring, S. (1999). Interactional coherence in CMC. *Journal of Computer-Mediated Communication, 4*. Retrieved February 4, 2004, from http://www.ascusc.org/jcmc/vol4/issue4/herring.html

———. (2001). Computer-mediated discourse. In D. Shiffman, D. Tannen, & H. Hamilton (Eds.), *The handbook of discourse analysis* (pp. 612–634). Malden, MA: Blackwell.

Herring, S. C., Kouper, I., Schiedt, L. A., & Wright, E. L. (2004). Women and children last: The discursive construction of weblogs. Retrieved July 5, 2004, from Into the Blogosphere website: http://blog.lib.umn.edu/blogosphere/women_and_children.html

Hewings, M., & Hewings, A. (2002). It is interesting to note that...: A comparative study of anticipatory "it" in student and published writing. *English for Specific Purposes, 21,* 367–383.

Holmevik, J. R. (2004). *TraceBack: MOO, open source, and the humanities.* Bergen, Norway: University of Bergen.

Honeycutt, L. (2001). Comparing e-mail and synchronous conferencing in online peer response. *Written Communication, 18,* 26–60.

Hopper, P. J. (1998). Emergent grammar. In M. Tomasello, (Ed.), *The new psychology of language: Cognitive and structural approaches to language structure.* Mahwah, NJ: Lawrence Erlbaum.

Hot Potatoes, V.6. [computer program] (2004). Retrieved August 11, 2004, from http://web.uvic.ca/hrd/hotpot/index.htm

Hourihan, M. (2002). What we're doing when we blog. Retrieved January 9, 2004, from the O'Reilly website: http://www.oreillynet.com/pub/a/javascript/2002/06/13/megnut.html

Howard, R. (1999). *Standing in the shadow of giants: Plagiarists, authors, collaborators.* Stamford, CT: Ablex.

Hunston, S. (2000). Evaluation and the planes of discourse: Status and value in persuasive texts. In S. Hunston & G. Thompson (Eds.), *Evaluation in text: Authorial stance and the construction of discourse* (pp. 176–207). Oxford, UK: Oxford University Press.

Hunston, S. (2000). *Corpora in applied linguistics.* Cambridge, UK: Cambridge University Press.

Hyland, K. (1998). *Hedging in scientific research articles.* Amsterdam: John Benjamins.

———. (2002a). *Teaching and researching writing.* Harlow, UK: Longman.

———. (2002b). Genre: Language, context, and literacy. *Annual Review of Applied Linguistics, 22,* 113–135.

———. (2002c). Activity and evaluation: New windows on academic writing. In J. Flowerdew (Ed.), *Academic discourse* (pp. 131–149). Harlow, UK: Longman.

———. (2002d). Specificity revisited: How far should we go now? *English for Specific Purposes, 21*, 385–395.

———. (2003a). Genre-based pedagogies: A social response to process. *Journal of Second Language Writing, 12*, 17–29.

———. (2003b). *Second language writing*. Cambridge, UK: Cambridge University Press.

Ibrahim, Y. (2006). Capital punishment and virtual protest: A case study of Singapore. *First Monday, 11*. Retrieved November 27, 2006, from http://www.firstmonday.org/issues/issue11_10/ibrahim/index.html

Ingram, A. L., Hathorn, L. G., & Evans, A. (2000). Beyond chat on the Internet. *Computers and Education, 35*, 21–35.

Janangelo, J. (1991). Technopower and technoppression: Some abuses of power and control in computer-assisted writing environments. *Computers and Composition, 9*, 47–64.

Jaszi, P. (1994). On the author effect: Contemporary copyright and collective creativity. In M. Woodmansee & P. Jaszi (Eds.), *The construction of authorship: Textual appropriation in law and literature* (pp. 29–56). Durham, NC: Duke University Press.

Johanyak, M. F. (1997). Analyzing the amalgamated electronic text: Bringing cognitive, social, and contextual factors of individual language users. *Computers and Composition, 14*, 91–110.

Johns, T. (1994). From printout to handout: Grammar and vocabulary teaching in the context of data-driven learning. In T. Odlin (Ed.), *Perspectives of pedagogical grammar* (pp. 293–313). Cambridge, UK: Cambridge University Press.

———. (1997). Contexts: The background, development, and trialing of a concordance-based CALL Program. In A. Wichmann, S. Fligelstone, T. McEnery, & G. Knowles (Eds.), *Teaching and language corpora* (pp. 100–115). London: Longman.

Johnson-Eilola, J. (1994). Reading and writing in hypertext: Vertigo and euphoria. In C. L. Selfe & S. Hilligoss (Eds.), *Literacy and computers: The complications of teaching and learning with technology* (pp. 195–219). New York: MLA.

———. (1997). *Nostalgic angels: Rearticulating hypertext writing*. Norwood, NJ: Ablex Publishing.

Johnson-Eilola, J., & Selber, S. (1996). Policing ourselves: Defining the boundaries of appropriate discussion in online forums. *Computers and Composition, 13,* 269–281.

Jones, R. H., Garralda, A., Li, D. C. S., & Lock, G. (2006). Interactional dynamics in on-line and face-to-face peer-tutoring sessions for second language writers. *Journal of Second Language Writing, 15,* 1–23.

Jones, S. G. (1995). Community in the information age. In S. G. Jones (Ed.), *Cybersociety: Computer-mediated communication and community* (pp. 10–35). Thousand Oaks, CA: Sage.

———. (1997). *Virtual culture: Identity and communication in cybersociety.* London: Sage.

Kaplan, R. B. (1966). Cultural thought patterns in intercultural education. *Language Learning, 16,* 1–20.

Katz, J. (2002). Here come the weblogs. In *We've got blog: How weblogs are changing our culture* (pp. 17–24). Cambridge, MA: Perseus Press.

Kay, A. (1996). Revealing the elephant: The role and misuse of computers in education. *Educom Review.* Retrieved October 1, 2002, from the Educause website: http://www.educause.edu/pub/er/review/review Articles/31422.html

Kemp, F. (1992). Who programmed this? Examining the instructional attitudes of writing-support software. *Computers and Composition, 9,* 9–24.

———. (1993). The origins of ENFI, network theory, and computer-based collaborative writing instruction at the University of Texas. In B. Bruce, J. K. Peyton, & T. Batson (Eds.), *Network-based classrooms: Promises and realities* (pp. 161–180). Cambridge, UK: Cambridge University Press.

———. (1998). Computer-mediated communication. In J. R. Galin & J. Latchow (Eds.), *The dialogic classroom: Teachers integrating computer technology, pedagogy, and research* (pp. 133–150). Urbana, IL: NCTE.

Kennedy, G. (1998). *An introduction to corpus linguistics.* London: Longman.

Kern, R. G. (1995). Restructuring classroom interaction with networked computers: Effects on quantity and characteristics of language production. *The Modern Language Journal, 79,* 457–476.

Kiesler, S., Siegal, J., & McGuire, T. W. (1984). Social psychological aspects of computer-mediated communication. *American Psychologist, 39,* 1123–1134.

Kim, H., & Papacharissi, Z. (2003). Cross-cultural differences in online self-presentation: A content analysis of personal Korean and US home pages. *Asian Journal of Communication, 13,* 100–119.

King, J., Grinter, R. E., & Pickering, J. M. (1997). The rise and fall of Netville: Construction boomtown in the great divide. In S. Kiesler (Ed.), *Culture of the Internet* (pp. 3–33). Mahwah, NJ. Lawrence Erlbaum.

Kramarae, C. (1988). Gotta go Myrtle, technology's at the door. In C. Kramarae (Ed.), *Technology and women's voices* (pp. 1–14). New York: Routledge & Kegan Paul.

Krause, S. D. (2005). When blogging goes bad: A cautionary tale about blogs. *Kairos, 9.1.* Retrieved February 22, 2005, from http://english.ttu.edu/kairos/9.1/binder.html?praxis/krause/index.html

Kraut, R., Kiesler, S., Boneva, B., Cummings, J., Hegelson, V., & Crawford, A. (2002). Internet paradox revisted. *Journal of Social Issues, 58,* 49–74.

Kraut, R., Mukhopadhyay, T., Szcypula, J., Kiesler, S., & Sherlis, B. (1999). Information and communication: Alternative uses of the Internet in households. *Information Systems Research, 10,* 287–303.

Kress, G. (1998). Visual and verbal modes of representation in electronically mediated communication: The potentials of new forms of text. In I. Snyder (Ed.), *Page to screen: Taking literacy into the electronic era* (pp. 53–79). New York: Routledge.

———. (1999). "English" at the crossroads: Rethinking curricula of communication in the context of the turn of the visual. In G. E. Hawisher & C. L. Selfe (Eds.), *Passions, pedagogies, and 21st century technologies* (pp. 66–88). Urbana, IL: NCTE.

———. (2003). *Literacy in the new media age.* London: Routledge.

Lakoff, G., & Johnson, M. (1980). *Metaphors we live by.* Chicago: University of Chicago Press.

Lam, W. S. E. (2000). L2 literacy and the design of self: A case study of a teenager writing on the Internet. *TESOL Quarterly, 34,* 457–482.

Lamb, B. (2004, September–October). Wide open spaces: Wikis ready or not. *Educause Review, 39*(5), 38–48. Retrieved August 31, 2004, from http://www.educause.edu/ir/library/pdf/erm0452.pdf

Lambert, J. (2003). *Digital storytelling cookbook and traveling companion.* Berkeley, CA: Digital Diner Press.

Landauer, T. K., Laham, D., & Folte, P. W. (2003). Automated scoring and annotation of essays with the Intelligent Essay Assessor™. In M. D. Shermis & J. Burstein (Eds.), *Automated essay scoring: A cross-disciplinary perspective* (pp. 87–115). Mahwah, NJ: Lawrence Erlbaum.

Landow, G. (1997). *Hypertext 2.0.* Baltimore: Johns Hopkins Press.

Langham, D. (1994). The common place MOO: Orality and literacy in virtual reality. *Computer-Mediated Communication Magazine, 1.* Retrieved February 4, 2004, from http://www.december.com/cmc/mag/1994/jul/moo.html

Langston, D. M., & Batson, T. W. (1990). The social shifts invited by working collaboratively on computer networks: The ENFI project. In C. Handa (Ed.), *Computers and community* (pp. 140-159). Portsmouth, NH: Boynton/Cook.

Lankshear, C., & Knobel, M. (2003). *New literacies: Changing knowledge and classroom learning.* Buckingham, UK: Open University Press.

Latour, B. (1988). *Science in action.* Cambridge, MA: Harvard University Press.

Latour, B., & Woolgar, S. (1986). *Laboratory life.* Princeton, NJ: Princeton University Press.

Lave, J., & Wenger, E. (1991). *Situated learning: Legitimate peripheral participation.* Cambridge, UK: Cambridge University Press.

LeCourt, D. (1998). Critical pedagogy in the computer classroom: Politicizing the writing space. *Computers and Composition, 15,* 275–295.

Lee, D., & Swales, J. (2006). A corpus-based EAP course for NNS doctoral students: Moving from specialized corpora to self-compiled corpora. *English for Specific Purposes, 25,* 56–75.

Leech, G. (1997). Teaching and language corpora: A convergence. In A. Wichmann, S. Fligelstone, T. McEnery, & G. Knowles (Eds.), *Teaching and language corpora* (pp. 1–22). London: Longman.

Lefevre, K. B. (1987). *Invention as a social act.* Carbondale: Southern Illinois University Press.

Lemke, J. L. (2004). Metamedia literacy: Transforming meanings and media. In C. Handa (Ed.), *Visual rhetoric in a digital world* (pp. 71–93). Boston: Bedford/St. Martin's.

Lessing, L. (1999). *Code and other laws of cyberspace.* New York: Basic Books.

———. (2001). *The future of ideas: The fate of the commons in a connected world.* New York: Random House.

Levy, M. (1997). *Computer assisted language learning.* Oxford, UK: Clarendon Press.

Li, X., & Xiong, L. (1996). Chinese researchers debate rash of plagiarism cases. *Science, 274,* 337–338.

Li, Y. L. (2000). Linguistic characteristics of ESL writing in task-based e-mail activities. *System, 28,* 229–245.

Liaw, M. L. (1998). Using electronic mail for English as a foreign language instruction. *System, 26,* 335–351.

Liu, J., & Hansen, J. G. (2002). *Peer response in the second language writing classroom.* Ann Arbor: University of Michigan Press.

Lowe, C., & Williams, T. (2004). Moving to the public: Weblogs in the writing classroom. Retrieved February 16, 2005, from the Into the Blogosphere website: http://blog.lib.umn.edu/blogosphere/moving_to_the_public.html

Lunsford, A. A. (2006). Writing, technologies, and the fifth canon. *Computers and Composition, 23,* 169–177.

Lunsford, A. A., & Ede, L. (1994). Collaborative authorship and the teaching of writing. In M. Woodmansee & P. Jaszi (Eds.), *The construction of authorship: Textual appropriation in law and literature* (pp. 417–438). Durham, NC: Duke University Press.

Lydon, C. (2003). The year that made Larry Lessing an optimist. Retrieved January 14, 2004, from http://blogs.law.harvard.edu/lydon/2003/12/18#a455

———. (2004). Christopher Lydon interviews… Retrieved January 26, 2004, from http://blogs.law.harvard.edu/lydon/

Malinowski, B. (1947). The problem of meaning in primitive languages. In C. K. Ogden & I. A. Richards (Eds.), *The meaning of meaning: A study of the influence of language upon thought and of the science of symbolism* (pp. 296–336). New York: Harcourt, Brace.

Mao, L. M. (1995). Individualism or personhood: A battle of locution or rhetoric? In J. F. Reynolds (Ed.), *Rhetoric, cultural studies, and literacy* (pp. 127–135). Mahwah, NJ: Lawrence Erlbaum.

Marcus, S. (1990). Invisible writing with a computer: New sources and recommendations. Retrieved February 8, 2004, from http://www.hu.mtu/~candc/archives/v8/8_1_3_Marcus.html

Markoff, J. (2005). *What the dormouse said: How the 60s counterculture shaped the personal computer.* New York: Viking Press.

Marsh, B. (2004). Turnitin.com and the scriptural enterprise of plagiarism detection. *Computers and Composition, 21,* 427–438.

McCullough, M. (2001). On typologies of situated interaction. *Human-Computer Interaction, 16,* 337–349.

McLuhan, M. H. (1962). *The Gutenberg galaxy: The making of typographic man.* Toronto, ON: University of Toronto Press.

Milton, J. (1997). Providing computerized self-access opportunities for the development of writing skills. In P. Benson & P. Voller (Eds.), *Autonomy and independence in language learning* (pp. 204–214). London: Longman.

———. (2000). WordPilot 2000 [computer program]. Hong Kong: Compulang. Retrieved March 21, 2004, from http://www.compulang.com

Mitchell, W. J. (2003). *Me++: The cyborg self and the networked city.* Cambridge: MIT Press.

Moran, C. (1995). Notes toward a rhetoric of e-mail. *Computers and Composition, 12,* 15–21.

———. (2003). Computers and composition 1983–2002: What we have hoped for. *Computers and Composition, 20,* 343–358.

———. (2005). Powerful medicine with long-term side effects. *Computers and Composition, 22,* 63–68.

Mortensen, T., & Walker, J. (2002). Blogging thoughts: Personal publication as an online research tool. In A. Morrison (Ed.), *Researching ICTs in context* (pp. 249–279). Oslo, Norway: University of Oslo. Retrieved January 26, 2004, from http://www.intermedia.uio.no/konferanser/skikt02/docs/Researching_ICTs_in_context.pdf

Myers, G. (1990). *Writing biology: Texts in the social construction of scientific knowledge.* Madison: University of Wisconsin Press.

Mynard, J. (2003). *Synchronous computer-mediated communication and learner autonomy in female Emirati learners of English.* Unpublished doctoral dissertation, University of Exeter, Exeter, UK.

Negroponte, N. (1995). *Being digital.* New York: Knopf.

Nelson, T. H. (1992). *Literary machines.* Sausalito, CA: Mindful Press.

Noble, D. (1998). Digital diploma mills: The automation of higher education. *First Monday.* Retrieved: November 28, 2002, from http://www.firstmonday.dk/issues/issue3_1/noble/index.html

North, S. (1987). *The making of knowledge in composition: Portrait of an emerging field.* Upper Montclair, NJ: Boynton/Cook.

Nydahl, J. (1991). Ambiguity and confusion in word-processing research. *Computers and Composition, 8,* 21–37.

Olson, D. R. (1995). Writing and the mind. In J. V. Wretsch, P. del Rio, & A. Alvarez (Eds.), *Sociocultural studies of the mind* (pp. 95–123). New York: Cambridge University Press.

Olson, G. A. (1999). Toward a post-process composition: Abandoning the rhetoric of assertion. In T. Kent (Ed.), *Post process theory: Beyond the writing process paradigm* (pp. 7–15). Carbondale: Southern Illinois University Press.

Ong, W. J. (1982). *Orality and literacy: The technologizing of the word.* London: Methuen.

————. (1997). The writer's audience is always a fiction. In V. Villanueva, Jr. (Ed.), *Cross-talk in comp theory: A reader* (pp. 55–76). Urbana, IL: NCTE.

O'Reilley, T. (2005). What is Web 2.0: Design patterns and business models for the next generation of software. Retrieved December 3, 2005, from the O'Reilley website: http://www.oreillynet.com/pub/a/oreilly/tim/news/2005/09/30/what-is-web-20.html?page=1

Palmquist, M., Kiefer, K., Hartvigsen, J., & Goodlew, B. (1998). *Transitions: Teaching writing in computer-supported and traditional classrooms.* Greenwich, CT: Ablex.

Paquet, S. (2002). Personal knowledge publishing and its uses in research. Retrieved April 10, 2003, from http://www.knowledgeboard.com/cgi-bin/item.cgi?id=96934&d=1&h=0&f=0&dateformat=%o%20%B%20%Y

Pawley, A., & Syder, F. H. (1983). Natural selection in syntax: Notes on adaptive variation and change in vernacular and literary grammar. *Journal of Pragmatics, 7,* 551–579.

Pax, S (2003). *Salam Pax: The clandestine diary of an ordinary Iraqi.* New York: Grove Press.

Pennycook, A. (2001). *Critical applied linguistics: A critical introduction.* Mahwah, NJ: Lawrence Erlbaum.

Petraglia, J. (1998). *Reality by design: The rhetoric and technology of authenticity in education.* Mahwah, NJ: Lawrence Erlbaum.

Phillipson, R. (1992). *Linguistic imperialism.* Oxford, UK: Oxford University Press.

Porter, J. (1986). Intertextuality and the discourse community. *Rhetoric Review, 1,* 34–47.

————. (2002). Why technology matters to writing: A cyberwriter's tale. *Computers and Composition, 20,* 375–394.

Postman, N. (1992). *Technopoly: The surrender of culture to technology.* New York: Knopf.

Raimes, A. (1983). Tradition and revolution in ESL teaching. *TESOL Quarterly, 4,* 535–550.

Rainie, L. (2005). The state of blogging. Retrieved January 11, 2005, from Pew Internet and American Life Project: http://www.pewinternet.org/pdfs/PIP_blogging_data.pdf

Ramanathan, V., & Atkinson, D. (1999). Individualism, academic writing, and ESL writers. *Journal of Second Language Writing, 8,* 45–75.

Raymond, E. (1998). The cathedral and the bazaar. *First Monday, 3.* Retrieved October 29, 2005, from http://www.firstmonday.org/issues/issue3_3/raymond/

Rea, A., & White, D. (1999). The changing nature of writing: Prose or code in the classroom. *Computers and Composition, 16,* 421–436.

Reid, E. (1995). Virtual worlds: Culture and imagination. In S. G. Jones (Ed.), *Cybersociety: Computer-mediated communication and community* (pp. 164–183). Thousand Oaks, CA: Sage.

———. (1999). Hierarchy and power: Social control in cyberspace. In M. A. Smith & P. Polluck (Eds.), *Communication in cyberspace* (pp. 197–133). London: Routledge.

Reid, S., & Findlay, G. (1986). Writer's workbench analysis of holistically scored essays. *Computers and Composition, 3,* 6–32.

Reiguluth, C. M. (1999). *Instructional design theories and models: An overview of their current status.* Mahwah, NJ: Lawrence Erlbaum.

Reppen, R. (2001). Review of MonoConc Pro and Wordsmith tools. *Language, Learning, & Technology, 5,* 32–36.

Rheingold, H. (1993). *The virtual community: Homesteading on the electronic frontier.* Reading, MA: Addison-Wesley.

———. (2003). *Smart mobs: The next social revolution.* Cambridge, MA: Perseus Press.

Richardson, W. (2006). *Blogs, Wikis, podcasts, and other powerful Web tools for classrooms.* Thousand Oaks, CA: Corwin Press.

Romano, S. (1993). The egalitarian narrative: Whose story? Which yardstick? *Computers and Composition, 10,* 5–28.

Rose, M. (1989). *Lives on the boundary: The struggles and achievements of America's underprepared.* New York: The Free Press.

Rouzer, J. (2005). Personal communication.

Salomon, G., Pea, R., Brown, J. S., & Heath, C. (1993). *Distributed cognitions: Psychological and educational considerations.* Cambridge, UK: Cambridge University Press.

Samuelson, P. (1999). Intellectual property and the digital economy: Why the anti-circumvention regulations need to be revised. *Berkeley Technology Law Journal, 14,* 519–566. Retrieved August 11, 2004, from http://www.law. berkeley.edu/journals/btlj/articles/vol14/Samuelson/html/reader.html

Sands, P. (2002). Inside outside, upside downside: Strategies for connecting online and face-to-face instruction in hybrid courses. *Teaching with Technology Today, 8.* Retrieved June 5, 2006, from http://www.uwsa. edu/ttt/articles/sands2.htm

Schmitt, N. (2000). *Vocabulary in language teaching.* New York: Cambridge University Press.

Schwartz, H. (1984). SEEN: A tutorial and user network for hypothesis testing. In W. Wresch (Ed.), *The computer in composition instruction: A writer's tool* (pp. 47–62). Urbana, IL: NCTE.

Scribner, S., & Cole, M. (1981). *The psychology of literacy.* Cambridge, MA: Harvard University Press.

SDIdeas announces intuitive WRITE~NOW software that helps students improve and enhance writing skills. (2003). Retrieved December 18, 2003, from http://home.businesswire.com/portal/site/google/index. jsp?ndmViewId=news_view&newsId=20031216005325&newsLang=en

Selber, S. (2004). *Multiliteracies for the digital age.* Carbondale, IL: Southern Illinois University Press.

Selfe, C. L. (1992). Preparing English teachers for the virtual age: The case for technology critics. In G. E. Hawisher & P. LeBlanc (Eds.), *Re-imaging computers and composition* (pp. 24–42). Portsmouth, NH: Boynton/Cook.

———. (1999). *Technology and literacy in the twenty-first century: The importance of paying attention.* Carbondale: Southern Illinois University Press.

Selfe, C. L., & Selfe, R. (1994). The politics of the interface: Power and its exercise in electronic contact zones. *College Communication and Composition, 45,* 480–504.

Shank, R. C., & Cleary, C. (1995). *Engines for education.* Mahwah, NJ: Lawrence Erlbaum.

Shirkey, C. (2003). Power laws, weblogs, and inequality. Retrieved January 4, 2006, from the Clay Shirkey's Writing about the Internet website: http://www.shirky.com/writings/powerlaw_weblog.html

Shiu, E., & Lenhart, A. (2004). How Americans use instant messaging. Retrieved December 23, 2004, from Pew Internet and American Life Project: http://www. Pewinternet.org/pdfs/PIP_Instantmessage_Report. pdf

Siegal, D. (1996). *Creating killer web sites*. Indianapolis, IN: Hayden Books.

Siemens, G. (2002). The art of blogging—part 1. Retrieved January 9, 2004, from the elearnspace website: http://www.elearnspace.org/Articles/blogging_part_1.htm

———. (2005). Connectivism: Learning in a digital age. Retrieved February 22, 2007, from www.elearnspace.org/Articles/connectivism.htm

Simons, H. W. (1990). *The rhetorical turn: Invention and persuasion in the conduct of inquiry*. Chicago: University of Chicago Press.

Simpson, R. C., Briggs, J., Ovens, S. L, & Swales, J. M. (2002). *The Michigan corpus of academic spoken English: MICASE*. Ann Arbor: The Regents of the University of Michigan. Retrieved August 11, 2004, from http://www.hti.umich.edu/m/micase/

Simpson-Vlach, R. C., & Leicher, S. (2006). *The MICASE handbook: A Resource for users of the Michigan Corpus of Academic Spoken English*. Ann Arbor: University of Michigan Press.

Sinclair, J. (1997). Corpus evidence in language description. In A. Wichmann, S. Fligelstone, T. McEnery, & G. Knowles (Eds.), *Teaching and language corpora* (pp. 27–39). London: Longman.

Smith, A. D. (1999). Problems of conflict management in virtual communities. In M. A. Smith & P. Kollak (Eds.), *Communities in cyberspace* (pp. 134–166). London: Routledge.

Smith, C. (2000). Nobody, which means anybody: Audience on the World Wide Web. In S. Gruber, (Ed.), *Weaving a virtual web: Practical approaches to new information technologies* (pp. 239–250). Urbana, IL: NCTE.

Smith, C. R., Kiefer, K. E., & Gingrich, P. S. (1984). Computers come of age in writing instruction. *Language Resources and Evaluation, 18*, 215–224.

Spiro, R. J., Feltovich, P. J., Jacobsen, M. J., & Coulson, R. L. (1995). Cognitive flexibility, constructivism, and hypertext: Random access instruction advance knowledge acquisition in ill-structured domains. In L. Steffe & J. Gale (Eds.), *Constructivism in education* (pp. 85–107). Mahwah, NJ: Lawrence Erlbaum.

Spivey, N. N. (1997). *The constructivist metaphor: Reading, writing, and the making of meaning*. San Diego, CA: Academic Press.

Sproull, L., & Kiesler, S. (1991). *Connections: New ways of working in networked organizations*. Cambridge: MIT Press.

———. (1993). Computers, networks, and work. In L. Harasim (Ed.), *Global networks: Computers and international communication* (pp. 105–120). Cambridge: MIT Press.

Stallman, R. (1999). The GNU operating system and the free software movement. In C. Dibona, S. Ockman, & M. Stone (Eds.), *Open sources: Voices from the open source revolution* (pp. 53–70). Sebastopol, CA: O'Reilly.

Stapleton, P. (2002). Critiquing voice as a viable pedagogical tool in L2 writing: Returning the spotlight to ideas. *Journal of Second Language Writing, 11,* 177–190.

————. (2005). Assessing the quality and bias of web-based sources: implications for academic writing. *Journal of English for Academic Purposes, 2,* 229–245.

Stevens, V. (2003). How the TESOL CALL Interest Section began. *Computer-Assisted Language Learning E-Section, 21*(1).

Street, B. (1984). *Literacy in theory and practice.* Cambridge, UK: Cambridge University Press.

Sun, H. T. (2004). *Expanding the scope of localization: A cultural usability perspective on mobile text messaging use in American and Chinese contexts.* Unpublished doctoral dissertation, Rensselaer Polytechnic Institute, Troy, NY.

Swales, J. M. (1990). *Genre analysis: English in academic and research settings.* Cambridge, UK: Cambridge University Press.

Swales, J. M., & Feak, C. B. (2000). *English in today's research world: A writing guide.* Ann Arbor: University of Michigan Press.

Takayoshi, P. (2000). Complicated women: Examining methodologies for understanding the uses of technology. *Computers and Composition, 17,* 123–138.

Terdiman, D. (2006). Second Life teaches life lessons. *Wired News.* Retrieved May 16, 2006, from http://www.wired.com/news/games/0,2101,67142,00. html

Thiesmeyer, E., & Thiesmeyer, J. (1990). *Editor.* New York: MLA.

Thompson, G. (2001). Corpus, concordance, culture: Doing the same things differently in different cultures. In M. Ghadessy, A. Henry, & R. L. Roseberry (Eds.), *Small corpus studies and ELT* (pp. 311–334). Amsterdam: John Benjamins.

Thompson, G., & Ye, Y. Y. (1991). Evaluation in reporting verbs used in academic papers. *Applied Linguistics, 12,* 365–382.

Thompson, P., & Tribble, C. (2001). Looking at citations: Using corpora in English for academic purposes. *Language Learning & Technology 5,* 91–105. Retrieved September 24, 2001, from http://llt.msu.edu/vol5num3/pdf/thompson.pdf

Thurston, J., & Candlin, C. N. (2002). *Exploring academic English: A workbook for student essay writing.* Sydney, Australia: NCELTR.

Tognini-Belloni, E. (2001). *Corpus linguistics at work.* Amsterdam: John Benjamins.

Toyoda, E., & Harrison, R. (2002). Categorization of text chat communication between learners and native speakers of Japanese. *Language Learning & Technology, 6,* 82–99.

Tribble, C. (2002). Corpora and corpus analysis: New windows on academic writing. In J. Flowerdew (Ed.), *Academic discourse* (pp. 131–149). Harlow, UK: Longman.

Trupe, A. L. (2002). Academic literacy in a wired world: Redefining genres for college writing courses, *Kairos, 7.* Retrieved December 5, 2002, from http://english.ttu.edu/kairos/7.2/binder.html?sectionone/trupe/WiredWorld.htm

Truscott, J., (1996). The case against grammar correction in L2 writing classes. *Language Learning, 46,* 327–369.

———. (1999). The case for "The case against grammar correction in L2 writing classes": A response to Ferris. *Journal of Second Language Writing, 8,* 111–122.

Tufte, E. (2003). PowerPoint is evil. *Wired, 11.* Retrieved December 28, 2003, from http://www.wired.com/wired/archive/11.09/ppt2.html

Turkle, S. (1995). *Life on the screen: Identity in the age of the Internet.* New York: Simon and Shuster.

Velma, R. (1994). Global communication through email: An ongoing experiment at Helsinki University of Technology. Retrieved August 15, 2001, from http://www.ruthvilmi.net/hut/autumn93/global.html#HDR%202%2017

von Glaserfield, E. (1995). A constuctivist approach to teaching. In L. Steffe & J. Gale (Eds.), *Constructivism in education* (pp. 3–15). Mahwah, NJ: Lawrence Erlbaum.

Wales, J. (2006, August). Plenary session at Wikimania 2006, Cambridge, MA. Retrieved August 6, 2006, from http://www.supload.com/listen?s=SIOOG2vN04i#

Warschauer, M. (1995). *E-mail for English teaching: Bringing the Internet and computer learning networks into the language classroom.* Alexandria, VA: TESOL.

———. (1999). *Electronic literacies: Language, culture, and power in online education.* Mahwah, NJ: Lawrence Erlbaum.

————. (2000). Online learning in second language classrooms. In M. Warschauer & R. Kern (Eds.), *Network-based language teaching: Concepts and practice* (pp. 41–58). Cambridge, UK: Cambridge University Press.

————. (2003). *Technology and social inclusion: Rethinking the digital divide.* Cambridge: MIT Press.

Warschauer, M., & Kern, R. (2000). *Network-based language teaching: Concepts and practice.* New York: Cambridge University Press.

Warschauer, M., Turbee, L., & Roberts, B. (1996). Computer learning networks and student empowerment. *System, 24,* 1–14.

Weasenforth, D., Biesenbach-Lucas, S., & Meloni, C. (2002). Realizing constructivist objectives through collaborative technologies: Threaded discussions. *Language Learning & Technology, 6,* 58–86. Retrieved November 28, 2002, from http://llt.msu.edu/vol6num3/WEASENFORTH/

Weigle, S. C., & Nelson, G. L. (2004). Novice tutors and their ESL tutees: Three case studies of tutor roles and perceptions of tutorial success. *Journal of Second Language Writing, 13,* 203–225.

Weinberger, D. (2003). *Small pieces loosely joined: A unified theory of the Web.* Cambridge, MA: Perseus Press.

What is copyleft? (1999). Retrieved February 22, 2005, from the GNU Project website: http://www.gnu.org/copyleft/

What is technorealism? (1998). Retrieved January 24, 2004, from the Berkman Center for Internet & Society at Harvard Law School website: http://cyber.law.harvard.edu/technorealism/panel1.html

White, N. (2006). Blogs and community: Launching a new paradigm for online community? Retrieved November 29, 2006, from The Knowledge Tree website: http://kt.flexiblelearning.net.au/edition-11-editorial/blogs-and-community-%E2%80%93-launching-a-new-paradigm-for-online-community

Wickliffe, G., & Yancey, K. B. (2001). The perils of creating a class web-site: It was the best of times, it was the…. *Computers and Composition, 18,* 177–186.

Wiley, D. A. (2001). Connecting learning objects to instructional design theory: A definition, a metaphor, and a taxonomy. In D. Wiley (Ed.), *The instructional use of learning objects* (pp. 1–35). The Agency for Instructional Technology & The Association for Educational Communications and Technology. Retrieved April 22, 2004, from http://reusability.org/read/chapters/wiley.doc

Windschitl, M., & Sahl, K. (2002). Tracing teachers' use of technology in a laptop computer school: The interplay of teacher beliefs, social dynamics, and institutional culture. *American Educational Research Journal, 39,* 165–205.

Winterowd, R. (1975). *The contemporary writer.* New York: Harcourt.

Woodmansee, M. (1994). On the author effect: Recovering collectivity. In M. Woodmansee & P. Jaszi (Eds.), *The construction of authorship: Textual appropriation in law and literature* (pp. 15–28). Durham, NC: Duke University Press.

Woodmansee, M., & Jaszi, P. (1995). The law of texts: Copyright in the academy. *College English, 57,* 769–787.

WordSmith Tools Version 3.0 [computer program] (n.d.). Oxford, UK: Oxford University Press.

Wrede, O. (2003, October). *Weblogs and discourse: Weblogs as a transformational technology for higher education and academic research.* Paper presented at the Blogtalk Conference, Vienna, Austria. Retrieved April 24, 2004, from http://weblogs.design.fh-aachen.de/owrede/publikationen/weblogs_and_discourse

Wresch, W. (1984). *The computer in composition instruction: A writer's tool.* Urbana, IL: NCTE.

Yagelski, R. F., & Powley, S. (1996). Virtual connections and real boundaries: Teaching writing and preparing writing teachers on the Internet. *Computers and Composition, 13,* 25–36.

Yoon, H., & Hirvela, A. (2004). ESL student attitudes toward corpus use in L2 writing. *Journal of Second Language Writing, 13,* 257–283.

Young, R. E. (1978). Paradigms and problems: Needed research in rhetorical invention. In C. R. Cooper & L. Edell (Eds.), *Research on composing* (pp. 29–48). Urbana, IL: NCTE.

Young, R. E., & Liu, Y. M. (1994). *Rhetorical invention in writing.* Davis, CA: Hermagoras Press.

Yuan, Y. (2003). The use of chat rooms in an ESL setting. *Computers and Composition, 20,* 194–206.

Zamel, V. (1983). The composing process of advanced ESL students: Six case studies. *TESOL Quarterly, 17,* 165–187.

Zittrain, J., & Edelman, B. (2003). Empirical analysis of Internet filtering in China. Retrieved October 24, 2006, from http://cyber.law.harvard.edu/filtering/china/

Subject Index

Author Index